S

D0085671

Training in Inter-Personal Skills

TIPS for Managing People at Work

Stephen P. Robbins
San Diego State University

Phillip L. Hunsaker
University of San Diego

Prentice Hall, Upper Saddle River, New Jersey 07458

Library of Congress Cataloging-in-Publication Data
ROBBINS, STEPHEN P., [date]
  Training in interpersonal skills: TIPS for managing people at
work / STEPHEN P. ROBBINS, PHILLIP L. HUNSAKER.—2nd ed.
      p.   cm.
  Includes bibliographical references (p.).
  ISBN 0-13-435827-9
  1. Supervision of employees. 2. Interpersonal communication.
I. Hunsaker, Phillip L. II. Title.
HF5549. 12.R63   1996
658.3'02—dc20   95-33975

Acquisitions editor: *David A. Shafer*
Associate editor: *Lisamarie Brassini*
Project management: *Edie Riker*
Cover design: *Bruce Kenselaar*
Cover photo illustration: *"People Joining Hands," Tim Grajek/Stock Works*
Buyer: *Vincent Scelta*
Editorial assistant: *Nancy Kaplan*

Printed in the Unted States of America

10 9 8 7 6 5 4 3 2 1

ISBN 0-13-435827-9

Prentice Hall International, (UK) Limited, *London*
Prentice-Hall of Australia Pty. Limited, *Sydney*
Prentice-Hall Canada Inc., *Toronto*
Prentice-Hall Hispanoamericana, S.A., *Mexico*
Prentice-Hall of India Private Limited, *New Delhi*
Prentice-Hall of Japan, Inc., *Tokyo*
Simon & Schuster Asia Pte. Ltd., *Singapore*
Editora Prentice-Hall do Brasil, Ltda., *Rio de Janeiro*

CONTENTS

PREFACE

TIPS was one of the first interpersonal skills training packages for management students. Since its original publication, management faculty in colleges and universities have increasingly come to recognize the importance of developing interpersonal skill competencies in their students. Dr. Milton Blood, a former professor and now an executive with the American Association of Collegiate Schools of Business, recently explained why skills training has gained in popularity, over more traditional theory building:

> Leadership sounds like an applied topic, but its classroom presentation can leave students no better prepared to lead . . . The business school graduate needs to lead, not trace the history of leadership research. [Similarly] the graduate needs to motivate, not compare and contrast six different theories of motivation.[1]

By developing and practicing the interpersonal skills in this book, students can learn to lead and motivate others.

OVERVIEW OF THE SECOND EDITION

The first edition of *TIPS* was widely used in courses such as Interpersonal Relations, Organizational Behavior, Management, Human Relations, Supervision, and Organizational Development. It was also used with practicing managers in executive development programs. The second edition includes

---

[1]M.R. Blood, "The Role of Organizational Behavior in the Business School Curriculum," in J. Greenberg (ed.) *Organizational Behavior: The State of Science*, (Hillsdale, N.J.: Lawrence Erlbaum, 1994), p. 216.

a number of significant additions and changes resulting from our experiences in the classroom, new research findings, and the feedback from colleagues, reviewers, and students.

The major changes are highlighted below:

1. We've modified the TIPS learning model. It now contains ten components which ask students to: (1) assess their basic skill level; (2) review key concepts that are relevant to applying the skill; (3) test their conceptual knowledge; (4) identify on a checklist the specific behavioral dimensions that they need to learn for each skill; (5) observe how to apply the skill through watching others in a modeling exercise; (6) practice the skill in small groups; (7) use a summary checklist to identify deficiencies; (8) answer application questions to cement practical understanding of the concepts; (9) do reinforcement exercises outside of the classroom; and (10) develop an action plan for ongoing skill improvement in their own lives.

2. New chapters on Empowering People, Coaching, Team Building, Negotiating, and Interviewing have been added.

3. Material in previous chapters on Performance Appraisal, Disciplining, and Delegating, has been integrated as applications or subsections in new more comprehensive chapters such as Empowering People, Interviewing, or Persuading.

4. Application questions and action plans have been added to the learning model for each chapter.

5. Many role plays, cases, and exercises have been added, replaced, and revised to enhance the chapters.

6. Concepts, research references, and examples have been updated.

7. The *Instructor's Manual* has been revised and expanded to provide more complete guidance based upon the cumulative experience and feedback from instructors using the first edition.

ACKNOWLEDGMENTS

We want to express our appreciation to the many reviewers of the previous edition who assisted us in this revision. These include Diana Page, Alison Konrad, Raymond Shea, John Wells, and Bill Zachary.

We are grateful to our students who offered us open and honest feedback about what did and did not work for them. They also contributed many ideas for improvements. The same was true for Jo Hunsaker and Sarah Hunsaker, from professorial, student, and other perspectives.

Finally, special thanks to Lisamarie Brassini and David Shafer at Prentice Hall. Lisamarie guided this revision in its development stage. Edie Riker managed the book through the production process.

Stephen P. Robbins
Phillip L. Hunsaker

Chapter *1*

SKILLS: AN INTRODUCTION

Today's business graduates have an abundance of technical knowledge. They can do linear programming problems, calculate a discounted rate of return, develop a sophisticated marketing plan, and crunch numbers on a computer spreadsheet. They're technically solid, but most lack the interpersonal and social skills necessary to manage people. If there is an area where business schools need to improve, it's in developing the "people skills" of their graduates.

—A corporate recruiter

This is not an isolated criticism of business programs. In recent years, industry (AACSB, 1993), the media (*Business Week*, 1986), teaching faculty (Cummings, 1990; Finney and Siehl, 1985-86), and the accrediting agencies of business programs (AACSB 1980; Porter and McKibbin, 1988) have all noted the weakness in interpersonal skills among recent business graduates. But in which interpersonal skills are graduates deficient, and if these skills can be identified, what are the best ways for business schools to teach them?

INTERPERSONAL SKILLS AND EFFECTIVE MANAGEMENT BEHAVIOR

Studies seeking to identify what it is that differentiates effective managers from ineffective ones have determined that there are fifty-one behaviors that successful managers engage in. Of course managers must be motivated to engage in these behaviors and they must have the skills to effectively implement them.

1

Behaviors

Through aggregation, researchers condensed the fifty-one behaviors of effective managerial into six role sets (Morse and Wagner, 1978). These are summarized below.

1. **Controlling the organization's environment and its resources**. This set of behaviors includes the ability to be proactive and stay ahead of environmental changes both in long-range planning and on-the-spot decision making. It also involves basing resource decisions on clear, up-to-date, accurate knowledge of the organization's objectives.

2. **Organizing and coordinating**. In this role, the manager organizes subordinate's behaviors around tasks and then coordinates interdependent relationships to accomplish common goals.

3. **Information handling**. This set of behaviors comprises using information and communication channels for identifying problems, understanding a changing environment, and making effective decisions.

4. **Providing for growth and development**. The manager's role is to provide for his or her own personal growth and development, as well as for the personal growth and development of subordinates through continual learning on the job.

5. **Motivating employees and handling conflict**. In this role, the manager enhances the positive aspects of motivation so that employees feel impelled to perform their work and concurrently eliminates those conflicts that may inhibit employees' motivation.

6. **Strategic problem solving**. The manager's role is to take responsibility for his or her own decisions and to ensure that subordinates effectively use their decision-making skills.

The researchers found that these six behaviors explained a more than 50 percent of a manager's effectiveness. Even if managers understand the necessity of doing these things, they will not engage in these specific behaviors unless they are motivated to do so.

Motivation

Desire to be a manager is another factor which influences managerial effectiveness. Research has found seven subcategories that make up the *motivation to manage* (Miner and Smith, 1982). They are summarized below.

1. **Authority acceptance.** A desire to accept the authority of superiors.
2. **Competitive games.** A desire to engage in competition with peers involving games or sports.
3. **Competitive situations.** A desire to engage in competition with peers involving occupational or work activities.
4. **Assertiveness.** A desire to behave in an active and assertive manner.
5. **Imposing wishes.** A desire to tell others what to do and to utilize sanctions in influencing others.
6. **Distinctiveness.** A desire to stand out from the group in a unique and highly visible way.
7. **Routine functions.** A desire to carry out the routine, day-to-day activities often associated with managerial work.

Research has demonstrated that more successful managers tend to achieve higher motivation-to-manage scores on inventories measuring these desires. If these seven factors are things that you enjoy and are willing to do, they are a fairly good predictor of your willingness to engage in effective managerial behaviors.

Skills

Even if you know the behaviors that effective managers engage in and have the motivation to do them, you still need the appropriate skills to implement them effectively. The most popular approach to managerial effectiveness has been to break the manager's job down into critical roles or skills (Katz, 1974; Mintzberg, 1980). Such efforts generally conclude that the effective manager must be competent in four different skill areas (Pavett and Lau, 1983):

1. **Conceptual skills.** The mental ability to coordinate all of the organization's interests and activities.
2. **Human skills.** The ability to work with, understand, and motivate other people, both individually and in groups.
3. **Technical skills.** The ability to use the tools, procedures, and techniques of a specialized field.
4. **Political skills.** The ability to enhance one's position, build a power base, and establish the right connections.

Do managers need competence in all these skills to be successful? The answer is a qualified yes. All four were found to be important for managerial success (Pavett and Lau, 1983). Research has indicated, however, that conceptual skills are required to a greater extent at the chief executive level. It has also been found that human skills—such as the ability to listen, verbally communicate, show patience, and understand subordinates' needs—are most important for success at any managerial level.

Conclusion

Of the three components of managerial effectiveness—appropriate behaviors, motivations, and skills—this book concentrates on developing the interpersonal skills component of managerial success. In terms of effective managerial behaviors, communicating, developing employees, motivating others, and handling conflicts all involve interpersonal skills. Individuals who have a high motivation to manage manifest this desire through the application of their interpersonal skills in competitive activities with peers, by taking charge in groups and by exercising power over others. Finally, the human and political skills found to be necessary at all levels of management are clearly interpersonal in nature.

Given that competent interpersonal skills are an important, if not the *most important*, attribute for managerial effectiveness, it is clear why constituencies such as business corporations, the media, teaching faculty, and business accrediting bodies are disturbed by the number of business graduates who are deficient in these skills. College graduates who aspire to a career in management may have the motivation to manage and a conceptual understanding of the behaviors required to be effective, but if they have poorly developed interpersonal skills they are ill-equipped for their future. Sending motivated business school graduates into the work place with only a cognitive grasp of the behaviors necessary for managerial success allows them to talk a good game but does not prepare them to be proficient players (Bowen, 1987).

DEFINING THE KEY INTERPERSONAL SKILLS

Given the general agreement that interpersonal skills are necessary for managerial success, what specifically are the skills required? A number of studies have sought to identify interpersonal skills (Lewis, 1973; Porras and Anderson, 1981; Boyatzis, 1982; Levine, 1982; Whetton and Cameron, 1984; AACSB, 1984, 1987, 1993; and Clark et al., 1985). A careful review of these studies indicates that, despite the widely varying terminology, certain skills tend to surface on most lists. For instance, handling conflicts, running meetings, coaching, team building, and empowering are regarded as key interpersonal skills by most studies. Communication is also important, but it is dissected differently in different studies. The elements of effective communication that show up in most studies are listening, interviewing, and providing feedback. Similarly, motivating employees is included in most lists, although it's rarely stated as simply "motivation." Rather, it's broken down into parts, such as goal setting, persuading, empowering people, and providing feedback.

KEY INTERPERSONAL SKILLS

Listening	Persuading
Goal setting	Politicking
Providing feedback	Running meetings
Empowering people	Resolving conflicts
Coaching	Negotiating
Interviewing	Building teams

This table represents a synthesis of what these studies have found to be the interpersonal skills required for effective managerial performance. Although the table may omit some skills that are important, it represents our best selection of the skills that research and practice suggest are important for success in managing people. Given our current state of knowledge, these are the interpersonal skills that most "experts" believe effective managers have and prospective managers need to develop.

THE LEARNING OF SKILLS

Can interpersonal skills be taught? If so, *what* teaching methods should be used? Any objective discussion of skills must eventually—either explicitly or implicitly—deal with these complex issues (Porter, 1983). This section summarizes our current knowledge regarding these questions.

Can Interpersonal Skills Be Taught?

Some social scientists view interpersonal skills as essentially personality traits that are deeply entrenched and not amenable to change (Fiedler, 1965). Just as some people are naturally quiet while others are outgoing, the antitraining side argues that some people can work well with others while many others simply cannot. That is, it's a talent you either have or you don't. Most of their evidence is of an anecdotal variety but can be intuitively appealing when they single out individuals with highly abrasive interpersonal styles and propose that no amount of training is likely to convert them into "people-oriented" types.

On the other hand, the skills advocates have an increasing body of empirical research to support their case. There is evidence that training programs focusing on the human relations problems of leadership, supervision, attitudes toward employees, communication, and self-awareness produce improvements in managerial performance (Burke and Day, 1986). This research has convinced business and public-sector organizations to spend tens of millions—maybe hundreds of millions—of dollars each year on development programs to improve their managers' interpersonal skills.

Nothing in the research suggests that skills training can magically transform every very interpersonally incompetent manager into a highly effective leader, but that should not be the test of whether interpersonal skills can be taught. The evidence strongly demonstrates that these skills can be learned. Although people differ in their baseline abilities, the research shows that training can result in better skills for most people who want to improve.

The Importance of Teaching Skills

In universities, instruction in human behavior runs the gamut from highly theoretical, research-based reviews of the behavioral literature to entirely experientially based courses where students learn about work group behavior by experiencing it. Textbooks reflect this diversity (see, for example, Dunham, 1984; and Kolb, Rubin, McIntyre, 1984). But skill building—through cases, role-plays, structured exercises, work simulations, and the like—has become an accepted added dimension of many college and university courses in human behavior.

Why is this important? You wouldn't want to submit yourself to an appendectomy if your surgeon had read everything available on the appendix and its removal but had never actually removed one before. You'd also be apprehensive if your surgeon had years of experience operating but had never studied the sciences of physiology and anatomy. Just as competent surgeons need both a sound understanding of how the body works and surgical skills finely honed through practice and experience, college and university instructors have come to believe that competent managers need a sound understanding of human behavior and the opportunity to hone their "people skills" through practice and experience.

If these skills are not taught in college and university programs that are designed to prepare people for managerial careers, where will they be taught? They seem too important to be left to on-the-job learning. As a recent report from the American Assembly of Collegiate Schools of Business concluded:

> business curricula should begin to address [interpersonal skills and personal characteristics] in a manner more nearly approximating the same explicit and systematic approach that characterizes the cognitive category if students are to be comprehensively prepared at the point of graduation for the managerial challenges ahead. (AACSB, 1984, p. 3)

How Do You Teach Skills?

"I hear and I forget. I see and I remember. I do and I understand." This famous quote, attributed to Confucius, is frequently used to support the value of learning through experience. The saying has some truth to it, but contemporary research on learning suggests that a more accurate rephrasing would be: "I understand best when I hear, see, and do!"

The lecture format continues to be the most popular method of teaching. It's a proven, effective means for increasing student awareness and understanding of concepts. As such, it probably should be part of any comprehensive system for learning skills. But it should be only a part! A skill, by definition, is "the ability to demonstrate a system and sequence of behavior that is functionally related to attaining a performance goal" (Boyatzis, 1982, p. 33). No single action constitutes a skill. For example, the ability to write clear communications is a skill. People who have this skill know the particular sequence of actions to be taken to propose a project or summarize a report. They can separate primary from secondary ideas. They can organize their thoughts in a logical manner. They can simplify convoluted ideas. But none of these acts is by itself a skill. A skill is a system of behavior that can be applied in a wide range of situations.

To become competent at any skill, a person needs to understand it both conceptually and behaviorally; have opportunities to practice it; get feedback on how well he or she is performing the skill; and use the skill often enough so that it becomes integrated into his or her behavioral repertoire (Johnson and Johnson, 1975, pp. 8–10). Kolb (1984, pp. 29–31) has developed a model that encompasses most of these learning dimensions.

The Experiential Learning Model

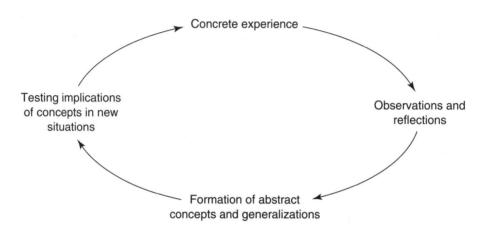

Source: David A. Kolb, Irwin M. Rubin, and James M. McIntyre, *Organizational Psychology: Readings on Human Behavior in Organizations*, 4th ed. (Englewood Cliffs, NJ.: Prentice Hall, 1984), p. 128. With permission.

This figure illustrates Kolb's experiential learning model. Consistent with social-learning theory (Bandura, 1977), it emphasizes that the development of behavioral skills comes from observation and practice.

According to the Kolb model, comprehensive learning encompasses four elements: active participation in a new experience (*concrete experience*); examination of that experience (*reflective observation*); integration of conclusions based on the new experience into workable theories (*abstract conceptualization*); and application of the theories to new situations (*active experimentation*). If this model is taken as a guide, the learning of skills is maximized when students get the opportunity to combine watching, thinking, and doing (Latham and Saari, 1979b; Manz & Sims, 1981; Decker, 1982; Clark et al., 1985).

Using Kolb's model and well-known learning principles, we propose the ten-step TIPS learning model for acquiring interpersonal skills as illustrated by the table below.

Training in InterPersonal Skills

1. Self-Assessment Exercise

2. Skill Concepts

3. Concept Quiz

4. Behavioral Checklist

5. Modeling Exercise

6. Group Exercises

7. Summary Checklist

8. Application Questions

9. Reinforcement Exercises

10. Action Plan

First, an individual needs to assess his or her baseline skill. Carl Rogers (1961) would call this step "self-discovery." Each skill chapter in this book begins with a self-assessment questionnaire, followed by a scoring key and an interpretation. The self assessment quiz is not meant to be a refined or highly valid measurement device. Rather, it is intended to give the individual insights into how much he or she already knows about the skill in question. Second, a person needs to learn the basic concepts underlying the skill. This is achieved by reviewing the published materials available on the skill. The third step is providing feedback to ensure that the basic concepts are understood. In our model, this is accomplished by a short quiz. The next step is the identification of specific skill behaviors that the individual desires to learn. This behavioral checklist, derived from the skill concepts, clarifies what specific behaviors the individual needs to acquire and is also used by others for evaluating how well the individual has learned the behaviors in question. Because research on decision making tells us that people have difficulty working with more than about seven pieces of information (Miller, 1956), the number of these specific behaviors needs to be limited. The importance of this behavioral checklist can't be overstated. It contains the sole criteria by which actual behavioral performance will be judged. By keeping evaluation focused only on the behaviors identified in the checklist, we reduce the likelihood that appraisals will veer off to include personality variables, personal styles, or similar extraneous factors.

The fifth step is a modeling exercise that allows the learner to observe others exhibiting the desired skill behaviors. In the sixth step, students form small groups and practice their newly acquired skills. Individuals not actively involved in a group exercise learn and contribute through observation and evaluation. The seventh step—completing a summary checklist—requires the learner to identify which, if any, behaviors he or she is deficient in. This appraisal comes from self-assessment and evaluations made by others. Deficiency feedback should be used to focus on where further practice is needed. Application questions provide opportunities to check understanding of how skill behaviors relate, and reinforcement exercises facilitate the transfer of classroom learning to real-life situations. Finally, the action plan provides the development of specific changes to implement.

SUMMARY AND COMING ATTRACTIONS

This text has been developed to help college and university programs teach their students the interpersonal skills necessary for successful careers in business and management. There is general agreement today on what the most important interpersonal skills are. Further, our knowledge of how people learn provides us with a solid basis for designing interpersonal skill-learning modules. We have used this knowledge to create an interpersonal skills book—TIPS—that can be used alone or as a supplement to cognitive textbooks in organizational behavior, human relations, applied psychology, principles of supervision, or similar courses that aim to improve students' "people skills."

In the belief that before you can understand others you need to know yourself, Chapter 2 provides a battery of self-assessment tests. After you've completed and scored the tests, you'll have a realistic evaluation of your own assets and liabilities, including insights into your values, needs, assertiveness level, and interpersonal style in dealing with others. Many skill programs (AACSB, 1984; Whetton and Cameron, 1984; Verderber and Verderber, 1986) stress the importance of such "self-objectivity" as a personal characteristic and as an essential part of an individual's interpersonal skills development.

Chapters 3 through 14 cover the twelve interpersonal skills identified in the table on page 5. You'll find that, for the most part, the chapters follow our ten-step skill development model. The last chapter gives you an opportunity to integrate the skills you have learned. It includes a comprehensive exercise that ties together many of the skills that you'll have already practiced.

Chapter *2*

SELF-AWARENESS: A POINT OF DEPARTURE

In order to improve your interpersonal skills, you need to know yourself. The more you know about yourself, the better you'll be able to understand how you're perceived by others and why they respond to you the way they do. To the degree that this examination indicates things about yourself that you don't like or that are hindering your interpersonal effectiveness, you may want to change certain things about yourself. But nothing in this chapter is meant to suggest that you need to change. Its contents are designed only to help you gain expanded insights into yourself.

We all want to protect, maintain, and enhance our self-concepts and the images others have of us. But, we also have fears, inadequacies, self-doubts, and insecurities that we don't want to reveal to others. Many of these we may not even want to admit to ourselves.

But as reasoning and complex human beings, we balance a need to know with a fear of knowing. None of us is perfect and insights into our strengths and weaknesses can help us gain insights into what areas we want to change and improve in.

Most of us have a tendency to avoid self-awareness. Opening ourselves up to honest self-appraisal may result in seeing things we don't want to see. But the more you know about your unique personal characteristics, the more insight you'll have concerning your basic behavioral tendencies and inclinations for dealing with others. The intention of this chapter is not to psychoanalyze you but to help you become more aware of what you do and its impact on others so that you can choose to try out new behaviors if you wish.

Which of your many personal characteristics are most likely to affect the way you deal with others? Since *values* are the foundation of our behavioral choices, an assessment of your inherent assumptions about people will help you understand why you feel and relate to others as you do. Your interpersonal *needs* determine what you want from your interactions with others and your level of *assertiveness* indicates how you go about getting what you want. Finally, interpersonal *styles* that worked for you in the past influence how you treat others you interact with today. The following questionnaires have been designed to measure each of these characteristics. Take the time now to complete them. When you're finished, you'll find directions for scoring the questionnaires and a discussion of what the results say about you.

SELF-AWARENESS QUESTIONNAIRES

SAQ 1

Interpersonal Values Questionnaire

This questionnaire is designed to help you better understand the assumptions you make about people and human nature. There are ten statements. Assign a weight from 0 to 10 to *each* statement to show the relative strength of your belief in the statements *in each pair*. The points assigned for each pair *must* total 10. Be as honest as you can and resist the natural tendence to respond as you would "like to think things are."

1. It's only human nature for people to do as little work
   as they can get away with.   _____(a)

   When people avoid work, it's usually because their
   work has been deprived of meaning.   _____(b)
                                                                    10

2. If employees are allowed access to any information
   they want, they tend to have better attitudes and to
   behave more responsibly.   _____(c)

   If employees have access to more information
   than they need to do their immediate tasks,   _____(d)
   they will usually misuse it.   10

3. One problem in asking employees for ideas is that
   their perspective is too limited for their suggestions
   to be of much practical value.   _____(e)

   Asking employees for their ideas broadens their
   perspective and results in the development of useful   _____(f)
   suggestions.   10

4. If people don't use much imagination and ingenuity on the job, it's probably because relatively few people have much of either. _____(g)

   Most people are imaginative and creative but may not show it because of limitations imposed by supervision and the job itself. _____(h)
   10

5. People tend to raise their standards if they are account-able for their own behavior and for correcting their own mistakes. _____(i)

   People tend to lower their standards if they are not punished for their misbehavior and mistakes. _____(j)
   10

6. It's better to give people both good and bad news be-cause most employees want the whole story, no matter how painful. _____(k)

   It's better to withold unfavorable news about business because most employees really want to hear only the good news. _____(l)
   10

7. Because a supervisor is entitled to more respect than those below him in the organization, it weakens his prestige to admit that a subordinate was right and he was wrong. _____(m)

   Because people at all levels are entitled to equal respect, a supervisor's prestige is increased when he supports this principle by admitting that a subordinate was right and he was wrong. _____(n)
   10

8. If you give people enough money, they are less likely to be concerned with such intangibles as responsibility and recognition. _____(o)

   If you give people interesting and challenging work, they are less likely to complain about such things as pay and supplemental benefits. _____(p)
   10

9. If people are allowed to set their own goals and stand-ards of performance, they tend to set them higher than the boss would. _____(q)

   If people are allowed to set their own goals and stand-ards of performance, they tend to set them lower than the boss would. _____(r)
   10

10. The more knowledge and freedom a person has regarding his job, the more controls are needed to keep him in line. _____(s)

The more knowledge and freedom a person has regarding his job, the fewer controls are needed to ensure satis-factory job performance. _____(t)

10

Source: Adapted from M. Scott Myers, *Every Employer a Manager,* 2nd. ed. (New York: McGraw-Hill, 1981), as included in David A. Kolb, Irwin M. Rubin, and James M. McIntyre, *Organizational Psychology: An Experiential Approach to Organizational Behavior,* 4th ed. (Englewood Cliffs, N.J.: Prentice Hall, 1984), pp. 519–520. With permission.

SAQ 2

Interpersonal Needs Questionnaire (FIRO-B)

For each statement below, decide which of the following answers best applies to you. Place the number of the answer at the left of the statement.

1. Usually **2.** Often **3.** Sometimes **4.** Occasionally **5.** Rarely **6.** Never

_____ 1. I try to be with people.

_____ 2. I let other people decide what to do.

_____ 3. I join social groups

_____ 4. I try to have close rela-tionships with people.

_____ 5. I tend to join social orga-nizations when I have an opportunity.

_____ 6. I let other people strongly influence my actions.

_____ 7. I try to be included in informal social activities.

_____ 8. I try to have close, per-sonal relationships with people.

_____ 9. I try to include other people in my plans.

_____ 10. I let other people control my actions.

_____ 11. I try to have people around me.

_____ 12. I try to get close and per-sonal with people.

_____ 13. When people are doing things together, I tend to join them.

_____ 14. I am easily led by peo-ple.

_____ 15. I try to avoid being alone.

_____ 16. I try to participate in group activities.

For each of the next group of statements, choose one of the following answers:

1. Most people   **2.** Many people   **3.** Some people
4. A few people   **5.** One or two people   **6.** Nobody

_____17. I try to be friendly to people.

_____18. I let other people decide what to do.

_____19. My personal relationships with people are cool and distant.

_____20. I let other people take charge of things.

_____21. I try to have close relationships with people.

_____22. I let other people strongly influence my actions.

_____23. I try to get close and personal with people.

_____24. I let other people control my actions.

_____25. I act cool and distant with people.

_____26. I am easily led by people.

_____27. I try to have close, personal relationships with people.

For each of the next group of statements, choose one of the following answers:

1. Most people   **2.** Many people   **3.** Some people
4. A few people   **5.** One or two people   **6.** Nobody

_____28. I like people to invite me to things.

_____29. I like people to act close and personal with me.

_____30. I try to influence strongly other people's actions.

_____31. I like people to invite me to join in their activities.

_____32. I like people to act close toward me.

_____33. I try to take charge of things when I am with people.

_____34. I like people to include me in their activities.

_____35. I like people to act cool and distant toward me.

_____36. I try to have other people do things the way I want them done.

_____37. I like people to ask me to participate in their discussions.

_____38. I like people to act friendly toward me.

_____39. I like people to invite me to participate in their activities.

_____40. I like people to act distant toward me.

For each of the next group of statements, choose one of the following answers:

1. Usually **2.** Often **3.** Sometimes **4.** Occasionally **5.** Rarely **6.** Never

_____41. I try to be the dominant person when I am with people.

_____42. I like people to invite me to things.

_____43. I like people to act close toward me.

_____44. I try to have other people do things I want done.

_____45. I like people to invite me to join their activities.

_____46. I like people to act cool and distant toward me.

_____47. I try to influence strongly other people's actions.

_____48. I like people to include me in their activities.

_____49. I like people to act close and personal with me.

_____50. I try to take charge of things when I'm with people.

_____51. I like people to invite me to participate in their activities.

_____52. I like people to act distant toward me.

_____53. I try to have other people do things the way I want them done.

_____54. I take charge of things when I'm with people.

Source: William C. Schutz, _FIRO: A Three Dimensional Theory of Interpersonal Behavior_ (New York: Rinehart & Co., 1958). Permission granted from the author for historical purposes only. _FIRO-B_ has been recently revised and updated. Its replacement, ELEMENT B, is described in Will Schutz, _The Truth Option_ (Tenspeed, 1984) and is available from WSA, Box 259, Muir Beach, Calif. 94965. Items in this instrument are not be reproduced.

SAQ 3

Assertiveness Questionnaire

For each statement below, decide which of the following answers best applies to you. Place the number of the answer to the left of the statement.

1. Never true   **2.** Sometimes true   **3.** Often true   **4.** Always true

_____ 1. I respond with more modesty than I really feel when my work is complimented.

_____ 2. If people are rude, I will be rude right back.

_____ 3. Other people find me interesting

_____ 4. I find it difficult to speak up in a group of strangers.

_____ 5. I don't mind using sarcasm if it helps me make a point.

_____ 6. I ask for a raise when I feel I really deserve it.

_____ 7. If others interrupt me when I am talking, I suffer in silence.

_____ 8. If people criticize my work, I find a way to make them back down.

_____ 9. I can express pride in my accomplishments without being boastful.

_____ 10. People take advantage of me.

_____ 11. I tell people what they want to hear if it helps me get what I want.

_____ 12. I find it easy to ask for help.

_____ 13. I lend things to others even when I don't really want to.

_____ 14. I win arguments by dominating the discussion.

_____ 15. I can express my true feelings to someone I really care for.

_____ 16. When I feel angry with other people, I bottle it up rather than express it.

_____ 17. When I criticize someone else's work, they get mad.

_____ 18. I feel confident in my ability to stand up for my rights.

Source: Douglas T. Hall, Donald D. Bowen, Roy J. Lewicki, and Francine S. Hall, *Experiences in Management and Organizational Behavior*, 2nd ed. (New York: John Wiley & Sons, 1982), p. 101. With permission.

SAQ 4

Interpersonal Style Questionnaire

For each of the following eighteen pairs of statements, distribute three points between the two alternatives A and B, based on how you usually interact with others in everyday situations. Although some pairs of statements may seem equally true for you, assign more points to the alternative that is more representative of your behavior most of the time.

If A is very characteristic of you and B is very uncharacteristic, write 3 next to A and O next to B.

If A is more characteristic of you than B, but you engage in B sometimes, write 2 next to A and 1 next to B.

If B is more characteristic of you than A, but you engage in A sometimes, write 2 next to B and 1 next to A.

If B is very characteristic of you and A is very uncharacteristic, write 3 next to B and O next to A.

Be sure that the numbers that you assign to each pair of statements add up to 3.

1A _____ I am ususally open to getting to know people personally and establishing relationships with them.

1B _____ I am usually not open to getting to know people personally and establishing relationships with them.

2A _____ I usually react slowly and deliberately.

2B _____ I usually react quickly and spontaneously.

3A _____ I am usually guarded about other people's use of my time.

3B _____ I am usually open to other people's use of my time.

4A _____ I usually introduce myself at social gatherings.

4B _____ I usually wait for others to introduce themselves to me at social gatherings.

5A _____ I usually focus my conversations on the interests of the parties involved, even if this means that the conversations stray from the business or subject at hand.

5B _____ I usually focus my conversations on the tasks, issues, business, or subject on hand.

6A _____ I am usually not assertive, and I can be patient with a slow pace.

6B _____ I am usually assertive, and at times I can be impatient with a slow pace.

7A _____ I usually make decisions based on facts or evidence.

7B _____ I usually make decisions based on feelings, experiences, or relationships.

8A _____ I usually contribute frequently to group conversations.

8B _____ I usually contribute infrequently to group conversations.

9A _____ I usually prefer to work with and through others, providing support when possible.

9B _____ I usually prefer to work independently or dictate the conditions in terms of how others are involved.

10A _____ I usually ask questions or speak more tentatively and indirectly.

10B _____ I usually make emphatic statements or directly express opinions.

11A _____ I usually focus primarily on the idea, concept, or results.

11B _____ I usually focus primarily on the person, interaction, and feelings.

12A _____ I usually use gestures, facial expressions, and voice intonation to emphasize points.

12B _____ I usually do not use gestures, facial expressions, and voice intonation to emphasize points.

13A _____ I usually accept others' points of view (ideas, feelings, and concerns).

13B _____ I usually do not accept others' point of view (ideas, feelings, and concerns).

14A _____ I usually respond to risk and change in a cautious or predictable manner.

14B _____ I usually repond to risk and change in a dynamic or unpredictable manner.

15A _____ I usually prefer to keep my personal feelings and thoughts to myself, sharing only when I wish to do so.

15B _____ I usually find it natural and easy to share and discuss my feelings with others.

16A _____ I usually seek out new or different experiences and situations.

16B _____ I usually choose known or similar situations and relation-ships.

17A _____ I usually am responsive to others' agendas, interests, and concerns.

17B _____ I usually am directed toward my own agendas, interests, and concerns.

18A _____ I usually respond to conflict slowly and indirectly.

18B _____ I usually respond to conflict quickly and directly.

Source: Tony Alessandra and Michael J. O'Connor, *Behavioral Profiles: Self-Assessment* (San Diego: Pfeiffer & Company, 1994). Permission granted from the author.

SCORING THE QUESTIONNAIRES

Scoring SAQ 1

SAQ 1 taps your basic assumptions about the nature of people at work. It's based on Douglas McGregor's (1960) Theory X and Theory Y. To get your scores, add up the points you assigned to the following:

Your Theory X score is the sum of

(a),(d),(e),(g),(j),(1),(m),(o),(r), and (s).

Your Theory Y score is the sum of

(b),(c),(f),(h),(i),(k),(n),(p),(q), and (t).

Put your scores in the appropriate boxes:

Theory X = [ ]   Theory Y = [ ]

Scoring SAQ 2

SAQ 2 is known as the Fundamental Interpersonal Relations Orientation-Behavior [FIRO-B] questionnaire (Schutz, 1958). The theory underlying this questionnaire is that there are three interpersonal needs that vary among individuals. The first is *inclusion*—the need to establish and maintain a relationship with other people. Inclusion concerns how you balance the desire to be part of a group against the desire for solitude. The second is *control*—the need to maintain a satisfactory balance of power and influence in relationships. Control concerns the trade-offs we have to make between the desire for structure and authority versus the desire for freedom. Finally, there is the need for *affection*—the need to form close and personal relationships with others. Affection concerns how you balance the desire for warmth and commitment against the desire to maintain distance and independence.

Each of these three needs has two subdimensions—the *expressed* desire to give the need and the *wanted* desire to receive the need from others. So, for instance, the questionnaire measures both your need to include others and your need to be included by others. The result is that the SAQ 2 generates six separate scores. To calculate your scores, refer to the table below. Note that there are six columns. Each column refers to one of the boxes in the 2 x 3 matrix on page 22. The term Item in the column refers to question numbers on the SAQ 2 questionnaire; Key refers to answers on each of those items. If you answered an item using any of the alternatives in the corresponding key column, circle the item number below. When you have checked all of the items for a single column, count up the number of circled items and place that number in the corresponding box in the matrix. These numbers will tell you the strength of your interpersonal need in each of the six areas. Your score in each box will range between 0 and 9. Your total interpersonal needs score is calculated by summing the numbers in all six boxes. That overall summation score should be placed in the small box next to the matrix at the top of page 22.

Expressed Inclusion		Wanted Inclusion		Expressed Control		Wanted Control		Expressed Affection		Wanted Affection	
ITEM	KEY	ITEM	KEY	ITEM	KEY	ITEM	KEY	ITEM	KEY	ITEM	KEY
1	1-2-3	28	1-2	30	1-2-3	2	1-2-3-4	4	1-2	29	1-2
3	1-2-3-4	31	1-2	33	1-2-3	6	1-2-3-4	8	1-2	32	1-2
5	1-2-3-4	34	1-2	36	1-2	10	1-2-3	12	1	35	5-6
7	1-2-3	37	1	41	1-2-3-4	14	1-2-3	17	1-2	38	1-2
9	1-2	39	1	44	1-2-3	18	1-2-3	19	4-5-6	40	5-6
11	1-2	42	1-2	47	1-2-3	20	1-2-3	21	1-2	43	1
13	1-2	45	1-2	50	1-2	22	1-2-3-4	23	1-2	46	5-6
15	1	48	1-2	53	1-2	24	1-2-3	25	4-5-6	49	1-2
16	1	51	1-2	54	1-2	26	1-2-3	27	1-2	52	5-6

	Inclusion	Control	Affection
Expressed behavior toward others			
Wanted behavior from others			

Scoring SAQ 3

SAQ 3 evaluates your basic interpersonal style in terms of the emphasis you place on passive, aggressive, and assertive behaviors (Bowen, 1982). *Passive behavior* is inhibited and submissive. Individuals who score high in passive behavior seek to avoid conflicts and tend to sublimate their own needs and feelings in order to satisfy other people. *Aggressive behavior* is the opposite of passiveness; it is domineering, pushy, self-centered, and without regard for the feelings or rights of others. Bowen (1982) argues that both passive and aggressive behaviors hinder effective interpersonal relations because neither facilitates openness and receptiveness. The preferred style, according to Bowen, is *assertive behavior*. People who score high in assertiveness express their ideas and feelings openly, stand up for their rights, and do so in a way that makes it easier for others to do the same. The assertive person, therefore, is straightforward, yet sensitive to the needs of others. Assertiveness improves interpersonal communication because the more assertive you are, the more assertive you encourage others to be. So assertiveness facilitates more effective interactions because it lessens defensiveness, domination, putting down other people, "wishy-washiness," and similar dysfunctional behaviors.

To calculate your assertiveness style scores, refer back to the responses you gave on the SAQ 3. Sum up your answers to items 1, 4, 7, 10, 13, and 16. That is your Passive score. Put that number in the appropriate box below. Your Aggressive score is the total of your answers to items 2, 5, 8, 11, 14, and 17. Your Assertive score is the total of your answers to items 3, 6, 9, 12, 15, and 18.

Put these scores in the appropriate box below. Your score in each box will range between 6 and 24.

Passive = ☐   Aggressive = ☐   Assertive = ☐

Scoring SAQ 4

We develop habitual ways of relating to others based on what behaviors were reinforced when we were growing up. A behavioral habit is something we do when we interact with others without even thinking about it. Our predominant behavioral habits can be understood by looking at how open or self-contained we are, and how direct or indirect we are.

To determine your degrees of openness and directness, transfer your scores from SAQ 4 to the table below. Then, total each column to get your O, S, D, and I scores.

INTERPERSONAL STYLE SCORING SCHEET

O			
S			
D			
I			
1A			
1B			
2B			
2A			
3B			
3A			

Compare the O and S scores. Which is higher? Write the higher score in the blank below and circle the corresponding letter:

_____ O S

Compare the D and I scores. Which is higher? Write the higher score in the blank below and circle the corresponding letter:

_____ D I

In the first dimension, O stands for Open and S stands for Self-Contained. An Open person is relationship oriented, supportive of other's needs, and shares feelings readily. A Self-Contained person is task oriented, aloof, and not prone to share feelings. The letter you circled ("O" or "S") indicates where on this continuum your main tendencies lie.

On the second continuum, D stands for direct and I stands for indirect. Direct people are extroverted and express their thoughts and feelings quite forcefully. Indirect people hold back and appear more introverted. On SAQ 3, Direct people can be thought of as ranging from highly assertive to aggressive, while Indirect people go the other way from moderately assertive to passive. The letter you circled, "D" or "I," indicates where on this continuum your tendencies lie.

Four different behavioral styles, or habits of relating to others, can be discerned by how direct and open you are. To learn more about your behavioral style, plot your scores on the graph on page 19 which also provides a summary of the characteristics of each style. If your scores are highest on open and direct, you are an assertive and relationship-oriented Socializer. If your scores are highest on self-contained and direct, your are an assertive and task-oriented Director. If your scores are highest on indirect and self-contained, you are a task-oriented and low assertive Thinker. If your scores are highest on indirect and open, you are a low assertive and relationship-oriented Relater.

INTERPRETING YOUR SELF-AWARENESS PROFILE

You now have calculated your scores for interpersonal values, needs, style, and habits. Together they make up your Self-Awareness Profile. In this section, we'll analyze your scores and attempt to interpret what they say about you.

Interpreting Your Values Score (SAQ 1)

McGregor (1960) proposed that a manager's view of the nature of human beings tends to fall into one of two sets. In the first, which is called Theory X, managers assume

1. Employees inherently dislike work and, whenever possible, will attempt to avoid it.
2. Since employees dislike work, they must be coerced, controlled, or threatened with punishment to achieve goals.
3. Employees will shirk responsibility and seek formal direction whenever possible.
4. Most workers place security above all other factors associated with work and will display little ambition.

In contrast to these negative views about the nature of human beings, McGregor listed four other assumptions that constituted what he called Theory Y:

1. Employees can view work as natural as rest or play.
2. People will exercise self-direction and self-control if they are committed to the objectives.
3. The average person can learn to accept, and even seek, responsibility.
4. The ability to make innovative decisions is widely dispersed throughout the population and is not necessarily the sole province of those in management positions.

Do you see people as basically lazy and irresponsible or as industrious and trustworthy? Look at your Theory X and Y scores. In which box did you score highest? Now, subtract your low score from your highest. The larger this number is, the more strongly you hold to the assumptions of the higher category. Conversely, the lower the number, the more flexibility you show. That is, the closer each of your Theory X and Y scores is to 50, the less intensity you have about the fixed nature of human behavior. You regard some people as hard-working and trustworthy but see *others* as irresponsible and needing direction.

If you scored high only on Theory X assumptions (above 65 points), you don't have much confidence in others—an attitude that is likely to show itself in behaviors like unwillingness to delegate, authoritarian leadership, and excessive concern with closely monitoring and controlling the people who work for you. A similar high score on Theory Y assumptions indicates a great deal of confidence in other people and may lead, at the extreme, to ineffective managerial performance. How? Excessive delegation of authority, inadequate coordination of subordinates' activities, and unawareness of problems that need attention are some of the possible dysfunctional outcomes of an unrealistic confidence in one's employees.

Interpreting Your Needs Score (SAQ 2)

Look back to page 22 for your total interpersonal needs score. It's in the box to the right of the 2 x 3 matrix. Your score will fall somewhere between 0 and 54. According to national studies, the average person scores 29.3, and 50 percent of adult respondents' scores fell between 20 and 38 (Whetton and Cameron, 1993, pp. 59–60). A high score indicates that you have strong interpersonal needs. You have a strong desire to interact with others and are probably outgoing and gregarious. A low score means you don't mind being alone a lot of the time and are more reserved around others.

What is the significance of your score? Business school students have been found to have different scores depending upon their majors (Hill, 1974). Marketing and human resource majors had above average scores while accounting and systems analysis students had lower than average scores. These findings indicate that students with higher interpersonal needs tend to select people-oriented careers and vice versa. The findings do not necessarily predict your success as a manager, however, because that depends to a large degree on the types of work and people you are supervising.

There is no "right" score. The value of this information is that it lets you know your own interpersonal tendencies and inclinations. Your scores are also good indicators of how others are likely to see you. You can use this information to hone your interpersonal skills.

One way to know yourself better is to examine your scores on each need category as they relate to each other. Your highest individual scores, for example, indicate which interpersonal needs are least satisfied and probably dominate your relationships with others. To fine-tune a little, the range of scores for each need is 0–9, so 4.5 is the median, which rougly equates to the average of national scores, although they do vary for each category. You might examine if you are significantly higher or lower than average on the six different interpersonal need scores. If so, how are these differences probably perceived by others and do you behave in ways you want to change.

Another valuable use of your scores is to compare them to the scores of persons with whom you relate. Are you compatible, that is, one person wants what the other expresses, or incompatible, that is, one person expresses something another does not want? Other problems can arise when both parties want to express the same thing, for example, control, or neither wants to express something that is necessary, for example, control. Finally, what do you think happens when two people emphasize the same need, for example, affection, as opposed to situations where they emphasize different needs, for example, control, versus affection?

As you have probably surmised, incompatible interpersonal needs may be responsible for a host of problems from seeing interactions from different points of view, to conflict and lack of need satisfaction. On the other hand, research has confirmed that compatible individuals usually like each other more and work better together (DiMarco, 1974; Liddell & Slocum, 1976). By being aware of your interpersonal needs and those of others, you can increase your interpersonal effectiveness by redefining issues, letting others have opportunities to satisfy their needs, and adapting your own behaviors to be more consistant with the needs of others.

Interpreting Your Style Score (SAQ 3)

SAQ 3 assessed your assertiveness level. You may wonder if you are too passive or too agressive. Or are you assertive enough in your interpersonal relations?

A high Passive score indicates an unwillingness to confront problems. You're likely to be perceived as a "wimp" who can be bullied by others. Your desire to please other people may also result in your being viewed as inconsistent. In the effort to please everyone, the passive person may please no one. But a high Aggressiveness score causes equally troublesome problems. Here you're likely to be seen as "the little dictator." Your desire to take command and dominate others is often interpreted as pushy. Both excessive passiveness and excessive aggressiveness negatively affect interpersonal relations.

The higher your Assertiveness score, the more open and self-expressive you are. You confront issues in a straightforward manner. You say what you mean, but you're not rude or thoughtless. You're sensitive to the needs of others and receptive to what they have to say. Generally speaking, assertiveness is a desirable quality in that it tends to facilitate effective interpersonal relations.

If, for example, you score low on assertiveness and high on aggressiveness, recognize how you are likely to be perceived by others. When you sit down to set goals jointly with an employee, you'll need to work extra hard to sublimate your desire to control the goal-setting session and impose your standards on the employee. The first step toward being open and effective in your interpersonal relations is to know your strengths and limitations.

Interpreting Your Interpersonal Style Score (SAQ 4)

As you can see on the following "Summary of Behaviorial Characteristics," each of the four different interpersonal style types have different ways of seeing the world and communicating with other people. Now that you understand the basic differences and are aware of your own habits, you can see how you come across to others. You can also appreciate how each of the other types prefers to communicate. Consequently, you can adapt your own style to match the expectations of others to speak *their* style language. Following are some guidelines to make your style more effective when interacting with others with different interaction habits.

If you are a Socializer, you can usually be more effective in dealing with others if you can control your time and emotions better; develop more of an objective mindset; spend more time checking, verifying, specifying, and organizing the things you want to do; concentrate on the task; and take a more logical approach to projects and issues. If you are another style and want to get along better with a Socializer, you can allow their discussion to occasionally go off on tangents; be interested in their ideas and dreams; avoid conflict and arguments; compliment their appearance and charisma; allow them to "get things off their chests."

If you are a Director, you can usually be more effective in dealing with others if you practice active listening; project a more relaxed image; develop patience, humility, and sensitivity. You should show a concern for others, use more caution, verbalize the reasons for your conclusions, become more of a team player. If you are another style and want to get along better with a Director better, you should concentrate on being businesslike and achieving the desired results as efficiently as possible; be precise, efficient, and well organized; provide executive summaries of problems and ideas; argue facts, not feelings, when disagreements occur.

If you are a Thinker, you can usually be more effective in dealing with others if you show concern and appreciation of others more openly, occasionally try shortcuts and time-savers, and try to adjust more readily to change and disorganization. Others will also appreciate you more if you are more timely in decision making, initiate more new projects, compromise occasionally with those with opposing points of view, and use policies more as guidelines than as rigid decrees. If you are another style and want to get along better with a Thinker, be thorough and well prepared, provide solid, tangible, factual evidence, support their organized thoughtful approach, allow time for deliberation and analysis, and compliment the accuracy and quality of everything they do.

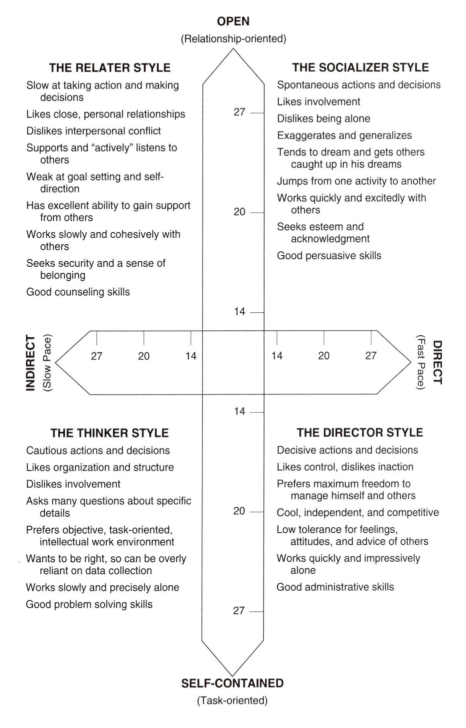

OPEN
(Relationship-oriented)

THE RELATER STYLE

Slow at taking action and making decisions

Likes close, personal relationships

Dislikes interpersonal conflict

Supports and "actively" listens to others

Weak at goal setting and self-direction

Has excellent ability to gain support from others

Works slowly and cohesively with others

Seeks security and a sense of belonging

Good counseling skills

THE SOCIALIZER STYLE

Spontaneous actions and decisions

Likes involvement

Dislikes being alone

Exaggerates and generalizes

Tends to dream and gets others caught up in his dreams

Jumps from one activity to another

Works quickly and excitedly with others

Seeks esteem and acknowledgment

Good persuasive skills

INDIRECT (Slow Pace)   **DIRECT** (Fast Pace)

27   20   14   14   20   27

THE THINKER STYLE

Cautious actions and decisions

Likes organization and structure

Dislikes involvement

Asks many questions about specific details

Prefers objective, task-oriented, intellectual work environment

Wants to be right, so can be overly reliant on data collection

Works slowly and precisely alone

Good problem solving skills

THE DIRECTOR STYLE

Decisive actions and decisions

Likes control, dislikes inaction

Prefers maximum freedom to manage himself and others

Cool, independent, and competitive

Low tolerance for feelings, attitudes, and advice of others

Works quickly and impressively alone

Good administrative skills

SELF-CONTAINED
(Task-oriented)

SUMMARY OF BEHAVIORAL CHARACTERISTICS

If you are a Relater, you can usually be more effective in dealing with others if you attend more to completing tasks on time, delegate more to others, and show your commitment to important values by saying no occasionally. If you are another style and want to get along better with a Relater, be warm and sincere with them, actively listen to their concerns and feelings, and compliment them on their teamwork and ability to get along with others.

GROUP EXERCISE

Form small groups with three or four class members you do not know well. The following activities take approximately forty minutes to complete and should be conducted within these groups.

1. Each group member spends three to five minutes introducing him- or herself. Highlight your background, career goals, and most important accomplishments to date, and briefly describe what you believe are your interpersonal strengths and limitations.

2. After all group members have completed their introductions, discuss this statement: "First impressions provide me with a lot of insight into people."

3. Group members share their scores on each of the four assessment profiles and discuss how closely they think the profiles align with their previous self-images.

4. Group members give each other feedback about how closely they see assessment profile scores aligning with each persons behaviors exhibited in steps 1 and 2 of this exercise.

We recommend doing steps 3 and 4 in round robin fashion. One person volunteers to be the focus and shares his or her scores and feelings about their accuracy (step 3). Then group members provide their feedback to the focus as described in step 4. After the focus clarifies this feedback, another person volunteers to be the focus and the process continues until all group members have shared and received feedback.

Summary Sheet

Summarize your self-assessment profile in the spaces provided on this page. Then tear out the page and turn it in to your instructor. Do not put your name on the sheet. Your instructor will aggregate your class's scores and summarize your interpersonal profiles.

From page 20, Values Scores:

Theory X _____

Theory Y _____

From page 22, Interpersonal Needs Scores:

Total interpersonal needs _____

Check your highest interpersonal need:

Need	Expressed	Wanted
Inclusion	_____	_____
Control	_____	_____
Affection	_____	_____

From page 22, Assertiveness Level:

Passive _____

Aggressive _____

Assertive _____

From page 29, Behavior Style:

Dominant style _____

Chapter *3*

LISTENING

SELF-ASSESSMENT EXERCISE

For each of the following questions, select the answer that best describes your listening habits.

	Usually	Sometimes	Seldom
1. I maintain eye contact with the speaker.	☐	☐	☐
2. I determine whether or not a speaker's ideas are worthwhile solely by his or her appearance and delivery.	☐	☐	☐
3. I try to understand the message from the speaker's point of view.	☐	☐	☐
4. I listen for specific facts rather than for "the big picture."	☐	☐	☐
5. I listen for both factual content and the emotion behind the literal words.	☐	☐	☐
6. I ask questions for clarification and understanding.	☐	☐	☐

	Usually	Sometimes	Seldom
7. I withhold judgment of what the speaker is saying until he or she is finished.	☐	☐	☐
8. I make a conscious effort to evaluate the logic and consistency of what is being said.	☐	☐	☐
9. While listening, I think about what I'm going to say as soon as I have my chance.	☐	☐	☐
10. I try to have the last word.	☐	☐	☐

Scoring Key and Interpretation

For questions 1, 3, 5, 6, 7, and 8, give yourself 3 points for "Usually," 2 points for "Sometimes," and 1 point for "Seldom."

For questions 2, 4, 9, and 10, give yourself 3 points for "Seldom," 2 points for "Sometimes," and 1 point for "Usually."

Sum up your total points. A score of 27 or higher means you're a good listener. A score of 22 to 26 suggests you have some listening deficiencies. A score below 22 indicates that you have developed a number of bad listening habits.

SKILL CONCEPTS

Many communication problems develop because listening skills are ignored, forgotten, or just taken for granted (Kharbanda & Stallworthy, 1991). We confuse hearing with listening. Hearing is merely picking up sound vibrations. Listening is making sense out of what we hear. That is, listening requires paying attention, interpreting, and remembering sound stimuli. As we'll show in this chapter, listening is a skill that can be learned. While it's something we've done all our lives, paradoxically, few of us do it well.

Why begin our review of interpersonal skills with listening? Is there some logic for considering it first? The answer is yes.

If we want to consider interpersonal skills in order of importance, we could make a good case that listening tops the list. For instance, a survey of personnel directors in three hundred organizations found that effective listening was ranked highest among the skills defined as most important in becoming a manager (Crocker, 1978). Listening is also a vital ingredient for learning the remaining skills. Throughout this book, you'll be asked to participate in and observe interpersonal exercises. You'll need effective listening skills to do this. So another reason to begin with listening is that if you aren't an effective listener, you're going to have consistent trouble developing all the other interpersonal skills.

Active versus Passive Listening

Effective listening is active rather than passive. In passive listening, you are much like a tape recorder, but not nearly as accurate. You try to absorb as much of the information presented as possible. Even if the speaker provides you with a clear message and makes his or her delivery interesting enough to keep your attention, however, your comprehension of a presentation two or more days previously will always be incomplete and usually inaccurate (Goldhaber, 1980).

Active listening requires you to empathize with the speaker so that you can understand the communication from his or her point of view. As you'll see, active listening is hard work. You have to concentrate and you have to want to fully understand what a speaker is saying. Students who use active listening techniques for an entire fifty-minute lecture are almost as tired as their instructor when that lecture is over because they have put as about as much energy into listening as the instructor put into speaking.

There are four essential requirements for active listening. You need to listen with (1) intensity, (2) empathy, (3) acceptance, and (4) a willingness to take responsibility for completeness (Rogers & Farson, 1976).

Our brain is capable of handling a speaking rate of about four times the speed of the average speaker (Nichols and Stevens, 1957). That leaves a lot of time for idle mind wandering while listening. The active listener concentrates intensely on what the speaker is saying and tunes out the thousands of miscellaneous thoughts (about work deadlines, money, sex, parties, friends, getting the car fixed, and the like) that create distractions. What do active listeners do with their idle brain time? Summarize and integrate what has been said! They put each new bit of information into the context of what has preceded it.

Empathy requires you to put yourself in the speaker's shoes. You try to understand what the *speaker* wants to communicate rather than what *you* want to understand. Notice that empathy demands both knowledge of the speaker and flexibility on your part. You need to suspend your own thoughts and feelings and adjust what you see and feel to your speaker's world. In that way, you increase the likelihood that you will interpret the message being spoken in the way the speaker intended.

An active listener demonstrates acceptance. He or she listens objectively without judging content. This is no easy task. It is natural to be distracted by the content of what a speaker says, especially when we disagree with it. When we hear something we disagree with, we begin formulating our mental arguments to counter what is being said. Of course, in doing so, we miss the rest of the message. The challenge for the active listener is to absorb what is being said and to withhold judgment on content until the speaker is finished.

The final ingredient of active listening is taking responsibility for completeness. That is, the listener does whatever is necessary to get the full intended meaning from the speaker's communication. Two widely used active listening techniques to achieve this end are listening for feelings as well as for content and asking questions to ensure understanding.

Active listeners listen with their ears, their eyes, and their mind. They take in the objective information by listening to the literal words that are spoken. But every spoken message contains more than words. Speakers also communicate subjective information—their feelings and emotions—through other vocal sounds and nonverbal signals. These include verbal intonations like loudness, emphasis, hesitations, voice inflections, and the rate of speaking. Nonverbal signals encompass the speaker's eye movements, facial expressions, body posture, and hand gestures. By listening for feelings and emotions, as well as for literal words, you can grasp the total meaning behind the speaker's message. Yet, no matter how good you become at listening for total meaning, there still remains the potential for misunderstanding. That's why the active listener verifies completeness by asking questions. The use of questions can uncover distortions and clarify misunderstandings. Again, notice that questioning is consistent with taking a positive and responsible role in the communication process. The success of a verbal communication does not rest solely with the speaker. By seeking clarification, active listeners ensure that they are receiving and understanding the message as the speaker intended.

What We Know about Effective Listening

The active listening model forms the foundation for making you an effective listener. In this section, we'll summarize fourteen specific characteristics or techniques used by effective listeners. Some of these characteristics are explicit behaviors that can be directly observed. For instance, asking questions is a directly observable behavior. Others, such as listening without judging content, are cognitive processes that can only be evaluated indirectly. As we review these fourteen characteristics, ask yourself whether each represents an observable behavior. For those that don't, try to determine what you might look for that could tell you indirectly if someone is using the technique.

1. Be motivated. If a listener is unwilling to exert the effort to hear and understand, no amount of additional advice is likely to improve listening effectiveness. As we previously noted, active listening is hard work. So your first step toward becoming an effective listener is a willingness to make the effort.

2. Make eye contact. How do you feel when somebody doesn't look at you when you're speaking? If you're like most people, you're likely to interpret this as aloofness or disinterest. It's ironic that while "you listen with your ears, people judge whether you are listening by looking at your eyes" (Hunsaker and Alessandra, 1986, p. 123). Making eye contact with the speaker focuses your attention, reduces the likelihood that you will become distracted, and encourages the speaker.

3. Show interest. The effective listener shows interest in what is being said (Murphy, 1987). How? Through nonverbal signals. Affirmative head nods and appropriate facial expressions, when added to good eye contact, convey to the speaker that you're listening.

4. Avoid distracting actions. The other side of showing interest is avoiding actions that suggest your mind is somewhere else. When listening, *don't* look at your watch, shuffle papers, play with your pencil, or engage in similar distractions. They make the speaker feel you're bored or uninterested. Maybe more importantly, they indicate that you *aren't* fully attentive and may be missing part of the message that the speaker wants to convey.

5. Empathy. We said the active listener tries to understand what the speaker sees and feels by putting him- or herself in the speaker's shoes. Don't project your own needs and intentions onto the speaker. When you do so, you're likely to hear what you want to hear. So ask yourself: Who is this speaker and where is he coming from? What are his attitudes, interests, experiences, needs, and expectations?

6. Take in the whole picture. The effective listener interprets feelings and emotions as well as factual content (Murphy, 1987). If you listen to words alone and ignore other vocal cues and nonverbal signals, you will miss a wealth of subtle messages. To test this point, read the script of a play. Then go and see that play live in a theater. The characters and the message take on a much richer meaning when you see the play acted on stage.

7. Ask questions. The critical listener analyzes what he or she hears and asks questions. This behavior provides clarification, ensures understanding, and assures the speaker that you're listening.

8. Paraphrase. Paraphrasing means restating what the speaker has said in your *own words*. The effective listener uses phrases such as: "What I hear you saying is . . . " or "Do you mean . . .?" Why rephrase what's already been said? Two reasons! First, it's an excellent control device to check on whether you're listening carefully. You can't paraphrase accurately if your mind is wandering or if you're thinking about what you're going to say next. Second, it's a control for accuracy. By rephrasing what the speaker has said in your own words and feeding it back to the speaker, you verify the accuracy of your understanding.

9. Don't interrupt. Let the speaker complete his or her thought before you try to respond. Don't try to second-guess where the speaker's thoughts are going. When the speaker is finished, you'll know it!

10. Integrate what's being said. Use your spare time while listening to better understand the speaker's ideas. Instead of treating each new piece of information as an independent entity, put the pieces together. Treat each part of the message as if it were an additional piece of a puzzle. By the time the speaker has finished, instead of having ten unrelated bits of information, you'll have ten integrated pieces of information that form a comprehensive message. If you don't, you should ask the questions that will fill in the blanks.

11. Don't overtalk. Most of us would rather speak our own ideas than listen to what someone else says. Too many of us listen only because it's the price we have to pay to get people to let us talk. While talking may be more fun and silence may be uncomfortable, you can't talk and listen at the same time. The good listener recognizes this fact and doesn't overtalk (Murphy, 1987).

12. Confront your biases. Evaluate the source of the message. Notice things such as the speaker's credibility, appearance, vocabulary, and speech mannerisms. But don't let them distract you. For instance, all of us have "red flag" words that prick our attention or cause us to draw premature conclusions. Examples might include terms like *racist, gay, chauvinist, conservative, liberal, feminist, environmentalist,* and *Religious Right.* Use information about the speaker to improve your understanding of what he or she has to say, but don't let your biases distort the message.

13. Make smooth transitions between speaker and listener. As a student sitting in a lecture hall, you find it relatively easy to get into an effective listening frame of mind. Why? Because communication is essentially one-way: The teacher talks and you listen. But the teacher-student dyad is atypical. In most work situations, you're continually shifting back and forth between the roles of speaker and listener. The effective listener, therefore, makes transitions smoothly from speaker to listener and back to speaker. From a listening perspective, this means concentrating on what a speaker has to say and practicing, not thinking about what you're going to say as soon as you get your chance.

14. Be natural. An effective listener develops a style that is natural and authentic. Don't try to become a compulsive good listener. If you exaggerate eye contact, facial expressions, the asking of questions, showing of interest, and the like, you'll lose credibility. A good listener is not a manipulator. Use moderation and develop listening techniques that are effective and fit well with your interpersonal style.

CONCEPT QUIZ

Take the following ten-question, true-false quiz. The answers are at the end of the quiz. If you read the previous material carefully, you should get them all correct. If you miss any, go back and find out why you got them wrong.

Circle the right answer:

True or False   1. Active listening is hard work.

True or False   2. One of the essential requirements for being an active listener is to anticipate what the speaker is going to say.

True or False   3. Empathy means reading nonverbal as well as verbal messages.

True or False   4. The first step toward effective listening is the motivation to make the effort.

True or False   5. The effective listener maintains constant penetrating eye contact with the speaker.

True or False   6. The efficient listener listens to what is being said and, at the same time, develops his or her response.

True or False   7. If you can't paraphrase a speaker's message, something was missing from the speaker's explanation.

True or False   8. You should let a speaker complete his or her thought before you try to respond.

True or False   9. The effective listener uses idle brain time to get the "big picture" from the speaker's message.

True or False   10. A speaker's looks or accent can enhance the content and your understanding of his or her message.

Answers: (1) True; (2) False; (3) False; (4) True; (5) False; (6) False; (7) False; (8) True; (9) True; (10) True.

BEHAVIORAL CHECKLIST

The following represents the most important behaviors related to effective listening. These are the specific behaviors you will want to look for when evaluating your listening skills and those of others.

THE EFFECTIVE LISTENER

- Makes eye contact

- Exhibits affirmative head nods and appropriate facial expressions

- Avoids distracting actions or gestures that suggest boredom

- Asks questions

- Paraphrases using his or her own words

- Avoids interrupting the speaker

- Doesn't overtalk

- Makes smooth transitions between the role of speaker and that of listener

MODELING EXERCISE

Modeling exercises are done in front of the class. They give you an opportunity to observe participants performing specific skill behaviors and to learn from that observation. After a modeling exercise has been completed, the entire class rates and discusses the participants' performance using the behavioral checklist for that skill.

There are two responsibilities for you as a participant in a role-play. First, read *only* the background information on the exercise and *your* role. Reading your counterpart's role will lessen the effectiveness of the exercise. Of course, if you're the observer in an exercise, you should read everything pertaining to the role-play. Second, get into the character. Role-playing is acting. The role description establishes your character. Follow the guidelines it establishes. Don't change or omit the facts you're given.

Actors: LEE WILSON—College recruiter for Procter & Gamble. M.B.A. from a prestigious business school. Two years experience. CHRIS BATES—Job candidate. Graduating M.B.A.

Situation: Preliminary interview (in a college placement center) for a marketing management trainee position with Procter & Gamble. A brief job description and Chris' résumé follow.

LEE WILSON's role: You will be interviewing approximately 150 students over the next six weeks to fill four trainee positions. You're looking for candidates who are bright, articulate, ambitious, and have management potential. The P&G training program is two years in length. Trainees will be sales representatives calling on retail stores and will spend the first fifteen weeks taking formal P&G classes at the head office. The compensation to start is $32,000 a year plus a car. You are to improvise other information as needed.

Questions you might ask include: Where do you expect to be in five years? What's important to you in a job? What courses did you like best in your M.B.A. program? Like least? What makes you think you would do well in this job?

Abbreviated Job Description

Title: Marketing Management Trainee—Consumer Products Group
Reports to: District Marketing Manager
Duties and Responsibilities: Completes formal training program at headquarters in Cincinnati. Thereupon;

- Calls on retail stores
- Introduces new products to store personnel
- Distributes sales promotion materials
- Stocks and arranges shelves in stores
- Takes sales orders
- Follows up on complaints or problems
- Completes all necessary sales reports

Abbreviated Résumé

Name: Chris Bates

Age: 24

Education: B.A. in Economics; G.P.A. = 3.8 (out of 4.0); M.B.A., with specialization in marketing; G.P.A. = 3.95.

Work Experience: Worked summers, during undergraduate days, at The Gap and Walden Books.

Honors: Top graduating M.B.A. student in marketing; Graduate assistantship; Dean's Honor Roll.

Extracurricular activities: Intercollegiate tennis team (undergraduate); Vice President, Graduate Business Students Association; College Marketing Club.

CHRIS BATES's role: Review your résumé. You are a top student whose previous work experience has been limited to selling in retail stores in the summer months during your undergraduate collegiate days. This is your first interview with P&G, but you're very interested in their training program. Fill in any voids in information as you see fit.

Time: Not to exceed fifteen minutes.

Modeling Exercise Observations Two members of the class will be selected to play the roles of Lee and Chris. On completion of the exercise, class members are to rate each player's listening behaviors. Use the following scale to rate each player between 1 and 5. Write in concrete examples in the space for comments to use in explaining your feedback.

	1	2	3	4	5
	Unsatisfactory	Weak	Adequate	Good	Outstanding

LISTENING BEHAVIORS	LEE RATING	COMMENTS	CHRIS RATING	COMMENTS
Makes eye contact	_____		_____	
Gives affirmative responses	_____		_____	
Avoids distractions	_____		_____	
Asks questions	_____		_____	
Paraphrases	_____		_____	
Avoids interrupting	_____		_____	
Doesn't overtalk	_____		_____	
Makes smooth transitions	_____		_____	

GROUP EXERCISES

The class will be divided into groups of three. (Some groups of four may be necessary to ensure that everyone is assigned.) Each of the following exercises will have two participants. The remaining group member(s) will be an observer. The roles will change in each exercise so that every group member gets to be both a participant and an observer. When you're playing a specific actor, do not read the other actor's role!

Group Exercise 1

Actors: PAT DRIVER (Actor A) is the Manufacturing Manager in a company with a hundred employees. SANDY BABSON (Actor B) is a supervisor and one of ten people who work for Pat.

Situation: In Pat's office. Pat has scheduled a meeting with Sandy to discuss Pat's decision on filling the position of Assistant to the Manufacturing Manager.

PAT DRIVER's role: You've decided to appoint Dave to the Assistant's position. Both Dave and Sandy have bachelor's degrees in engineering and have been with the company for four years. Both have approximately two and a half years' experience as production supervisors. Dave and Sandy's job performance evaluations have been consistently excellent. You've chosen Dave over Sandy essentially because he has completed about one-third of the requirements for an M.B.A. by taking courses at night. You know Sandy has wanted this promotion badly, both for the added responsibility and the extra money. Sandy, a single parent with two small children whose spouse died in a car accident last year, could probably really use the additional pay. You expect Sandy to be quite disappointed with your decision.

SANDY BABSON's role: You have a B.S. degree in industrial engineering. You've been with this company for four years, spending more than half that time as a production supervisor. You have consistently received outstanding performance evaluations. You figure that the only other supervisor with similar qualifications is Dave, a workaholic bachelor who even attends night school to work towards an M.B.A. degree. You're ambitious and want to move ahead in the company. Part of your motivation is to earn more money to help with the expenses of raising two children alone since the death of your spouse a year ago in a car accident. You have told Pat that you think you're the best candidate for the recently created position of Pat's assistant. You hope this meeting is going to bring the good news.

OBSERVER's role: Turn to page 48 and use this rating sheet to evaluate both actors.

Time: Not to exceed ten minutes.

Group Exercise 2

Situation: A debate. Actor A can choose any contemporary issue. Some examples: business ethics, value of unions, prayer in schools, stiffer college grading policies, gun control, money as a motivator. Actor B then selects a position on that issue. Actor A must automatically take the counterposition. The debate is to proceed, with only one catch. Before each speaks, he or she must first summarize, in his or her *own* words and without notes, what the other has said. If the summary doesn't satisfy the speaker, it must be corrected until it does.

OBSERVER's role: In addition to rating both debaters on the rating sheet, the observer should remind each debater to paraphrase the other's statements until acknowledged as correct, before stating their own points.

Time: Ten minutes.

Group Exercise 3

Situation: ALEX JACOBS (Actor A) is the corporate controller for a restaurant chain, responsible for financial and information control. Over the past weekend, the computer system at one of the restaurants went down. The restaurant's manager called DALE TRAYNOR (Actor B), who reports to Alex and oversees the chain's computer operations. Dale authorized an emergency service call. Because it was a weekend, local people were not available, and the computer firm had to fly in a repair person from six hundred miles away. Alex has just learned about the emergency call in a casual conversation with the restaurant manager.

ALEX JACOBS's role: You have phoned the computer firm and found out that the cost of the service call is $1400. You're fuming. Not only is $1400 a large unexpected expenditure, but also Dale's authority limit is only $500. You can't figure out why you were neither advised of the problem nor asked to approve the expenditure. You have called Dale to your office.

DALE TRAYNOR's role: You have been called into your boss's office. You expect it has to do with the weekend computer breakdown. The restaurant manager had called you, as she is supposed to do when there is a computer problem. Because it was Sunday morning and you expected Sunday to be a busy day at the restaurant, you decided against going to the backup manual system until a local repair person could go out on Monday. Instead, you authorized an overtime emergency call. You expected the cost to be within your $500 authority, although you did not ask for an estimate.

OBSERVER's role: Use the rating sheet below.

Time: Not to exceed ten minutes.

OBSERVER'S RATING SHEET

For the exercise in which you are an observer, evaluate both participants on a 1 to 5 scale (5 being highest).

Exercise: 1   2   3   (Circle one)

ACTOR A		BEHAVIOR	ACTOR B	
COMMENTS	RATING		RATING	COMMENTS
	_____	Makes eye contact	_____	
	_____	Paraphrases	_____	
	_____	Gives affirmative responses	_____	
	_____	Avoids interrupting	_____	
	_____	Avoids distractions	_____	
	_____	Doesn't over-talk	_____	
	_____	Makes smooth transitions	_____	
	_____	Asks questions	_____	

SUMMARY CHECKLIST

Take a few minutes to reflect on your performance and look over others' ratings of your skill. Now assess yourself on each of the key learning behaviors. Make a check (✓) next to those behaviors on which you need improvement.

I make effective eye contact. _____

I exhibit affirmative head nods and appropriate expressions. _____

I avoid distracting actions or gestures that suggest boredom. _____

I ask questions. _____

I paraphrase using my own words. _____

I avoid interrupting the speaker. _____

I don't overtalk. _____

I make smooth transitions from being a speaker to listener. _____

APPLICATION QUESTIONS

1. "Symbols, not meanings, are transferred from sender to receiver." Discuss this statement and its ramifications for effective listening.

2. How do your personal values distort your interpretation of meaning? What are some examples?

3. Does everyone you work with and everything they have to say deserve your exhibiting effective listening skills? Explain.

4. Have you taken a formal speech course? If so, did it include listening skills? Is there a bias in our society toward speaking over listening?

5. Who do you find it easiest to listen to? Why? Is this person a good listener also? What behaviors make you think so?

REINFORCEMENT EXERCISES

The following suggestions are activities you can do to practice and reinforce the listening techniques you learned in this chapter. You may want to adapt them to the Action Plan you will develop next, or try them independently.

1. In another class—preferably one with a lecture format—practice active listening. Ask questions, paraphrase, exhibit affirming non-verbal behaviors. Then ask yourself: Was this harder for me than a normal lec-

ture? Did it affect my note taking? Did I ask more questions? Did it improve my understanding of the lecture's content? What was the instructor's response?

2. During your next telephone conversation, close your eyes and concentrate on being an effective listener; for example, ask questions, paraphrase. Then ask yourself: Did I get more out of the conversation?

3. Spend an entire day fighting your urge to talk. Listen as carefully as you can to everyone you talk to and respond as appropriately as possible to understand, not to make your own point.

ACTION PLAN

1. Which behavior do I want to improve the most?

_____

_____

2. Why? What will be my payoff?

_____

_____

3. What potential obstacles stand in my way?

_____

_____

4. What are the specific things I will do to improve? (For examples, see the Reinforcement Exercises.)

_____

_____

5. When will I do them?

_____

_____

6. How and when will I measure my success?

_____

_____

Chapter *4*
GOAL SETTING

SELF-ASSESSMENT EXERCISE

For each of the following questions, select the answer that best describes your relationship with subordinates. Remember to respond as you have behaved or *would* behave, not as you think you *should* behave. If you have no managerial experience, answer the questions assuming you are a manager.

THE PEOPLE WHO WORK FOR ME HAVE:

	Usually	Sometimes	Seldom
1. Complete autonomy to set their own goals.	☐	☐	☐
2. Goals for all key areas relating to their job performance.	☐	☐	☐
3. Challenging goals which are beyond their current ability to make them stretch.	☐	☐	☐
4. The opportunity to participate in setting their goals.	☐	☐	☐

	Usually	Sometimes	Seldom
5. A say in deciding how to implement their goals.	☐	☐	☐
6. To determine when they would like to accomplish the goals assigned to them on their own.	☐	☐	☐
7. Sufficient skills and training to achieve their goals.	☐	☐	☐
8. Sufficient resources (i.e., time, money, equipment) to achieve their goals.	☐	☐	☐
9. Feedback on how well they are progressing toward their goals.	☐	☐	☐
10. Rewards (i.e., pay, promotions) allocated to them according to how hard they try to reach their goals.	☐	☐	☐

Scoring Key and Interpretation

For questions 2, 4, 5, 7, 8, and 9, give yourself 3 points for "Usually," 2 points for "Sometimes," and 1 point for "Seldom." For questions 1, 3, 6, and 10, reverse the scale.

Sum up your total points. Scores of 26 or higher demonstrate a strong understanding of goal-setting techniques. A score of 21 to 25 indicates you can improve your goal-setting skills. Scores of 20 or less suggest that you have significant room for improvement.

SKILL CONCEPTS

Employees should have a clear idea of what they're trying to accomplish in their jobs. Further, managers have the responsibility for seeing that this is achieved by helping employees set work goals. These two statements seem obvious. Employees need to know what they're supposed to do, and it's the manager's job to provide this guidance. Simple? Hardly!

Goal setting is frequently dismissed by managers as self-evident (Latham and Locke, 1979). It's not! Setting goals is a sophisticated skill that many managers perform poorly. But when managers follow the goal-setting sequence that we'll describe in this chapter, they can expect improved employee performance (Locke, Shaw, Saari, and Latham, 1981). They're also likely to hear comments such as, "Finally, I know what you expect from me on this job!"

The Basics of Effective Goals

There are five basic rules that should guide you in defining and setting goals. The goals should be (1) specific, (2) challenging, (3) set with a time limit for accomplishment, (4) participatively established, and (5) designed to provide feedback to the employee. Let's elaborate on each of these points.

1. Specific. Goals are only meaningful when they're specific enough to be verified and measured. This is best achieved by stating them in quantitative terms: "Drill three new wells" rather than "Drill wells"; "Limit spending to $10 million" rather than "Be frugal"; "Increase sales in my territory by 10 percent" rather than "Try to improve sales"; or "I'm going to get at least three A's and two B's this term" rather than "I'm going to do my best" (Locke and Latham, 1984). When there is no confusion over the desired result, the likelihood of its being achieved is increased.

2. Challenging. Goals should be set so as to require the employee to stretch to reach them. If they're too easy, they offer no challenge. If set unrealistically high, they create frustration and are likely to be abandoned. So the employee should view goals as challenging yet reachable. Keep in mind, however, that one person's "*challenging*" is another person's "*impossible*." It's a question of perception. "Hard goals are more likely to be perceived as challenging rather than impossible if the person has a high degree of self-assurance and has previously had more success in goal attainment than failures" (Latham and Yukl, 1975, p. 835).

3. Time limits. Open-ended goals are likely to be neglected because there is no sense of urgency associated with them. Whenever possible, therefore, goals should include a specific time limit for accomplishment (Latham and Locke, 1979). So instead of stating, "I'm going to complete the bank management training program, with at least a score of 85," a time-specific goal would state, "I'm going to complete the bank management training program, with at least a score of 85, by February 1st of next year."

4. Employee participation. Goals can typically be set two ways: they can be assigned to the employee by the boss or they can be participatively determined in collaboration between the boss and employee. The research comparing the effects of participatively set and assigned goals on employee performance has not resulted in strong or consistent relationships (Latham and Saari, 1979a). When goal difficulty is held constant, assigned goals are frequently achieved as well as participatively determined ones (Latham and Yukl, 1975). Participation does seem to increase a person's goal aspiration level and leads to the setting of more difficult goals (Latham, Mitchell, and Dossett, 1978). Also, participatively set goals are often more readily accepted, and accepted goals are more likely to be achieved (Locke and Schweiger, 1979). So while assigned goals may be achieved as effectively as participative ones, collaboration is likely to result in more ambitious goals and more acceptance of those goals by those who must implement them. Participation actually makes the whole goal-setting process more acceptable. Employees are less likely to question or resist a process in which they actively participate than one that is imposed upon them from above.

5. Feedback. Feedback lets people know if their level of effort is sufficient or needs to be increased. It can also induce them to raise their goal level after attaining a previous goal and inform them of ways in which to improve their performance. Ideally, feedback on goal progress should be self-generated rather than provided externally (Ivancevich and McMahon, 1982). When an employee is able to monitor his or her own progress, the feedback is less threatening and less likely to be perceived as part of a management control system.

How to Set Goals

Seven steps need to be followed to obtain the optimum results from goal setting (Locke and Latham, 1984, pp. 27–37).

1. Specify the general objective and tasks to be done. Goal setting begins by defining what it is that you want your employees to accomplish. The best source for this information is each employee's job description, if one is available. It details what tasks an employee is expected to perform, how these tasks are to be done, what outcomes the employee is responsible for achieving, and the like.

2. Specify how the performance in question will be measured. Once an employee's tasks are defined, you can determine how the outcomes from these tasks are to be measured. Typically, work outcomes are measured in physical units (i.e., quantity of production, number of errors), time (i.e., meeting deadlines, coming to work each day), or money (i.e., profits, sales, costs). Of course, for many jobs, developing valid individual measures of performance is difficult or even impossible. For example, upper-level management jobs are complex and often defy clear measurement. Similarly, when employees are part of a work team, it is often difficult to single out their individual contributions. In such cases, the available outcome measures can be combined with inputs (behaviors) that are controllable by the employee and that are assumed to lead to successful outcomes. So a senior executive might be evaluated on criteria such as, "listens to employees' concerns" or "explains how changes will affect employees" in addition to "completes monthly forecast by the 25th of the preceding month."

3. Specify the standard or target to be reached. The next step requires identifying the *level* of performance expected. In step 2, it might be determined that one of the criteria by which a salesperson will be judged is customer returns. In this step, you need to specify a target; for example, monthly returns will not represent more than 1 percent of that month's sales. If properly selected, the target will meet the requirements of being both specific and challenging for the employee.

4. Specify the time span involved. After the targets are set, deadlines for each goal need to be put in place. Typically, the time span increases at upper levels of management. So while the goals of operative employees tend to be in the range of one day to several months, middle managers' goals are more likely to fall into the three-months-to-a-year range, and top-level managers' goals will often extend to two, three, or five years.

While putting a time target on each goal is important because it reduces ambiguity, keep in mind that deadlines should not be chosen arbitrarily. The reason is that people tend to stress whatever time span is attached to any given goal. If daily goals are assigned, the time focus will be one day. If quarterly goals are set, actions will be directed accordingly. The message here is twofold. First, to rephrase Parkinson's Law, effort toward a goal will be expended to fill the time available for its completion. Give people a month to complete a task that requires a week, and they'll typically take the full month. Second, overemphasis on short-term goals can undermine long-term performance. Short-range time targets encourage people to do *whatever is necessary* to get immediate results, even if it's at the expense of achieving long-term goals.

5. Prioritize goals. When someone is given more than one goal, it is important to rank the goals in order of importance. The purpose of this step is to encourage the employee to take action and expend effort on each goal in proportion to its importance.

6. Rate goals as to their difficulty and importance. Goal setting should *not* encourage people to choose easy goals in order to ensure success. While it is an extreme illustration, no employee should be able to say, "My goal was to do nothing and I'm pleased to say I achieved it!!" Goal setting needs to take into account the difficulty of the goals selected and whether individuals are emphasizing the right goals.

In step 6, each goal should be rated for its difficulty and importance. When these ratings are combined with the actual level of goal achievement, you will have a more comprehensive assessment of overall goal performance. This procedure gives credit to individuals for trying difficult goals even if they don't fully achieve them. So an employee who sets very easy goals and exceeds them might get a lower overall evaluation than one who sets hard goals and partially attains them. Similarly, an employee who reaches only low-priority goals and neglects those with high priorities could be evaluated lower than one who tries for important goals and only partially achieves them.

7. Determine coordination requirements. Is the achievement of any person's goals dependent on the cooperation and contribution of other people? If so, there is a potential for conflict. It is important in such cases to ensure that these goals are coordinated. Failure to coordinate interdependent goals can lead to territorial fights, abdication of responsibility, and overlapping of effort.

Obtaining Goal Commitment

The mere existence of goals is no assurance that employees accept and are committed to them. However, certain actions by managers can increase acceptance and commitment (Latham and Locke, 1979).

1. Managerial support. Managers need to create a supportive climate where goals are seen as a device for clarifying employee expectations rather than as a manipulative tool for threatening and intimidating subordinates. Managers exhibit support by helping employees select challenging goals and by reducing barriers that stand between employees and the attainment of their goals. This means, for example, making sure employees have the necessary equipment, supplies, time, and other resources to complete their tasks. A manager is supportive when subordinates view him or her as a goal facilitator.

2. Use participation. Employee participation in goal setting is a key to getting goals accepted. To be effective, however, the participation must be authentic. That is, employees must perceive managers as truly seeking their input. If a manager merely "goes through the motions" of soliciting employee input, participation will not succeed. Employees are not stupid. If a manager attempts to co-opt them—pretending to want their participation when, in fact, he or she has specific goals, levels of performance, and target dates firmly in mind—the employees will be quick to label the process for what it is: assigned goals from above.

3. Know your subordinates' capabilities. Individuals differ in terms of their skills and abilities. If these differences are taken into consideration, each person's goals will realistically reflect his or her capabilities. Further, matching goal difficulty and an individual's capabilities increases the likelihood that the employee will see the goals as fair, realistic, attainable, and acceptable. Where a person's abilities aren't adequate to meet the minimally satisfactory goals, this matching effort may signal the need for additional skill training for that employee.

4. Use rewards. There's an old saying: What's worth doing is worth doing for money. Offering money, promotions, recognition, time off, or similar rewards to employees contingent on goal achievement is a powerful means to increase goal commitment. When the going gets tough on the road toward meeting a goal, people are prone to ask themselves, "What's in it for me?" Linking rewards to the achievement of goals helps employees answer that question.

CONCEPT QUIZ

After answering the following quiz, remember to go back and check your understanding of any questions you missed.

Circle the right answer:

True   or   False   1. Specific goals reduce ambiguity about what an employee is expected to do.

True   or   False   2. Goals should be set just a little beyond what a person can realistically achieve to maximize motivation.

True   or   False   3. Hard goals are more likely to be perceived as challenging rather than impossible if the person has a college degree.

True   or   False   4. Participation reduces employee commitment to goals.

True   or   False   5. Feedback on goal progress is best if self-generated.

True   or   False   6. Everything an employee does on his or her job can and should be quantified and have a goal set for it.

True   or   False   7. In goal setting, short-term goals take priority over long-term goals.

True   or   False   8. Coming up short in trying to achieve a difficult goal should always be evaluated more positively than fully achieving an easy goal.

True   or   False   9. Managers are able to facilitate employee goal attainment.

True   or   False   10. People accept goals more readily when the goals are tied to rewards they desire.

Answers: (1) True; (2) False; (3) False; (4) False; (5) True; (6) False; (7) False; (8) False; (9) True; (10) True.

BEHAVIORAL CHECKLIST

Look for these specific behaviors when evaluating your goal-setting skills and those of others.

THE EFFECTIVE GOAL SETTER

- Identifies an employee's key job tasks

- Establishes specific and challenging goals for each key task

- Specifies deadlines for each goal

- Allows the subordinate to actively participate

- Prioritizes goals

- Rates goals for difficulty and importance

- Builds in feedback mechanisms to assess goal progress

- Commits rewards contingent on goal attainment

MODELING EXERCISE

Actors: ROBIN GORDON and LOU MILLAN.

Situation: Kelly Frum has recently been promoted to the position of operations officer at one of the largest branches of State Bank of Vermont. His/her staff includes three supervisors who report directly to him/her, and another thirty-five or so operatives who are responsible to the supervisors. One of these supervisors is responsible for directing the fifteen tellers, while the others direct customer relations and the computer functions. Kelly reports to the bank manager, who, in turn, works under the State Bank of Vermont's president.

Kelly has suggested to all three supervisors that they establish goals for themselves and their employees.

One supervisor, Robin Gordon, who is responsible for the tellers, has set up a meeting with his/her most senior teller—Lou Millan—to begin the goal-setting process.

Objective: Establish goals for Lou. They might address issues such as prompt attention to customer needs, showing courtesy to customers, selling bank services such as Christmas Club accounts, keeping the cash drawer in balance, or taking bank-sponsored courses to improve skills.

Time: Not to exceed fifteen minutes.

The class is to evaluate Robin Gordon's goal-setting skills on a 1 to 5 scale (5 being highest).

- Identifies key tasks   ____

- Sets specific and challenging goals   ____

- Sets deadlines   ____

- Provides for subordinate participation   ____

- Prioritizes goals   ____

- Rates for difficulty and importance   ____

- Builds in feedback   ____

- Commits rewards   ____

Comments: _____

_____

_____

_____

_____

_____

GROUP EXERCISES

Break into groups of three and perform the three role plays that follow. Remember that observers are to evaluate goal setting skills using the behaviors on the Observer's Rating Sheet on page 66.

Group Exercise 1

Actors: TERRY DONAHUE and CHRIS ESPO.

Situation: Terry Donahue is a Probation Supervisor. Chris Espo is a newly hired Juvenile Probation Officer. The following describes the job of Juvenile Probation Officer and gives Chris's qualifications. Both are currently in Terry's office.

JUVENILE PROBATION OFFICER

Tasks	Conditions	Standards
Meets with probationers weekly to assess their current behavior	Caseload of not more than 60 appointments scheduled by receptionist; supervisor will help with difficult cases; use procedures stated in rules and regulations	All probationers must be seen weekly; those showing evidence of continued criminal activity or lack of a job will be reported to supervisor
Prepares presentence reports on clients	When requested by the judge; average of 5 per week, per instructions issued by judge; supervisor will review and approve	Your reports will be complete and accurate as determined by judge; he/she will accept 75 percent of presentence recommendations

Skills, Knowledge, and Abilities Required

- Knowledge of the factors contributing to criminal behavior
- Ability to counsel probationers
- Ability to write clear and concise probation reports
- Knowledge of judge's sentencing habits for particular types of offenders and offenses
- Knowledge of law concerning probation

Source: Adapted from Donald E. Klingner, "When the Traditional Job Description Is Not Enough." Reprinted with the permission of Personnel Journal, Inc., Costa Mesa, Calif., all rights reserved, 1979.

TERRY DONAHUE's role: You are happy to have been allocated a new Juvenile Probation Officer because your department is understaffed and has a heavy caseload. Chris Espo seems like a bright and capable addition to your staff who desires to learn the job quickly. You are concerned that his/her recent business degree has not provided some of the essential knowledge and skills desired for the job, but with some extra classes and training, that can be upgraded. Everyone in your agency has read about Chris's golf championships and he/she is quite a hero in your small town. You want to set goals for Chris's job and professional development.

CHRIS ESPO's role: You are happy to have the Juvenile Probation Officer job because, next to golf, you really like working with kids. It was a tough decision to stay off of the pro golf tour but you married your high school sweetheart two years ago and just had a new baby. Both of your families still live in the small town you've grown up in, and you feel OK about your trade-offs as long as you can use your spare time to practice and to compete in amateur golf tournaments.

Time: Not to exceed twenty minutes.

OBSERVER's role: Provide feedback to the student playing Terry Donahue using the "Observer's Rating Sheet" on page 66.

Group Exercise 2

Actors: LEE DAVIS and JAN REEVES.

Situation: It's the first week of the fall semester at your college. Lee Davis recently received a doctorate from a prestigious Eastern university and has been hired as a new faculty member by the psychology department. Lee's major area is social psychology and his/her dissertation was on how norms impact on decision making in groups. Lee's department head, Jan Reeves, has invited Lee to sit down and discuss Lee's future plans.

The following advertisement appeared in psychology journals for the position that Lee accepted.

POSITION AVAILABLE: Entry-level Assistant Professor of Psychology. Teach in areas of introductory psych., social psych., and industrial psych. Ph.D. required. Strong research/publication interest. Teaching load: three courses per term. University service and active involvement in professional associations expected. Contact Dr. Jan Reeves.

JAN REEVES's role: You strongly believe that every faculty member should have goals for all areas of responsibility. This is especially true of junior staff who are often so concerned about new class preparations that they forget about their service and publication responsibilities. You believe new faculty must be particularly concerned with excellence in the classroom and publishing articles that will reinforce the prestigious reputation of the department and university.

LEE DAVIS's role: You are looking forward to a productive academic career as a teacher and scholar. As most new faculty members, you are very concerned about preparing well for your new courses and getting started publishing some research. You have a good start with your dissertation data, but know that you must start some new experiments to generate new data. This is a prestigous "publish or perish" university with a reputation for teaching excellence.

Suggestion: Before starting the role-play, Jan Reeves should jot down ideas on what makes an effective faculty member.

Time: Not to exceed fifteen minutes.

Group Exercise 3

Actors: R. J. SIMPSON, Athletic Director at State College; and PAT BELL, new women's basketball coach at State.

Situation: R. J. Simpson made a recent offer to Pat Bell to join State College as the college's new women's basketball coach at a salary of $65,000 a year. Pat has accepted. Pat will replace the previous coach, who held the job for three years and had a combined record of twenty wins and forty-two losses. Pat previously was head women's basketball coach at a junior college where he/she won 92 percent of his/her games and two national JC championships.

State College has twelve thousand students and is a member of the ten-school Northwest Athletic Conference. During the past three years, State College has finished no higher than sixth in the conference and has not been in any postseason tournaments. The team averages fifteen hundred fans for its home games in the college's arena, which has a capacity of nine thousand. The women's basketball program, which last year had a budget of $150,000, was responsible for a loss of $60,000 to the college's overall athletic program.

This meeting is to set goals for the women's basketball program's coming season. These goals will be used to judge Pat's performance and as a basis for allocating performance-based bonuses, provided by alums and athletic boosters, of up to $20,000 annually.

R.J. SIMPSON's role: You are delighted to have hired Pat Bell who has such an excellent record from a very competitive JC league. State College is at a crucial juncture with its womens' basketball program this year after losing $60,000 last year. If you can't get at least a break-even this year, the Board of Governors is insisting that the program be dropped which means you will face women's rights protests, possible discrimination lawsuits, and problems in meeting NCAA requirements that universities spend equally (excluding football) on men and women's intercollegiate sports programs. You want to make sure that Pat has extremely clear-cut goals and is motivated to achieve them.

PAT BELL's role   You feel that you are at the right place at the right time. You were very fortunate over the last two years at JC to have some extraordinary talent playing for you. Nevertheless, you have to pat yourself on the back because you were able to capitalize on your teams' skills by implementing some creative strategies during the national championsnhip playoffs. You have enjoyed the complete independence and freedom to do as you choose as a coach. If you can get the right recruits and do things your way, you feel that you can turn State's record around, improve the school's prestige, and boost your career.

Time: Not to exceed twenty minutes.

OBSERVER'S RATING SHEET

For the exercise in which you are an observer, evaluate key goal-setting behaviors on a 1 to 5 scale (5 being highest).

RATING	BEHAVIOR	RATING	BEHAVIOR
_____	Identifies key tasks	_____	Sets deadlines
_____	Prioritizes goals	_____	Builds in feedback
_____	Sets specific and challenging goals	_____	Provides for subordinate participation
_____	Rates for difficulty and importance	_____	Commits rewards

Comments: _____

_____

_____

_____

SUMMARY CHECKLIST

Review your performance and look over others' ratings of your skill. Now assess yourself on each of the key learning behaviors. Put a check (✓) next to those behaviors on which you need improvement.

I identify key tasks in employees' jobs. _____

I establish specific and challenging goals for each key task. _____

I specify deadlines for each goal. _____

I allow subordinates to actively participate. _____

I prioritize goals. _____

I rate goals for difficulty and importance. _____

I build in feedback mechanisms to assess goal progress. _____

I commit rewards contingent on goal attainment. _____

APPLICATION QUESTIONS

1. Does goal setting emphasize short-term results at the expense of long-term effectiveness?

2. How does goal setting deal with employees who have multiple goals, some of which are conflicting?

3. What barriers in an organization can you identify that may limit the effectiveness of a goal-setting program? How can these barriers be overcome?

4. Explain what an instructor can do to use goal setting with his or her students in a classroom.

REINFORCEMENT EXERCISES

The following suggestions are activities you can do to practice and reinforce the goal-setting techniques you learned in this chapter.

1. Where do you want to be in five years? Write out three specific goals you want to achieve in five years. Make sure they are specific, challenging, and verifiable. Share your goals with a classmate and get feedback.

2. Set specific and challenging goals for yourself in this class. Do the same for your other classes.

3. Set ten personal and academic goals that you want to achieve by the end of this year. Prioritize and rate them for difficulty.

ACTION PLAN

1. Which behavior do I want to improve the most?

   _____

   _____

   _____

2. Why? What will be my payoff?

   _____

   _____

   _____

3. What potential obstacles stand in my way?

_____

_____

_____

4. What are the specific things I will do to improve? (For examples, see the Reinforcement Exercises.)

_____

_____

_____

5. When will I do them?

_____

_____

_____

6. How and when will I measure my success

_____

_____

_____

Chapter 5

PROVIDING FEEDBACK

SELF-ASSESSMENT EXERCISE

For each of the following questions, select the answer that best describes you. Remember to respond as you *have* behaved or *would* behave, not as you think you *should* behave.

WHEN GIVING FEEDBACK TO ANOTHER PERSON:

	Usually	Sometimes	Seldom
1. I focus my comments on specific, job-related behaviors.	☐	☐	☐
2. I keep my comments descriptive rather than evaluative.	☐	☐	☐
3. I prefer to save up comments so they can be presented and discussed in detail during the person's annual performance review.	☐	☐	☐
4. I ensure that my feedback is clearly understood.	☐	☐	☐

5. I supplement criticism with suggestions on what the person can do to improve.

☐ ☐ ☐

6. I tailor the type of feedback to reflect the person's past performance and future potential.

☐ ☐ ☐

Scoring Key and Interpretation

For questions 1, 2, 4, 5, and 6, give yourself 3 points for "Usually," 2 points for "Sometimes," and 1 point for "Seldom."

For question 3, give yourself 3 points for "Seldom," 2 points for "Sometimes," and 1 point for "Usually."

Sum up your total points. A score of 16 points or higher indicates excellent skills at providing feedback. Scores in the 13 to 15 range suggest some deficiencies in providing feedback. Scores below 13 indicate considerable room for improvement.

SKILL CONCEPTS

Ask a manager how much feedback he or she gives subordinates and you're likely to get a qualified answer. If the feedback is positive, it's likely to be given promptly and enthusiastically. Negative feedback, however, is often treated very differently. Managers, like most of us, don't particularly enjoy being the bearers of bad news. They fear offending or having to deal with defensiveness by the recipient. The result is that negative feedback is often avoided, delayed, or substantially distorted (Fisher, 1979). The purposes of this chapter are to show you the importance of providing both positive and negative feedback and to identify specific techniques to make your feedback more effective.

What do we mean by the term *feedback*? It's any communication to a person that gives him or her information about some aspect of his or her behavior and its effect on you (Mill, 1976). Although our concern in this chapter is predominantly with performance feedback, the skill techniques presented here are generalizable to most types of interpersonal feedback. When you tell someone sitting at an adjacent table in a restaurant that his or her cigarette smoking is bothering you, you're providing that person with feedback.

The Value of Feedback

An important reason to be skilled at giving feedback is because it can increase employee performance (Komaki, Collins, and Penn, 1982; Locke and Latham, 1984). There are a number of reasons why.

First, feedback can induce a person who previously had no goals to set some. And, as we demonstrated in the previous chapter, goals act as motivators to higher performance. Second, where goals exist, feedback tells people how well they're progressing toward those goals. To the degree that the feedback is favorable, it acts as a positive reinforcer. Third, if the feedback indicates inadequate performance, this knowledge may result in increased effort. Further, the content of the feedback can suggest ways—other than exerting more effort—to improve performance. Fourth, feedback often induces people to raise their goal sights after attaining a previous goal. Finally, providing feedback to employees conveys that others care how they're doing. So feedback is an indirect form of recognition that can motivate people to higher levels of performance (Coffey, Cook, and Hunsaker, 1994).

Positive versus Negative Feedback

We said earlier that managers treat positive and negative feedback differently. So, too, do recipients. You need to understand this fact and adjust your style accordingly.

Positive feedback is more readily and accurately perceived than negative feedback. Further, while positive feedback is almost always accepted, the negative variety often meets resistance (Ilgen, Fisher, and Taylor, 1979). Why? The logical answer seems to be that people want to hear good news and block out the bad. Positive feedback fits what most people wish to hear and already believe about themselves

Does this mean you should avoid giving negative feedback? No! What it means is that you need to be aware of potential resistance and learn to use negative feedback in situations where it is most likely to be accepted (Bartolome, 1986–87). What are those situations? Research indicates that negative feedback is most likely to be accepted when it comes from a credible source or if it is objective in form. Subjective impressions carry weight only when they come from a person with high status and credibility (Halperin et al., 1976). This suggests that negative feedback that is supported by hard data—numbers, specific examples, and the like—has a good chance of being accepted. Negative feedback that is subjective can be a meaningful tool for experienced managers, particularly those high in the organization who have earned the respect of their employees. From less experienced managers, those in the lower ranks of the organization, and those whose reputation has not yet been established, negative feedback is not likely to be well received.

What We Know about Providing Feedback

Now it's time to look at basic feedback techniques. The following should guide you in determining how and when to provide feedback.

1. Focus on specific behaviors. Feedback should be specific rather than general (Coffey, Cook, and Hunsaker, 1994). Avoid statements like "You have a bad attitude" or "I'm really impressed with the good job you did." They're vague, and while they provide information, they don't tell the recipient enough to correct the "bad attitude" or on *what basis* you concluded that a "good job" had been done. Suppose you said something like "Bob, I'm concerned with your attitude toward your work. You were a half hour late to yesterday's staff meeting, and then told me you hadn't read the preliminary report we were discussing. Today you tell me you're taking off three hours early for a dental appointment"; or "Jan, I was really pleased with the job you did on the Phillips account. They increased their purchases from us by twenty-two percent last month and I got a call a few days ago from Dan Phillips complimenting me on how quickly you responded to those specification changes for the MJ-7 microchip." Both of these statements focus on specific behaviors. They tell the recipient *why* you are being critical or complimentary.

2. Keep it impersonal. Feedback, particularly the negative kind, should be descriptive rather than judgmental or evaluative (Alessandra and Hunsaker, 1993). No matter how upset you are, keep the feedback job-related and never criticize someone personally because of an inappropriate action. Telling people they're "stupid," "incompetent," or the like is almost always counterproductive. It provokes such an emotional reaction that the performance deviation itself is apt to be overlooked. When you're criticizing, remember that you're censuring a job-related behavior, not the person. You may be tempted to tell someone he or she is "rude and insensitive" (which may well be true); however, that's hardly impersonal. Better to say something like "You interrupted me three times, with questions that were not urgent, when you knew I was talking long distance to a customer in Scotland."

3. Keep it goal-oriented. Feedback should not be given primarily to "dump" or "unload" on another (Mill, 1976). If you have to say something negative, make sure it's directed toward the *recipient's* goals. Ask yourself whom the feedback is supposed to help. If the answer is essentially you— "I've got something I just want to get off my chest"—bite your tongue. Such feedback undermines your credibility and lessens the meaning and influence of future feedback.

4. Make it well-timed. Feedback is most meaningful to a recipient when there is a very short interval between his or her behavior and the receipt of feedback about that behavior (Mill, 1976). To illustrate, a football player who makes a mistake during a game is more likely to respond to his coach's suggestions for improvement right after the mistake, immediately following the game, or during the review of that game's films a few days later, rather than feedback provided by the coach several months later. If you have to spend time recreating a situation and refreshing someone's memory of it, the feedback you're providing is likely to be ineffective (Verderber and Verderber, 1986). Moreover, if you are particularly concerned with changing behavior, delays providing feedback on the undesirable actions lessen the likelihood that the feedback will be effective in bringing about the desired change (Bourne and Bunderson, 1963). Of course, making feedback prompt merely for promptness' sake can backfire if you have insufficient information, if you're angry, or if you're otherwise emotionally upset. In such instances, "well-timed" may mean "somewhat delayed."

5. Ensure understanding. Is your feedback concise and complete enough so that the recipient clearly and fully understands your communication? Every successful communication requires both transference and understanding of meaning. So if feedback is to be effective, you need to ensure that the recipient understands it (Mill, 1976). Consistent with our discussion of listening techniques, you should have the recipient rephrase the content of your feedback to see whether it fully captures the meaning you intended.

6. If negative, make sure the behavior is controllable by the recipient. There's little value in reminding a person of some shortcoming over which he or she has no control. Negative feedback, therefore, should be directed toward behavior the recipient can do something about (Verderber and Verderber, 1986). So, for example, to criticize an employee who is late because he forgot to set his wake-up alarm is valid. To criticize him for being late when the subway he takes to work every day had a power failure, trapping him underground for half an hour, is pointless. There is nothing he could do to correct what happened.

Additionally, when negative feedback is given concerning something that is controllable by the recipient, it may be a good idea to indicate specifically what can be done to improve the situation. This takes some of the sting out of the criticism and offers guidance to recipients who understand the problem but don't know how to resolve it.

7. Tailor the feedback to fit the person. Our final advice regarding feedback is to take into consideration the person to whom it's directed. You should consider the recipient's past performance and your estimate of his or her future potential in designing the frequency, amount, and content of performance feedback (Cummings, 1976). For high performers with potential for growth, feedback should be frequent enough to prod them into taking corrective action, but not so frequent that it is experienced as controlling and saps their initiative. For adequate performers who have settled into their jobs and have limited potential for advancement, very little feedback is needed because they have displayed reliable and steady behavior in the past, know their tasks, and realize what needs to be done. For poor performers— that is, people who will need to be removed from their jobs if their performance doesn't improve—feedback should be frequent and very specific, and the connection between acting on the feedback and negative sanctions such as being laid off or fired should be made explicit.

CONCEPT QUIZ

Take the following ten-question, true-false quiz. The answers are at the end of the quiz. If you read the previous material carefully, you should get them all correct. If you miss any, go back and find out why you got them wrong.

Circle the right answer:

True   or   False   1. Both the givers and the receivers of feedback tend to treat negative and positive feedback differently.

True   or   False   2. Managers should refrain from giving an employee negative feedback.

True   or   False   3. Feedback, by definition, is concerned only with an employee's performance and its effect on you.

True   or   False   4. Feedback tells people how well they're progressing toward their goals.

True   or   False   5. Negative feedback is more likely to be accepted when combined with positive feedback.

True   or   False   6. Objective negative feedback is more likely to be accepted then the subjective variety.

True   or   False   7. Specific feedback is more effective than general feedback.

True   or   False   8. Effective feedback avoids criticism of a person's personality or personal style.

True   or   False   9. Delays between a recipient's undesirable behavior and providing feedback on that behavior shoudl be avoided.

True   or   False   10. Don't give criticism unless it is desired by the recipient.

Answers: (1) True; (2) False; (3) False; (4) True; (5) False; (6) True; (7) True; (8) True; (9) True; (10) False.

BEHAVIORAL CHECKLIST

Look for these specific behaviors when evaluating your feedback skills and those of others.

PROVIDING EFFECTIVE FEEDBACK REQUIRES

- Supporting negative feedback with hard data

- Focusing on specific rather than general behaviors

- Keeping comments impersonal and job-related

- Ensuring the recipient has a clear and full understanding of the feedback

- Directing negative feedback toward behavior that is controllable by the recipient

- Adjusting the frequency, amount, and content of feedback to meet the needs of the recipient.

ATTENTION!

Don't read this or the following exercises until assigned to do so by your instructor.

MODELING EXERCISE

A class leader is to be selected (either a volunteer or someone chosen by the instructor). The class leader will preside over the following discussion and perform the role of administrator in the feedback session. The instructor is to leave the room.

Research has identified seven performance dimensions to the college instructor's job (Bernardin and Walter, 1977): instructor knowledge, testing procedures, student-teacher relations, organizational skills, communication skills, subject relevance, and utility of assignments. The leader is to use the class as a resource in helping him or her provide feedback to the instructor on each dimension. The leader has up to fifteen minutes to get input from the class and to prepare his or her ratings. (The leader should take notes for personal use but will not be required to give the instructor any written documentation.) After the fifteen-minute period is up, the leader should invite the instructor back into the classroom. The feedback session begins as soon as the instructor walks through the door, with the class leader becoming the administrator and the instructor playing him- or herself.

Time: Not to exceed fifteen minutes.

IMPORTANT NOTE

Your instructor understands that this is only an exercise and is prepared to accept criticism (and, of course, any praise you may want to convey). Your instructor also recognizes that the leader's feedback is actually a composite of many students' input. Be open and honest in your feedback and have confidence that your instructor will not be vindictive.

Observer's Guide

Evaluate the feedback skills of your classmate playing the role of the leader using a 1 to 5 scale (5 being highest).

- Provides support for negative feedback   _____
- Focuses on specific behaviors   _____
- Keeps comments impersonal and job-related   _____
- Makes sure recipient understands feedback   _____
- Criticizes only controllable behaviors   _____
- Adjusts feedback to needs and situation of recipient   _____

Comments:

_____

_____

_____

_____

GROUP EXERCISES

Group Exercise 1

Actors: DR. FARGO and ROBIN MUNSON.

Situation: Robin Munson is a graduate student at State College and supplements his/her income by acting as resident manager of one of the college dormitories. Robin is responsible for overseeing the dorm's four wing residents (undergraduates who receive a small monthly stipend) and 250 students. This essentially means ensuring that dorm rules are obeyed (visiting hours in rooms, quiet hours, etc.) and notifying the appropriate maintenance personnel when there are problems. Robin is provided with a free residential suite in the dorm and a salary of $350 a month. Robin reports to the college's Dean of Students, Dr. Fargo.

      This is Robin's first semester as a resident manager. Though only on the job for three months, Robin is aware that several complaints have been registered against him/her by students in the dorm. Robin knows this because Dr. Fargo called yesterday and said so. Dr. Fargo has asked Robin to come over and discuss the complaints.

ROBIN MUNSON's role: You graduated from college three years ago and decided to return for a graduate degree. But money is a problem, so you applied for and received a resident manager position. You were told the job would take little of your time. That was important because you were taking a full load of graduate courses and would have to spend almost all of your time studying. Dr. Fargo called yesterday and told you some students were displeased with the way you were running the dorm. You had no idea what Dr. Fargo was alluding to. You thought everything was going okay because none of the students had said anything to you. So far, you have liked the resident manager's job—mostly because you don't have to spend more than an hour or two a week on it.

DR. FARGO's role: Within the past two weeks, you've received visits from several groups of students living in Robin's dorm. On the positive side, the students complimented Robin for keeping the common areas clean and for making sure that maintenance problems are quickly attended to. But their main concern was that the noise level at night made studying impossible. The students said that attempts to talk to

Robin had been unsuccessful—the consensus was that Robin was never available. You called two of the four wing residents and they confirmed that they were having trouble keeping the noise level down and that Robin's studies clearly had priority over problems in the dorm.

You believe that problems should be addressed as they arise. Therefore, you have decided to have a discussion with Robin. Your position on resident managers is basically that they need to spend as much time as necessary to keep things running smoothly. If they can do the job in a few hours a week, great. But if it takes twenty hours a week, so be it! You hired Robin because he/she seemed responsible and came highly recommended by several faculty members in his/her graduate department. You were impressed with Robin during the job interview and thought he/she would be a good addition to the staff. In retrospect, you may not have been as honest as you should have been about the demands of the job, but you've had trouble in past years getting and keeping good dorm resident managers.

Time: Not to exceed fifteen minutes.

Observer's role: Provide feedback to the student playing Dr. Fargo using the following "Observer's Rating Sheet." Make sure that you use the same behaviors contained on the rating sheet when you give your own feedback to the observee.

Group Exercise 2

Actors: KELLY KING and FRAN THOMAS.

Situation: Kelly King is a shift manager at a McDonald's restaurant. Kelly has been in this position for eighteen months and supervises twenty people (counter clerks and cooks) on the day shift. One of these people is Fran Thomas.

Fran is a nineteen-year-old high school graduate. Fran's prior work experience includes being an attendant at a laundromat and selling jewelry in a small department store. Kelly hired Fran three months ago from among half a dozen job applicants. What impressed Kelly about Fran was (1) the high school diploma; (2) the prior work experience; and (3) references that reported Fran was dependable, honest, good with numbers, and followed directions well.

McDonald's employees are on probation for their first three months, after which they are considered permanent. Fran has completed the three-month probationary period and Kelly is now required to give a performance review. It's 10 A.M., the restaurant is quiet, and Kelly has asked Fran to sit down in a booth and talk.

KELLY KING's role: Your job is hectic. Supervising twenty people in a busy fast-food restaurant allows little time for planning. You often feel that all you do each day is run around "putting out fires." Because of your hectic pace, you haven't had time to point out to Fran a few of his/her problems. As with other employees, you plan to use the three-month review as an opportunity to tell Fran that his/her job performance has been satisfactory on the whole, but two things concern you. First, Fran has long hair and is required by health regulations to wear a hair net at all times. You've had to remind him/her three or four times to wear the hair net. Second, you're aware that Fran has been dating Terry—another employee in the restaurant. You don't consider the fact that they're dating to be your business, but what does concern you is that the two show demonstrative affection (touching and caressing) toward each other while working behind the counter. You've decided to extend Fran's probation for one more month and then give him/her a 25-cent-per-hour raise. (Fran's currently making $4.75 an hour and the standard three month raise is 50 cents an hour.)

FRAN THOMAS's role: You've been on your job three months. You find it strange that your boss—Kelly King—hasn't said one word to you about how well you've been performing. This lack of communication has been bothering you for a number of weeks, but you haven't brought it up because you think it's King's job to initiate such discussion. This lack of communication got so bad last week that you actually thought about quitting. The only reason you didn't is that Terry—a co-worker you've been dating—convinced you not to. Terry agreed with you that Kelly King is curt, thoughtless, and a lousy communicator. But you think you've been doing a good job, you like your co-workers, and the promotion opportunities at McDonald's are good. As you sit down to talk with Kelly King, you expect King to tell you you're one of his/her best employees and that you can expect a pay raise (you're currently making $4.75 an hour). After all, you're conscientious, energetic, and the only comments that Kelly has ever made to you that could even possibly be construed as negative were on the few occasions you forgot to wear a hair net to control your long hair. You remember that during your initial job interview King said you could count on a pay raise at the end of three months if your work proved satisfactory. While no figure was mentioned, you know that Terry got a 50-cent-an-hour increase after three months.

Time: Not to exceed fifteen minutes.

Group Exercise 3

Actors: BARRY IRWIN and DANA DOUGLAS.

Situation: Barry Irwin is a sales representative for Atlas Metals, a distributor of aluminum sheet and tubing. Atlas sells predominantly to large aerospace, automobile, and truck manufacturing firms. Barry has worked for Atlas for several years. Last year, Atlas's sales reached $12 million. Barry's sales manager is Dana Douglas.

BARRY IRWIN's role: You've been trying for eight months to get Boeing Aerospace as a customer. Last month you saw a real opportunity. They were taking bids for a specific size of aluminum tubing that your firm carries. The order wouldn't be too big, but you thought it could get you in the door at Boeing. You submitted a bid of $19,300 for the order. You did so without checking with your boss, but you didn't think it necessary since you have authorization to make bids up to $40,000 without approval from above. The catch, however, is that the company sales policy (which is specifically stated in the sales manual) is never to sell below cost. You knew that your bid would result in a small loss for the company, but you saw the potential for annual sales to Boeing of $2 million or $3 million. Atlas had never been able to get Boeing business before. You knew you were wrong in breaking company policy, but you also knew that Atlas has wanted Boeing as a customer for years. To avoid a debate with your boss, you decided to act on your own and go for the Boeing order even though it would generate a loss. You got the order. In your view, the potential long-term benefits from the order far exceed the short-term costs.

Dana Douglas has just called you into his/her office. The reason? Dana just received the monthly sales analysis and wants to talk to you about the Boeing order.

DANA DOUGLAS's role: Barry Irwin is one of your best salespeople. You admire Barry's drive and determination. You particularly value Barry's success in developing new accounts and expanding sales with established customers. Barry has, at times, bent the rules at Atlas but has never broken them.

Today you received the monthly sales analysis, broken down by salesperson and customer. You noticed that Barry got a small order—under $20,000—from Boeing. It's the first you heard of it. You have mixed feelings. On the one hand, it's the first time Atlas has gotten a Boeing order. Though Atlas has wanted their business for years, it has never gotten an order before. It might be the beginning of a very profitable relationship. On the other hand, the order generates a loss of $2600. Company policy (which Barry knows perfectly well) allows salespeople to approve, on their own, sales of up to $40,000; however, taking orders that produce a loss are strictly prohibited. You know you have to talk to Barry about this. You don't want to stifle Barry's initiative, but company policy needs to be followed. You're a reasonable person and salespeople like Barry are hard to find. Yet you know Atlas's president will be on your back if salespeople begin taking it upon themselves to break company policies whenever they see fit. You have called Barry into your office to discuss the problem.

Time: Not to exceed ten minutes.

OBSERVER'S RATING SHEET

For the exercise in which you are an observer, evaluate key feed-back behaviors on a 1 to 5 scale (5 being highest).

- Provides support for negative feedback   _____

- Focuses on specific behaviors   _____

- Keeps comments impersonal and job-related   _____

- Makes sure recipient understands feedback   _____

- Criticizes only controllable behaviors   _____

- Adjusts feedback to needs and situation
  of recipient   _____

Comments:

_____

_____

_____

_____

_____

_____

_____

SUMMARY CHECKLIST

Review your performance and look over others' ratings of your skill. Now assess yourself on each of the key learning behaviors. Make a check next to those behaviors on which you need improvement.

I provide hard data to support negative feedback   _____

I focus on specific behaviors   _____

I keep my comments impersonal and job-related   _____

I make sure the recipient understands my feedback   _____

I direct negative feedback to behaviors that
   are controllable by the recipient   _____

I adjust my feedback to the needs and
   situation of the recipient   _____

APPLICATION QUESTIONS

1. Contrast the effects from positive and negative feedback.
2. Relate the feedback concepts in this chapter to your knowledge of how parents are supposed to properly raise children.
3. Some jobs provide their incumbents with internal feedback, thus lessening the need for the manager to provide feedback. Give some examples of jobs that provide a lot of internal feedback. Now give some examples of jobs where the feedback responsibility falls heavily on the manager.
4. How do you tailor the feedback to fit the recipient?

REINFORCEMENT EXERCISES

The following suggestions are activities you can do to practice and reinforce the feedback techniques you learned in this chapter.

1. Think of three things that a friend or relative did well recently. Did you praise the person at the time? If not, why? The next time that person does something well, give him or her positive feedback.

2. You have a good friend who has a mannerism (speech, body movement, style of dress, or the like) that you think is inappropriate and detracts from the overall impression that he or she makes. Would you criticize this person? If not, why? If so, how?

3. During your instructor's office hours, stop by and provide him or her with feedback on how this course is going so far.

ACTION PLAN

1. Which behavior do I want to improve the most?

_____

_____

_____

2. Why? What will be my payoff?

_____

_____

_____

3. What potential obstacles stand in my way?

_____

_____

_____

4. What are the specific things I will do to improve? (For examples, see the Reinforcement Exercises.)

_____

_____

_____

5. When will I do them?

_____

_____

_____

6. How and when will I measure my success?

_____

_____

_____

Chapter 6
EMPOWERING PEOPLE THROUGH DELEGATION

SELF-ASSESSMENT EXERCISE

For each of the following questions, select the answer that best describes your approach to delegating tasks to subordinates. Remember to respond as you *have* behaved or *would* behave, not as you think you *should* behave. If you have no managerial experience, answer the questions assuming you are a manager.

WHEN DELEGATING TO A SUBORDINATE, I:

	Usually	Sometimes	Seldom
1. Explain exacly how the task should be accomplished.	☐	☐	☐
2. Specify the end results I expect.	☐	☐	☐
3. Feel that I lose control.	☐	☐	☐

	Usually	Sometimes	Seldom
4. Expect that I'll end up doing the task over again myself.	☐	☐	☐
5. Only delegate routine or simple tasks.	☐	☐	☐
6. Clarify to the subordinate the limits to his or her authority.	☐	☐	☐
7. Establish progress report dates with the subordinate.	☐	☐	☐
8. Inform all who will be affected that delegation has occurred.	☐	☐	☐

Scoring Key and Interpretation

For questions 2, 6, 7, and 8, give yourself 3 points for "Usually," 2 points for "Sometimes," and 1 point for "Seldom."

For questions 1, 3, 4, and 5, give yourself 3 points for "Seldom," 2 points for "Sometimes," and 1 point for "Usually."

Sum up your total points. A score of 20 or higher suggests superior delegation skills. A score of 15 to 19 indicates you have room for improvement. A score below 15 suggests that your approach to delegation needs substantial improvement.

SKILL CONCEPTS

Managers are typically described as individuals who get things done through other people. This description recognizes that there are limits to any manager's time and knowledge, and that employees need to be motivated to achieve assigned tasks. Effective managers empower subordinates to accomplish assigned goals by delegating responsibility and authority to them. *Empowerment* means increasing your employees' involvement in their work through greater participation in decisions that control their work and by expanding responsibility for work outcomes (Robbins, 1994).

What Is Delegation?

Delegation allows a subordinate to make decisions by transferring authority from one organizational level to another, lower one (Leana, 1986). Delegation should not be confused with participation, where there is a *sharing* of authority when making decisions. With delegation, subordinates make decisions on their own.

Delegation is frequently depicted as a four-step process: (1) allocation of duties; (2) delegation of authority; (3) assignment of responsibility; and (4) creation of accountability.

Allocation of duties. Duties are the tasks and activities that a manager desires to have someone else do. Before you can delegate authority, you must allocate to a subordinate the duties over which the authority extends.

Delegation of authority. The essence of the delegation process is empowering the subordinate to act for you. It is passing to the subordinate the formal right to act on your behalf.

Assignment of responsibility. When authority is delegated, you must assign responsibility. That is, when you give someone "rights," you must also assign to that person a corresponding "obligation" to perform. Ask yourself: Did I give my subordinate enough authority to get the materials, the use of equipment, and the support from others necessary to get the job done? Imbalances either way can cause problems. Authority in excess of responsibility creates opportunities for abuse; however no one should be held responsible for what he or she has no authority over.

Creation of accountability. To complete the delegation process, you must create accountability; that is, you must hold your subordinate answerable for properly carrying out his or her duties. So while responsibility means a subordinate is obliged to carry out assigned duties, accountability means the subordinate has to perform the assignment in a satisfactory manner. Subordinates are responsible for the completion of tasks assigned them and are accountable to you for the satisfactory performance of that work.

Delegation Is Not Abdication

If you dump tasks on a subordinate without clarifying exactly what is to be done, the range of the subordinate's discretion, the expected level of performance, when the tasks are to be completed, and similar concerns, you are abdicating responsibility and inviting trouble (Steinmetz, 1976). But don't fall into the trap of assuming that, to avoid the appearance of abdicating, you should minimize delegation. Unfortunately, this is the approach taken by many new and inexperienced managers. Lacking confidence in their subordinates, or fearful that they will be criticized for their subordinates' mistakes, they try to do everything themselves.

It may very well be true that you're capable of doing the tasks you delegate to your subordinates better, faster, or with fewer mistakes. The catch is that your time and energy are scarce resources. It's not possible for you to do everything yourself. You need to learn to delegate if you're going to be effective in your job (Pringle, 1986). This suggests two important points. First, you should expect and accept some mistakes by your subordinates. It's part of delegation. Mistakes are often good learning experiences for your subordinates, as long as their costs are not excessive. Second, to ensure that the costs of mistakes don't exceed the value of the learning, you need to put adequate controls in place. As we'll discuss later in this chapter, delegation without feedback controls that let you know when there are serious problems is abdication.

Why Delegate?

Perhaps the primary reason managers delegate is that they can't do everything themselves. But there are some other benefits that can also accrue from delegating.

1. Delegation frees up a manager's time. Every manager gets the same time resource with which to work: twenty-four hours a day, seven days a week, fifty-two weeks a year. The fact that managers differ so greatly in what they accomplish with this common time allocation attests to the value of time management. Delegation is one means by which managers can use their time more efficiently and effectively. Many decisions can be delegated with little or no loss in quality, thus allowing managers—especially those in the middle and upper ranks—to focus on overall direction and coordination.

2. Delegation can improve decision making. In many cases, decisions can actually improve as a result of delegation. Why? Delegation pushes decisions down in the organization. The decision maker, therefore, is closer to the problem and often has better and more complete information about it. This increases the likelihood that the final solution will be of higher quality. Also, because the subordinate is closer to the problem, he or she is able to respond more quickly. So delegation can improve both the quality and the speed of decisions.

3. Delegation helps develop subordinates. Delegation is an excellent device for stimulating subordinate growth and development. It encourages subordinates to expand their job capabilities and knowledge. Moreover, it helps them to develop their decision-making skills and prepares them for future promotion opportunities.

4. Delegation enhances subordinate commitment. No matter how good a decision is, it is likely to be less than fully successful if improperly implemented. One means to improve implementation is to increase the commitment of those who are going to do the implementing. Delegation positively influences commitment. That is, a subordinate is much more likely to enthusiastically embrace a decision that he or she personally made than one imposed from above.

5. Delegation improves manager-subordinate relations. The act of delegation shows that a manager has trust and confidence in the delegatee. This explicit demonstration of support for a subordinate often leads to better interpersonal relations between the manager and the subordinate.

Determinants of Delegation

In spite of all of these benefits of empowering employees through delegation, some managers still have a hard time doing it. Why? They oftentimes are afraid to give up control. "I like to do things myself," says Cheryl Munro Sharp of London Life, "because then I know it's done and I know it's done right." Lisa Flaherty of the Della Femina McNama advertising agency says, "I have to learn to trust others. Sometimes I'm afraid to delegate the more important projects because I like to stay hands-on." Although delegation increases a manager's effectiveness and when done properly still provides control, there are several other factors that determine whether a manager delegates.

The *organizational culture* tends to be a powerful influence on managers (Sapienza, 1985). If the organization is characterized by tolerance of risk, support for employees, and a high degree of autonomy for subordinates, managers will feel a great deal more comfortable delegating than they would in a risk-aversive, nonsupportive, and high-control culture.

Even within a supportive culture, however, managers vary in their propensity to delegate. Why? Research has identified three factors that influence managers (Leana, 1986). The most important is the manager's perception of a subordinate's competence. Managers consistently appear reluctant to delegate if they question their subordinates' capability, trustworthiness, or motivation to assume greater responsibility. The second factor is the *importance* of the decision. Managers tend to delegate the less important decisions. The third factor is the manager's *workload*. Heavy workloads put stress and time pressures on managers, which leads to more delegation of authority. This research also found that the manager's personality plays a relatively minor part in influencing the delegation decision. That is, an individual's personal predisposition toward subordinates is not a key factor.

The important implication of these findings for developing your delegation skills is that effective managers put delegation into context. So, for example, even if the organizational culture supports delegation and a manager strongly believes in its value, that manager is not likely to delegate if he or she doesn't feel that subordinates have the necessary ability and motivation.

Skill Dimensions

A number of actions differentiate the effective from the ineffective delegator. The following sections summarize these actions (McConkey, 1974; Steinmetz, 1976).

1. Clarify the assignment.   The place to begin is to determine *what* is to be delegated and to *whom*. You need to identify the person best capable of doing the task and then determine if he or she has the time and motivation to do the job.

Assuming you have a willing and able subordinate, it is your responsibility to provide clear information on what is being delegated, the results you expect, and any time or performance expectations you hold.

Unless there is an overriding need to adhere to specific methods, you should delegate only the end results. That is, get agreement on what is to be done and the end results expected, but let the subordinate decide on the means. By focusing on goals and allowing the employee the freedom to use his or her own judgment as to how those goals are to be achieved, you increase trust between you and the employee, improve that employee's motivation, and enhance accountability for the results.

2. Specify the subordinate's range of discretion.   Every act of delegation comes with constraints. You're delegating authority to act, but not *unlimited* authority. What you're delegating is authority to act on certain issues and, on those issues, within certain parameters. You need to specify what those parameters are so subordinates know, in no uncertain terms, the range of their discretion. When this has been successfully communicated, both you and the subordinate will have the same idea of the limits to the latter's authority and how far he or she can go without checking further with you.

How much authority do you give a subordinate? In other words, how tight do you draw the parameters? The best answer is that you should allocate enough authority to allow the subordinate to successfully complete the task.

3. Allow the subordinate to participate.   One of the best sources for determining how much authority will be necessary to accomplish a task is the subordinate who will be held accountable for that task. If you allow employees to participate in determining what is delegated, how much authority is needed to get the job done, and the standards by which they'll be judged, you increase employee motivation, satisfaction, and accountability for performance.

Be alert, however, that participation can present its own set of potential problems as a result of subordinates' self-interest and biases in evaluating their own abilities. Some subordinates, for example, are personally motivated to expand their authority beyond what they need and beyond what they are capable of handling. Allowing such people too much participation in deciding what tasks they should take on and how much authority they must have to complete those tasks can undermine the effectiveness of the delegation process.

4. Inform others that delegation has occurred.   Delegation should not take place in a vacuum. Not only do the manager and the subordinate need to know specifically what has been delegated and how much authority *has been* granted, but anyone else who may be affected by the delegation act also needs to be informed. This includes people outside the organization as well as inside it. Essentially, you need to convey what has been delegated (the task and amount of authority) and to whom. If you fail to follow through on this step, the legitimacy of your subordinate's authority will probably be called into question. Failure to inform others makes conflicts likely and decreases the chances that your subordinate will be able to accomplish the delegated task efficiently.

5. Establish feedback controls.   To delegate without instituting feedback controls is to invite problems. There is always the possibility that a subordinate will misuse the discretion that he or she has been delegated. The establishment of controls to monitor the subordinate's progress increases the likelihood that important problems will be identified early and that the task will be completed on time and to the desired specifications.

Ideally, controls should be determined at the time of the initial assignment. Agree on a specific time for completion of the task, and then set progress dates when the subordinate will report back on how well he or she is doing and any major problems that have surfaced. This can be supplemented with periodic spot checks to ensure that authority guidelines are not being abused, organization policies are being followed, proper procedures are being met, and the like. But too much of a good thing can be dysfunctional. If the controls are too constraining, the subordinate will be deprived of the opportunity to build self-confidence and much of the motivational properties of delegation will be lost. A well-designed control system permits your subordinate to make small mistakes but quickly alerts you when big mistakes are imminent.

6. When problems surface, insist on recommendations from the subordinate.   Many managers fall into the trap of letting subordinates reverse the delegation process: The subordinate runs into a problem and then comes back to the manager for advice or a solution. Avoid being sucked into reverse delegation by insisting from the beginning that when subordinates want to discuss a problem with you, they come prepared with a recommendation. When you delegate downward, the subordinate's job includes making necessary decisions. Don't allow the subordinate to push decisions back upward to you.

CONCEPT QUIZ

The following ten-question quiz is based on the previous material. If you miss any of these questions, be sure to go back and find out why you got them wrong.

Circle the right answer:

True or False   1. Delegation requires shifting decision-making authority to a lower-level employee in the organization.

True or False   2. Delegation is the sharing of authority between a manager and his or her subordinate.

True or False   3. Responsibility is the passing of formal rights to a subordinate so that person can act on a manager's behalf.

True or False   4. Authority should be equal to responsibility.

True or False   5. Accountability adds a performance requirement to responsibility.

True or False   6. Managers who delegate can never be accused of abdicating responsibility.

True or False   7. Delegation works because most subordinates can perform tasks better than their managers can.

True or False   8. The most important determinant of whether or not a manager delegates is how heavy the manager's workload is.

True or False   9. Reverse delegation is synonymous with participation.

True or False   10. Delegation can still be effective if subordinates make occasional mistakes.

Answers: (1) True; (2) False; (3) False; (4) True; (5) True; (6) False; (7) False; (8) False; (9) False; (10) True.

BEHAVIORAL CHECKLIST

Look for these specific behaviors when evaluating your delegating skills and those of others.

THE EFFECTIVE DELEGATOR

- Clarifies the assignment

- Specifies the subordinate's range of discretion

- Allows subordinate participation

- Informs others who may be affected that delegation has occurred

- Establishes feedback controls

ATTENTION!

Don't read this or the following exercises until assigned to do so by your instructor.

MODELING EXERCISE

Actors: CHRIS HALL and DALE MORGAN.

Situation: Chris Hall is Director of Research and Development for a large pharmaceutical manufacturer. Chris has six direct subordinates: Sue Traynor (Chris's secretary), Dale Morgan (the laboratory manager), Todd Connor (quality standards manager), Linda Peters (patent coordination manager), Ruben Gomez (market coordination manager), and Marjorie England (senior project manager). Dale is the most senior of the five managers and is generally acknowledged as the chief candidate to replace Chris when Chris is promoted.

CHRIS HALL's role: You have received your annual instructions from the CEO to develop next year's budget for your area. The task is relatively routine but takes quite a bit of time. In the past, you've always done the annual budget yourself. But this year, because your workload is exceptionally heavy, you've decided to try something different. You're going to assign budget preparation to one of your subordinate managers. The obvious choice is Dale Morgan. Dale has been with the company longest, is highly dependable, and, as your probable successor, is most likely to gain from the experience. The budget is due on your boss' desk in eight weeks. Last year it took you about thirty to thirty-five hours to complete. However, you had done a budget many times before. For a novice, it might take double that amount of time.

The budget process is generally straightforward. You start with last year's budget and modify it to reflect inflation and changes in departmental objectives. All the data that Dale will need are in your files or can be obtained from your other managers.

You have decided to walk over to Dale's office and inform him of your decision.

DALE MORGAN's role: You like Chris Hall. You think Chris is a first-rate boss and you've learned a lot from him/her. You also consider yourself Chris' heir apparent. To better prepare yourself to take Chris' job, you'd like to take on more of Chris' responsibilities.

Running the lab is a demanding job. You regularly come in around 7 A.M. and it's unusual for you to leave before 7 P.M. Four of the last five weekends, you've even come in on Saturday mornings to get your work done. But, within reasonable limits, you'd try to find the time to take on some of Chris' responsibilities.

As you sit behind your desk reviewing a lab report, Chris walks into your office.

Time: Ten minutes.

OBSERVER'S RATING SHEET

Evaluate the delegation skills of Chris Hall on a 1 to 5 scale (5 being highest).

- Clarifies the assignment   _____

- Specifies the subordinate's range of discretion   _____

- Allows subordinate participation   _____

- Informs others who may be affected that delegation has occurred   _____

- Establishes feedback controls   _____

Comments:

_____

_____

_____

_____

_____

GROUP EXERCISES

Group Exercise 1

Actors: DANA PORTER and C. J. STONE.

Situation: Dana Porter is the sales manager for Park City Toyota. Dana oversees a fifteen-member sales force at the dealership. In a typical week, Park City Toyota sells forty-five new cars and twenty used cars. Dana is responsible for supervising the sales force, approving all car sales, and handling customer relations.

DANA PORTER's role: You received a notice yesterday that you have been called for jury duty. You will have to appear in court next week and may be gone from work for as long as three weeks. Someone will have to take your place during your absence. No one is really fully qualified to handle your job. In past years, when you went on vacation or were called away from the dealership, the owner would cover for you. But he recently had a heart attack and can't work. You've decided that C. J. Stone, one of your salespeople, is the best person to cover for you. C. J. is young and has only been with the company for about eight months but is bright and assertive.

You have the authority to approve any and all sales. In fact, all new and used car sales require your approval. For instance, you decide on trade-in allowances and any discounts from the suggested list price. You're uncomfortable delegating such broad authority to C. J., so you've decided on a rather cumbersome arrangement. You propose to give C. J. total authority to sell any car at sticker (suggested retail) price, to allow price discounts up to 3 percent on new cars and 5 percent on used cars, and to accept trade-ins at prices not to exceed high wholesale bluebook. Whenever these limits are exceeded by one of the salespeople, C. J. will only be allowed to make a tentative commitment to the customer. You will come in every night after court lets out, review the exceptions, and either approve or reject them. If you have to reject a sale, you will leave a note for C. J. on how far to go to get the sale.

You've called C.J. into your office to discuss your plan.

C. J. STONE's role: You are a young and bright salesperson at Park City Toyota. You work for Dana Porter. You've been with the company for eight months and have been the number-one salesperson in six of those eight months. You've heard on the grapevine that Dana has been called for jury duty. It has crossed your mind that you might be selected to cover for Dana in his/her absence. You've decided that, if asked, you will accept; only you want full authority to approve all sales and resolve any customer complaints. You feel you understand the business and are capable of using good judgment. From your standpoint, any limits placed on a sales manager's discretion hinders the sales staff's ability to quickly close a sale. Moreover, you think it will be fun to call all the shots on the sales floor for a few weeks.

Time: Not to exceed fifteen minutes.

OBSERVER'S role: Use the "Observer's Rating Sheet" on page 104 to provide feedback to the student playing Donna Porter on his or her delegation skills.

Group Exercise 2

Actors: W. L. LAWRENCE and ALEX DREXEL.

Situation: W. L. Lawrence is president and CEO of Lawrence Electronics, a San Francisco firm with 5,000 employees and sales in excess of $800 million a year. Reporting directly to W. L. Lawrence are seven vice presidents. The Vice President for Finance is Alex Drexel.

W.L. LAWRENCE's role: The quarterly meeting of the American Electronics Manufacturers Association is scheduled for the early part of next week. The meeting will be held in Chicago and will last two days. Because of prior commitments, you realized a few days ago that you can't attend. But someone from Lawrence Electronics should be there to represent you. This person's duties would include attending two sessions of committees you belong to, entertaining several important customers, and presenting a short speech at one of the sessions. The speech has already been prepared by someone in the company's public relations department. While any of your vice presidents could handle the assignment, you think Alex Drexel is best qualified. Alex has been to several of these meetings before and knows the ropes. You sent a memo to Alex yesterday asking him/her to attend in your absence.

Alex has asked to see you to discuss the matter. Alex has just entered your office.

ALEX DREXEL's role: You're one of seven vice presidents at Lawrence Electronics. You've been with the firm for a dozen years and were promoted to vice president five years ago.

Yesterday you got a note from your boss, W. L. Lawrence, asking you to take his/her place at next week's American Electronics Manufacturing Association meeting in Chicago. You've been to two or three of these meetings before with W. L. They're incredibly boring. More important, you don't have the extra time to devote two days to the meeting. If pushed to the wall, you'll do it, but you really don't want to. You've called W. L.'s secretary and set up a meeting to discuss this with W. L. You are walking into W. L.'s office now.

Time: Not to exceed fifteen minutes.

Group Exercise 3

Actors: ADRIAN JACKSON and PAT BRENNAN.

Situation: Adrian Jackson is Director of the Sonoma County Hospital. Adrian's assistant is Pat Brennan. About six weeks ago, Adrian assigned Pat the job of developing a reorganization plan for the hospital and Pat enthusiastically accepted. It was agreed that Pat would complete the project in five weeks. The project is now one week past that deadline, and Adrian has heard nothing from Pat regarding the project or when it will be completed.

ADRIAN JACKSON's role: The hospital has grown a great deal in recent years. New departments have been added, while others have expanded considerably. To facilitate efficiency and coordination, you decided a reorganization was necessary. You delegated the reorganization plan to Pat six weeks ago. A memo was sent to all hospital personnel advising them of Pat's assignment and requesting their cooperation.

You're new in your job—you were hired only three months ago. Pat, a legacy from the previous director, has held the Assistant to the Director position at the hospital for six years. Because of Pat's experience, you assumed that he/she could do the reorganization plan with minimal supervision and that it would be completed by the agreed-upon deadline. But that deadline has come and gone. Moreover, you've heard nothing from Pat about how the project is going or when it will be completed. In retrospect, you realize you probably should have kept closer tabs on Pat, but because Pat had so much experience in the position, you were afraid that he/she would interpret almost any monitoring negatively.

You've decided to confront Pat. The monthly staff meeting has just ended. Pat was among the dozen or so in attendance. While everyone else is getting up to leave the conference room, you ask Pat to stay for a few minutes. Your intention is to find out the status of the reorganization plan.

PAT BRENNAN's role: You are the Assistant to the Director. You have held your position for six years, under three different Directors. Your current boss, Adrian, is new to the hospital. Adrian has been in the Director's job for only three months.

You're used to being left on your own. You have a number of routine tasks that you've been doing for years. For instance, you do the weekly bed-utilization report and the monthly departmental efficiency report. Occasionally, Directors have given you special assignments. About six weeks ago, Adrian asked you to develop a reorganization plan in response to the rapid growth the hospital has experienced. You agreed to have it completed in five weeks. A memo was sent out by Adrian to all hospital personnel advising them of your assignment and requesting their cooperation. You accepted the assignment with some reservations, although you didn't say anything to Adrian at the time. You had some ideas on how to reorganize the hospital, but it wasn't a project that especially interested you. Because you never heard anything from Adrian after receiving the initial assignment, you just let the plan sit in your in-basket.

The monthly staff meeting, which Adrian leads, has just concluded. As you are gathering your papers and preparing to leave, Adrian has asked you to stay for a few minutes. You don't know the purpose of this request. However, if it's to discuss the reorganization plan, you've decided to take a two-pronged approach. First, you will put Adrian on the defensive. If the reorganization plan was important, why hasn't he/she followed up on it with you? Second, you intend to throw the decision back at Adrian by asking him/her for possible suggestions.

Time: Not to exceed fifteen minutes.

OBSERVER'S RATING SHEET

For the exercise in which you were the observer, evaluate the delegator on the following behaviors:

- Clarifies the assignment   _____

- Specifies the subordinate's range of discretion   _____

- Allows subordinate participation   _____

- Informs others who may be affected   _____

- Establishes feedback controls   _____

Comments:

_____

_____

_____

SUMMARY CHECKLIST

Take a few minutes to reflect on your performance and look over others' ratings of your skill. Now assess yourself on each of the key learning behaviors. Make a check (✓) next to those behaviors on which you need improvement.

- I clarify assignments to my subordinates. _____

- I specify the subordinate's range of discretion. _____

- I allow subordinates to participate. _____

- I inform others who may be affected that delegation has occurred. _____

- I establish feedback controls. _____

APPLICATION QUESTIONS

1. Why do many managers who want to empower their subordinates find it difficult to delegate authority?

2. What can top management do to encourage managers to delegate to their subordinates?

3. When should a manager purposefully avoid delegation?

4. Which factor influences a manager's propensity to delegate more: the delegator's *personality* or the *organizational culture?* Why do you say this?

REINFORCEMENT EXERCISES

1. When watching a video of a classic movie which has examples of "managers" delegating assignments, pay explicit attention to the incidence of delegation. Was delegating done effectively? What was good about the practice? How might it have been improved? Examples of movies with delegation examples are *The Godfather, The Firm, Star Trek, James Bond, Nine-to-Five,* and *Working Girl.*

2. The next time you have to do a group project for a class, pay explicit attention to how tasks are delegated. Does someone assume a leadership role? If so, note how closely the delegation process is followed. Is delegation different in project or study groups than in typical work groups?

3. Do you delegate in your personal life? What? To whom? The next time you need to delegate, think through the delegation skills and use them to guide your behavior.

ACTION PLAN

1. Which behavior do I want to improve the most?

_____

_____

_____

2. Why? What will be my payoff?

_____

_____

_____

3. What potential obstacles stand in my way?

_____

_____

_____

4. What are the specific things I will do to improve? (For examples, see the Reinforcement Exercises.)

_____

_____

_____

5. When will I do them?

_____

_____

_____

6. How and when will I measure my success?

_____

_____

_____

Chapter 7
PERSUADING

SELF-ASSESSMENT EXERCISE

For each of the following statements, select the answer that best describes your approach to oral persuasion.

	Usually	Sometimes	Seldom
1. I have a clear objective in mind before I ask someone for something.	☐	☐	☐
2. I tailor my arguments to the personality of the person I'm trying to influence.	☐	☐	☐
3. When I want something from someone, I make it clear to that person how doing it will be in his or her self-interest.	☐	☐	☐

	Usually	Sometimes	Seldom
4. If I were manager, I'd expect my subordinates to obey my requests because of the authority in my position.	☐	☐	☐
5. If I want something from someone, I assume that person is intelligent and will respond to logic.	☐	☐	☐
6. When I want something from someone, I explain to the person why what I want is important.	☐	☐	☐
7. When I want something from someone, I try to use emotional appeals as well as logic.	☐	☐	☐

Scoring Key and Interpretation

For questions 1, 2, 3, 5, 6, and 7, give yourself 3 points for "Usually," 2 points for "Sometimes," and 1 point for "Seldom."

For question 4, give yourself 3 points for "Seldom," 2 points for "Sometimes," and 1 point for "Usually."

Sum up your total points. A score of 19 or higher indicates you make effective use of your persuasive resources. A score of 16 to 18 suggests you can be more persuasive in your interpersonal relations. A score below 16 indicates that you have room for significant improvement in your oral persuasion techniques.

SKILL CONCEPTS

If there is one skill that differentiates successful politicians from unsuccessful ones it is the ability to persuade others. They're able to make forceful arguments that appear logical and compelling. Successful politicians, of course, have no monopoly on this skill. We all know people whom we consider persuasive. They seem to know just what to say and when to say it. Were these people born with this skill? No! They were, however, probably exposed to people—parents, other relatives, teachers, friends—who were excellent role models for learning this skill. In this chapter, we'll review what it is that persuasive people do, and then we'll provide you with opportunities to practice these behaviors. Our objective is to equip you with techniques that will make you more persuasive in your interpersonal relations.

Definition

What is *persuasion?* It is the conscious manipulation of face-to-face communication to induce others to take action. How is persuasion different from authority or power? All three are means of influence. That is, they focus on getting other people to do what you want them to do. But power and authority are means of *making* someone else do something they otherwise would not have done, while persuasion preserves others' freedom to do whatever they want after you have tried to convince them to choose a certain course of action. "'Persuadees' feel they are acting of their own accord within the goals and guidelines set for them" (Lerbinger, 1972, p. 5).

Authority represents the rights that go with a managerial position and, for the most part, it's an effective device for gaining subordinates' compliance with requests. But it has its limitations. Authority is of little value in dealing with peers, superiors, or those outside your direct command; it's constrained by employees' perception of your legitimate rights; it's not likely to motivate employees; and it's more suitable for autocratic than democratic organizations.

Authority works well with subordinates. Unfortunately, your interpersonal relations in an organization are not confined to dealing with people who work directly for you. You'll need your boss' cooperation, but you can't get that through authority. You'll be in meetings where you'll need the support of other managers who are at the same level as you. That support can't be obtained through authority. At times, you'll undoubtedly find yourself needing the assistance of others—both inside and outside the organization—to get your job done. You may need a report from another department outside your chain of command or a favor from a supplier, for instance. Again, authority won't work. What you'll need in these varied situations is the ability to persuade.

Authority also has its limits. Every employee sets up a psychological line that defines his or her boss' authority. If you want your employees to do something that crosses that line— to work overtime, to assume an additional project, to take on an unpleasant task, or the like—authority isn't likely to be effective. Where authority won't work, persuasion can.

Even in situations where you have authority and know it will work, you may not want to use it. Why? Because it may have negative repercussions. Authority implies obligation. In contrast, when you persuade someone to do something—even though you have the authority to demand it instead—that person will be more likely to perform the task with commitment and enthusiasm. So persuasion may motivate employees better than authority. Remember, no matter how good your idea, its final effectiveness will depend on how well it's executed by others.

Finally, authority is inconsistent with humanistic-democratic values. Many organizations—especially small ones and those that employ a preponderance of professionals—are organized around participative principles. Authority and control are replaced by openness, trust, and democratic management practices. In such organizations, persuasion is the only viable means to get people to do what you want them to do.

Persuasion Strategies

There are three general strategies of persuasion. You can persuade through *credibility*, through *logical reasoning*, and through *emotional appeal* (Verderber and Verderber, 1986, pp. 163–169).

Credibility: You're more likely to persuade people when they like, trust, and have confidence in you. This credibility doesn't arise out of blind faith. It has to be earned. How? One source is *competence*. By demonstrating knowledge or ability, you establish credibility. A second source is having worthy *intentions*. When your motives are perceived as objective and honest by others, you will have credibility in their eyes. A third source is *character*. Are you ethical, industrious, dependable? If so, your credibility will be increased. Finally, credibility can be enhanced through your *personality*. If you strike others as friendly, caring, enthusiastic, having a positive outlook on life, and so forth, people will be drawn to you.

Credibility is not easy to attain, but it has controllable elements (Kouzes and Posner, 1993). For instance, while it takes time to develop a reputation for competence, you can help it along. How? By doing things like volunteering for projects that will increase your visibility and allow you to "show off" your talents. Similarly, you can concentrate on being friendly and thoughtful to others, conscientious in doing your work, and avoiding actions that might give the appearance of conflicts of interest.

Reasoning. You're more likely to persuade others when you can cite logical reasons for them to behave as you wish. People seek to be rational. Before they do something, they like to feel certain it's consistent with their goals. If that's not directly apparent, then you need to clarify *why* they should think or act the way you want. That is, you need to be prepared to answer the question, "Why?" This can be done by planning ahead and anticipating negative responses. You can prepare a number of possible reasons why a particular action is desirable and then advance the one that seems most appropriate for the particular situation. In this way, you make sure that you present the best argument possible.

You do not make an effective argument by using every reason you can possibly think of or find. Any reason you use should meet three tests (Verderber and Verderber, 1986, p. 168). First, it must really uphold what you're proposing. Second, it must be supportable by the facts. Third, the reason must have an impact on the person you're trying to persuade. The implications of these three criteria are self-evident. Take aim on your target with the precision of a rifle rather than with the overkill of a shotgun. If you're trying to persuade through logical argument, do your homework. Gather the facts to support your argument and, very importantly, get to know the "persuadees." The best-supported argument can fail if you haven't taken into consideration the goals, needs, and interests of the person you're trying to persuade.

Emotional appeal. You may be able to persuade people on the basis of good reasons alone. However, you're more likely to be effective if you also use language that touches their emotions. So, whenever you can, supplement good reasons with appeals to a person's fears, loves, joys, frustrations, and the like.

Why is a combination of logic and emotional appeal more effective than logic alone? The answer is that people can believe in the logic of an argument but still not act on that belief. What they need is a stimulus or kick that will move them from passive to active. An appeal to the emotions can be that stimulus.

Persuasion Tactics

Credibility, reason, and emotion provide three general strategies for persuading others. Now we want to get specific. Hultman (1981) has identified four tactics people can use in attempting to influence others. They are called *active facilitative, passive facilitative, active inhibiting,* and *passive inhibiting.* The first two tactics improve persuasive results; the latter two hinder effectiveness. Obviously, then, people rarely use inhibiting tactics deliberately. Rather, they are usually the unintended consequences of poor planning, lack of information, inadequate listening skills, or an inability to accurately assess one's impact on others. They're included here to dramatize how a tactic that may have begun as facilitative can backfire and actually hinder persuasive efforts.

Active facilitative.   If you actively engage in behavior that succeeds in influencing another person, you have used an active facilitative approach. Popular examples of this approach are being prepared and organized, stating views with conviction, providing information, asking for information, making recommendations, being willing to negotiate, taking the initiative, and paraphrasing (Hultman, 1981, p. 108). This approach is an effective means for clarifying facts; correcting mistaken, inaccurate, or incomplete beliefs; and modifying priorities.

Passive facilitative.   Sometimes the most effective way to persuade another is to do nothing. The passive facilitative approach recognizes that remaining silent, waiting patiently, letting others do the speaking, and similar passive actions can, at times, be highly effective means of influence. Victory doesn't always go to the loudest, the longest-winded, or the person armed with the most facts. The astute persuader knows when to say nothing and let someone else take the offensive.

Active inhibiting.   What kind of active behavior hinders persuasive effectiveness? Hultman (1981) offers some examples: trying to "wing it," stating views tentatively, being unwilling to negotiate, being aggressive, discouraging feedback, discouraging discussion, criticizing, changing the subject, rejecting ideas, and giving advice prematurely. This message should not be lost on those who want to become more effective persuaders: action, without thought, is very likely to be counterproductive.

Passive inhibiting.   The final category encompasses failures due to omission. According to Hultman (1981), these include withholding information, not paying attention, being submissive, ignoring others or their ideas, failing to respond with empathy, leaving issues ambiguous, failing to give praise or appreciation, refusing to grant recognition, withholding help or support, failing to ask for help or support, or allowing others to define your role.

Looking at persuasion through the prism of these four tactical categories drives home three points. First, there is always the potential for failure. Even with the best of intentions, you can fall flat on your face. Second, an active approach is not always preferable. There will be times when purposely "doing nothing" is likely to prove most effective. Third, whether you choose an active or a passive approach depends on whom you're trying to influence. If you have the necessary information about that person's needs, interests, goals, and the like, you can make a better decision about whether to use an active or a passive approach.

Improving Your Persuasive Skills

A review of the oral communication and persuasion research has identified a number of suggestions that can help you to improve your persuasive skills. They build on, and expand, the strategies and tactics previously discussed.

1. Establish your credibility. Nothing undermines persuasive efforts more than a lack of credibility. People don't want to listen to a person they don't trust and respect. By developing the following six dimensions you can enhance your credibility (Coffey, Cook, & Hunsaker, 1994, pp. 210–211).

Develop your *expertise* in the area in which you are trying to influence another. No one eagerly follows the advice of someone who doesn't know what he or she is talking about. By being *warm and friendly* and making sure that your information is *reliable*, you can develop *mutual* trust with influencees. A *dynamic presentation* style also helps as does a reputable *reputation* with others whom the influencee may consult about your ideas and intentions.

2. Use a positive, tactful tone. Assume the person you're trying to persuade is intelligent and mature. Don't talk down to that person. Be respectful, direct, sincere, and tactful. The worst thing that will happen if you follow this advice is that the person will respond in an immature manner and your persuasive effort will be for naught. But you will have advanced your credibility and laid the groundwork for a more effective response next time. On the other hand, if your tone is negative or if you treat the person as if he or she is stupid, you risk making that person defensive, failing in your effort to persuade, and undermining your credibility for future persuasive efforts. Unless you're a football coach—for whom talking down to players seems to be a role expectation—always speak to those you want to persuade in a tone that shows respect.

3. Make your presentation clear. In the event persuasion is successful, what exactly do you want to accomplish? This delineation of an objective should guide your presentation. That is, before you can convincingly articulate your view to someone else, you need to be clear about what it is you want. You'd be surprised how many people don't focus on what they want to accomplish before they jump in. No wonder potential "persuadees" are often confused and unclear about what is being asked of them.

Once your objective is clear, you should present your argument one idea at a time. Don't jump from issue to issue, and avoid unrelated topics. Focus on your end objective, and then present your ideas in a straight path that will lead the person to the conclusion you want and the objective you set.

4. Present strong evidence to support your position. You need to explain why what you want is important. Merely saying a request is important or urgent is not enough. Demanding compliance because "I'm the boss" has limited applicability, and even where it might be appropriate, relying on authority doesn't build credibility. You should demonstrate, with strong supporting evidence, why someone should do as you wish. And the responsibility for "building the case" lies with you.

5. Tailor your argument to the listener. Effective persuasion demands flexibility. You have to select your argument for your specific listener. To whom are you talking? What are his or her goals, needs, interests, fears, and aspirations? How much does the listener know about the subject you're discussing? Does he or she have preconceived views on this subject? If so, how do they align with yours? How does this person like to be treated? What is his or her behavioral style? Answering questions like these can help you define the right persuasion strategy.

Karlins and Abelson (1970, pp. 97–101) have found that an individual's personal characteristics influences his or her persuasibility. For instance, the research indicates that persons with high intelligence tend to be more easily influenced than people with low intelligence when exposed to persuasive communications that rely primarily on strong, logical arguments. However, highly intelligent people are *less* influenced by persuasive communications that rely primarily on unsupported generalities or false, illogical, irrelevant argumentation. High intelligence, in other words, seems to make people more receptive to logical reasoning and less susceptible to flawed logic. The research on authoritarianism reveals that authoritarian personalities—that is, those who believe that there should be status and power differences among people in organizations—are swayed by those in authority. In contrast, nonauthoritarian types are persuaded more by facts and credibility. Our overall conclusion, based on this research, is that you should alter your persuasive strategy to reflect the personal characteristics of the subject. Specifically, the higher a person's intelligence, the more logical and well documented your arguments should be; and you should rely more on facts than on your formal position in attempting to persuade nonauthoritarian types.

6. Appeal to the subject's self-interest. To effectively persuade someone, you need to understand what makes that person tick. Then you can put yourself into his or her position when you make a request. An individual's behavior is directed toward satisfying self-interest. You need to appeal to that self-interest by anticipating, before you make any demands, that the subject will ask, "What's in it for me?" Don't assume that other people will do what you want merely because you're a credible person or because you can articulate logical arguments. You also have to motivate people to action by showing them why it is in their best interests to do as you wish.

7. Use logic. While a logical, reasoned argument is not guaranteed to persuade the subject, if you lack facts and reasons to support your argument, your persuasiveness will almost certainly be undermined. So one test of your persuasive skills is your ability to present a logical argument.

8. Use emotional appeals. Presenting clear, rational, and objective evidence in support of your view is often not enough. You should also appeal to a person's emotions. Try to reach inside the subject and understand his or her loves, hates, fears, and frustrations. Then use that information to mold what you say and how you say it. The persuasiveness of most television evangelists lies in their abilities to understand their audience and to structure their oral presentations so as to appeal to their audience's emotions.

CONCEPT QUIZ

The following ten-question quiz is based on the previous material. If you miss any of these questions, go back and find out why you got them wrong.

Circle the right answer:

True or False   1. Authority is an effective means of influencing superiors.

True or False   2. Oral persuasion seeks to induce others to take action.

True or False   3. The evidence demonstrates that age and credibility are positively correlated.

True or False   4. An effective argument should include every possible reason you can find.

True or False   5. Oral persuasion works best when it focuses on logical reasoning and avoids appeals to emotions and feelings.

True or False   6. Persuasion encompasses both active and passive approaches.

True or False   7. An understanding of oral persuasion tactics ensures success.

True or False   8. You have nothing to gain by talking down to a person you are trying to persuade.

True or False   9. If a well-thought-out argument works with one person, it is likely to be effective with most people.

True or False   10. You should rely more on emotions than on your formal position when attempting to persuade nonauthoritarian types.

   Answers: (1) False; (2) True; (3) False; (4) False; (5) False; (6) True; (7) False; (8) True; (9) False; (10) False.

BEHAVIORAL CHECKLIST

Look for these specific behaviors when evaluating your oral persuasion skills and those of others.

AN EFFECTIVE PERSUADER

- Uses a positive, tactful tone
- Presents ideas one at a time
- Presents strong evidence to support position
- Tailors argument to the listener
- Appeals to the subject's self-interest
- Makes a logical argument
- Uses emotional appeals

ATTENTION!

Don't read this or the following exercises until assigned to do so by your instructor.

MODELING EXERCISE

Actors: PROFESSOR HATCH is a college instructor. DALE DILLON is one of Professor Hatch's former students.

Situation: Dale Dillon has come to Professor Hatch's office. Dale took the professor's course last semester and just received the grade report. It said Dale earned a "C." Dale has come to Hatch's office to persuade the professor to raise the grade to a "B."

DALE DILLON's role: You are a senior, majoring in management. You carried four courses last semester and also worked twenty hours a week. Your eighty-seven-year-old grandmother died last term, and attending her funeral required you to miss a week of class. Your grade-point average, with the "C" in Hatch's class, is 3.65 (out of 4.0). Hatch's "C" is the only "C" grade on your record. You're very disappointed with the grade. You made a "B" on both the midterm and the final, and a "B-" on the term paper. However, participation counted 20 percent and Hatch gave you a "D" in that category.

PROFESSOR HATCH's role: You pride yourself on being a fair instructor. If you make a mistake, you're willing to correct it. However, you don't think grades should be a political process. In the past five years, you've taught about a thousand students and have changed only three grades. In fact, on occasion, you've openly criticized colleagues who make a frequent practice of changing the grades of students who complain.

You perceive Dale Dillon as an exceptionally bright student who wasn't committed to your class last term. You gave Dale a "B" on both the midterm and final, and a "B-" on the term paper. However, participation counted 20 percent and you gave Dale a "D" in that category. Dale missed four of the thirty class sessions, two of them in one week. In contrast, no one else in the class missed more than two sessions. The quality of Dale's in-class contributions were at about the 75th percentile, but the quantity of those contributions was significantly below the class average.

Time: Not to exceed ten minutes.

OBSERVER'S RATING SHEET

Evaluate the oral persuasive performance of Dale Dillon on a 1 to 5 scale (5 being highest).

- Uses positive, tactful tone   _____
- Presents ideas one at a time   _____
- Gives strong supportive evidence   _____
- Tailors argument to listener   _____
- Appeals to subject's self-interest   _____
- Makes a logical argument   _____
- Uses emotional appeal   _____

Comments:

_____

_____

_____

GROUP EXERCISES

Break up into groups of three. Each group will perform three role-plays, allowing each member a chance to play persuader, subject, and observer. As the observer, you are to evaluate the persuader's skills using the seven behaviors identified in the "Observer's Rating Sheet" on page 121.

Group Exercises 1–3

Each exercise is not to exceed ten minutes in length. The subject is to choose any topic that he or she feels strongly about and state his or her position on the topic in thirty words or less. The persuader will then attempt to change the subject's mind. Both persuader and subject play themselves in each role-play.

Potential topics (the subject can choose *either* side of a topic) are

1. Current election issues.

2. Current events.

3. Controversial campus issues.

4. Management issues. Some examples are:

   a. Managing in the Middle East is significantly different from managing in North America.

   b. Employee turnover in an organization can be functional.

   c. Organizations should require all employees to undergo regular tests for AIDS.

   d. Organizations should require all employees to undergo regular drug tests.

   e. A degree in business prepares students for a career in the business world.

   f. Given current organizational practices, an employee's loyalty should be to him- or herself. An employee owes nothing more than a solid day's work to his or her employer.

OBSERVER'S RATING SHEET

For the exercise in which you were the observer, evaluate the persuader on the key oral persuasion behaviors on a 1 to 5 scale (5 being highest).

- Uses positive, tactful tone   _____

- Presents ideas one at a time   _____

- Gives strong supportive evidence   _____

- Tailors strong supportive evidence   _____

- Appeals to self-interest   _____

- Makes a logical argument   _____

- Uses emotional appeals   _____

Comments:

_____

_____

_____

SUMMARY CHECKLIST

Take a few minutes to reflect on your performance and look over others' ratings of your skill. Now assess yourself on each of the key learning behaviors. Make a check (✓) next to those behaviors on which you need improvement.

- I use a positive, tactful tone.   _____
- I present ideas one at a time.   _____
- I present strong evidence to support my position.   _____
- I tailor my argument to the listener.   _____
- I appeal to the subject's self-interest.   _____
- I make logical arguments.   _____
- I use emotional appeals.   _____

QUESTIONS FOR DISCUSSION

1. In what ways do television advertisements draw on the concepts in this chapter?
2. In what ways do effective persuasion skills parallel the skills necessary to be an effective salesperson?
3. Explain the differences between authority and persuasion.
4. Explain in what situations, and why, you would use each of the four persuasion tactics.

REINFORCEMENT EXERCISES

The following suggestions are activities you can do to practice and reinforce the oral persuasion techniques you learned in this chapter.

1. Persuade a person you know only in passing to lend you $10 for a week.
2. Convince a friend or relative to go with you to see a movie or play that you know the person doesn't want to see.
3. Go into a small retail store. Convince the proprietor, as a condition of purchase, to accept a price below that marked on an item.

ACTION PLAN

1. Which behavior do I want to improve the most?

_____

_____

_____

_____

2. Why? What will be my payoff?

_____

_____

_____

_____

3. What potential obstacles stand in my way?

_____

_____

_____

4. What are the specific things I will do to improve? (For examples, see the Reinforcement Exercises.)

_____

_____

_____

_____

5. When will I do them?

_____

_____

_____

6. How and when will I measure my success?

_____

_____

_____

Chapter *8*
POLITICKING

SELF-ASSESSMENT EXERCISE

For each of the following statements, circle the number that most closely resembles your attitude.

Statement	Disagree			Agree	
	A lot	A little	Neutral	A little	A lot
1. The best way to handle people is to tell them what they want to hear.	1	2	3	4	5
2. When you ask someone to do something for you, it is best to give the real reason for wanting it rather than reasons that might carry more weight.	1	2	3	4	5
3. Anyone who completely trusts someone else is asking for trouble.	1	2	3	4	5
4. It is hard to get ahead without cutting corners here and there.	1	2	3	4	5

Statement	Disagree			Agree	
	A lot	A little	Neutral	A little	A lot
5. It is safest to assume that all people have a vicious streak, and it will come out when they are given a chance.	1	2	3	4	5
6. One should take action only when it is morally right.	1	2	3	4	5
7. Most people are basically good and kind.	1	2	3	4	5
8. There is no excuse for lying to someone else.	1	2	3	4	5
9. Most people forget more easily the death of their father than the loss of their property.	1	2	3	4	5
10. Generally speaking, people won't work hard unless forced to do so.	1	2	3	4	5

Scoring Key and Interpretation

This exercise is designed to compute your Machiavellianism (Mach) score. Mach is a personality characteristic that taps people's power orientation. The high-Mach personality is pragmatic, maintains emotional distance from others, and believes that ends can justify means. To obtain your Mach score, add up the numbers you checked for questions 1, 3, 4, 5, 9, and 10. For the other four questions, reverse the numbers you have checked, so that 5 becomes 1, 4 is 2, 2 is 4, and 1 is 5. Then total both sets of numbers to find your score. A random sample of adults found the national average to be 25. Students in business and management typically score higher.

The results of research using the Mach test have found (1) men are generally more Machiavellian than women; (2) older adults tend to have lower Mach scores than younger adults; (3) there is no significant difference between high Machs and low Machs on measures of intelligence or ability; (4) Machiavellianism is not significantly related to demographic characterisitcs such as educational level or marital status; and (5) high Machs tend to be in professions that emphasize the control and maniuplation of people—for example, managers, lawyers, psychiatrists, and behavioral scientists.

Source: R. Christie and F. L. Geis, *Studies in Machiavellianism.* Academic Press, 1970. Reprinted by permission.

SKILL CONCEPTS

In the real world of organizations, the "good guys" don't always win. Demonstrating openness, trust, objectivity, support, and similar humane qualities in relationships with others doesn't always lead to improved managerial effectiveness. There will be times when, to get things done that you want done or to protect your interests against the maneuvering of others, you'll have to play "hard ball." That is, you'll have to engage in politicking. When is that? And how should you go about politicking? Those are the questions this chapter addresses.

What Is Politicking?

Politics relates to who gets what, when, and how. Politicking is the actions you can take to influence, or attempt to influence, the distribution of advantages and disadvantages within your organization (Farrell and Petersen, 1982).

Unlike such issues as goal setting and delegation, you don't learn much about politicking in the typical college program in business management. Why? One reason may be the prescriptive nature of business programs. They emphasize what managers *should* do rather than what they *actually* do (Robbins, 1977). Another reason may be the "underground" nature of politics (Yates, 1985). Much of it is subtle, disguised, or veiled in secrecy; and successful politicians in organizations are often highly adept at framing their political actions in nonpolitical terms. The result is that it is very difficult to get meaningful insights into the political process in organizations. This is unfortunate because political incompetence, political naiveté, and the inability or unwillingness to effectively perform required political tasks are all sources of management failure (Young, 1986).

Why Is There Politics in Organizations?

Can you conceive of an organization that is politics-free? It's possible but most unlikely.

Organizations are made up of individuals and groups with different values, goals, and interests (Pfeffer, 1981). This sets up the potential for conflict over resources. Departmental budgets, space allocations, project responsibilities, and salary adjustments are just a few examples of the resources about whose allocation organizational members will disagree.

Resources in organizations are also limited, which often turns potential conflict into real conflict. If resources were abundant, then all the various internal constituencies within the organization could satisfy their goals. But because they're limited, not everyone's interests can be provided for. Further, whether true or not, gains by one individual or group are often *perceived* as being at the expense of others within the organization. These forces create a competition among members for the organization's limited resources.

Maybe the most important factor leading to politics within organizations is the realization that most of the "facts" that are used to allocate the limited resources are open to interpretation. What, for instance, is *good* performance? What's a *good* job? What's an *adequate* improvement? The manager of any major league baseball team knows a .400 hitter is a high performer and a .125 hitter a poor performer. You don't need to be a baseball genius to know you should play your .400 hitter and send the .125 hitter back to the minors. But what if you have to choose between players who hit .280 and .290? Then other factors—less objective ones—come into play: fielding, attitude, potential, ability to perform in the clutch, and so on. Most managerial decisions in organizations more closely resemble choosing between a .280 and a .290 hitter than deciding between a .125 hitter and a .400 hitter. It is in this large and ambiguous middle ground of organizational life—where the facts *don't* speak for themselves—that politics takes place.

Finally, because most decisions have to be made in a climate of ambiguity—where facts are rarely fully objective, and thus are open to interpretation—people within the organization will use whatever influence they can to taint the facts to support their goals and interests. That, of course, creates the activities we call *politicking*.

Political Diagnostic Analysis

Before you consider your political options in any situation, you need to evaluate that situation. Political diagnostic analysis is a three-step process designed to make you a better evaluator.

1. Assess your organization's culture. The place to begin is with assessing your organization's culture to ascertain which behaviors are desirable and which aren't. Every organization has a system of shared meaning called its *culture* (Trice and Beyer, 1993). This culture is a set of unwritten norms that members of the organization accept and understand, and which guide their actions. For example, some organizations' cultures encourage risk taking, accept conflicts and disagreements, allow employees a great deal of autonomy, and reward members according to performance criteria. But there are cultures that differ by 180 degrees: They punish risk taking, seek harmony and cooperation at any price, minimize opportunities for employees to show initiative, and allocate rewards to people according to such criteria as seniority, effort, or loyalty. The point is that every organization's culture is somewhat different, and if a political strategy is to succeed, it must be compatible with the culture.

One of the fastest and most effective means for tapping an organization's culture is to learn as much as you can about the organization's performance-appraisal system and the criteria used for determining salary increases, promotions, and other rewards. Take a look at the organization's performance-appraisal form. What does it look like? What does it evaluate: traits, behaviors, goal accomplishments? How much emphasis is placed on factors like getting along with others, teamwork, and loyalty to the organization? Does style count as much as substance? Are people rated against absolute standards or against each other? How are people ranked? How often are appraisals required? How does top management view performance appraisal: to identify deficiencies, as a basis for reward allocations, or to facilitate employee growth and development? Then turn your attention to the reward system. Who gets the raises and promotions? Maybe more importantly, who doesn't? These reward-allocation decisions should tell you what behaviors "pay off" in your organization.

2. Assess the power of others. People are either powerful or they're not, right? Wrong! Power is differential. On some issues, a person may be very powerful. Yet that same person may be relatively powerless on other issues. What you need to do, therefore, is determine which individuals or groups will be powerful in a given situation.

Some people have influence as a result of their formal position in the organization. So that is probably the best place to begin your power assessment. What decision or issue do you want to influence? Who has formal authority to affect that issue? But that is only the beginning. After that, you need to consider others—individuals, coalitions, formal departments—who may have a vested interest in the decision's outcome. Who might gain or lose as a result of one choice being selected over another? This helps to identify the power players—those motivated to engage in politicking. It also pinpoints your likely adversaries.

Now you need to specifically assess the power of each player or group of players. In addition to each one's formal authority, you should evaluate the resources each controls (Pfeffer and Salancik, 1978) and his or her centrality in the organization (Brass, 1984). Research confirms that the control of scarce and important resources is a source of power in organizations.

Control and access to key information or expert knowledge and possession of special skills are examples of resources that may be scarce and important to the organization—and hence, potential means of influencing organizational decisions. It has also been found that centrality—being in the right place in the organization—can be a source of power. People or groups with network centrality gain power because their position allows them to integrate other functions or to reduce organization dependence. This explains, for instance, the frequent power of secretaries or the influence of the accounting department when a firm is experiencing a major financial crisis.

On a more micro level, you should not overlook assessing your boss' influence in any power analysis. What is his or her position on the issue under concern? For, against, or neutral? If it's for or against, how intense is your boss' stand? What is your boss' power status in the organization? Strong or weak? Answers to these questions can help you assess whether the support or opposition of your boss will be relevant. The support of a powerful boss can obviously be a plus. On the other hand, the support of a weak boss is likely to mean little and can even be harmful to your cause. If your boss is an "up-and-comer" with an expanding power base, you'll want to tread carefully. As an adversary, such a person can be a major hindrance to your future in the organization. However, as an ally, such a boss can open doors previously closed to you and possibly provide the vehicle to accelerate your rise in the organization. If your power assessment uncovers that your boss is widely perceived throughout the organization as "deadwood," your political strategy may need to include distancing yourself from him or her (remember guilt by association?).

3. Assess your power. After looking at others' power, you need to assess your own power base. What's your personal power? What power, if any, does your position in the organization provide? And where do you stand relative to others who hold power?

Some people project a personal charisma or magnetic personality that draws others to them. They have those hard-to-define "leadership qualities." They are often perceived as socially adept, popular, outgoing, self-confident, aggressive, and intelligent (Allen et al., 1979). If you happen to be seen in your organization as a *charismatic* leader, you'll find that others will want to know your position on issues, that your arguments will often be perceived as persuasive, and that your position is likely to carry considerable weight in others' decisions.

Few of us are charismatic leaders. We're more likely to develop a personal power base through our *expertise*. By controlling specialized information that others need, we increase others' dependence upon us. If there are lots of people in the organization who can do what you can do, or if your talent could be easily replaced by hiring an outsider, your expert power is low.

If you have neither charismatic nor expert power, possibly your *position* in the organization can be a source of power. If you're a manager, you'll have some reward and coercive powers derived solely from the authority of your position. So, for instance, you may be able to reassign people, approve time off, hand out salary increases, initiate suspensions, or even fire employees. In addition to formal authority, your position might also provide centrality, high visibility, access to important or guarded information, and the like. Depending on the issue, your position might prove an asset.

Finally, don't ignore the dynamics inherent in the relationship between you and other powerholders (Coplin, O'Leary, and Gould, 1985). Determine the degree to which players support or oppose you. Assess their power to influence the ultimate outcome. Then determine the priority they assign to your objective. In this way, you can identify where your allies are; who your opponents are likely to be; the intensity of support or opposition each can be expected to exert; and the personal, positional, and coalitional power you and your supporters can bring to bear to counter the resistance of opponents.

Politics in Action

Now we turn from analysis to action. We begin by offering some general guides and then propose specific strategies.

General Guidelines

1. Frame arguments in terms of organizational goals. Effective politicking requires covering up self-interest. No matter that your objective is self-serving; all the arguments you marshal in support of it must be framed in terms of the benefits that will accrue to the organization. People whose actions appear to blatantly further their own interests at the expense of the organization's are almost universally denounced, are likely to lose influence, and often suffer the ultimate penalty of being expelled from the organization.

2. Develop the right image. If you know your organization's culture, you understand what the organization wants and values from its managers—in terms of dress; associates to cultivate and those to avoid; whether to appear risk taking or risk aversive; the preferred leadership style; the importance placed on getting along well with others; and so forth. Then you are equipped to project the appropriate image. Because effectiveness in an organization is not a fully objective outcome, style as well as substance must be attended to. Impression management—that is, shaping a particular identity in the mind of others during an interaction (Goffman, 1959)—is an important part of political success.

3. Gain control of organizational resources. The control of organizational resources that are scarce and important is a source of power. Knowledge and expertise are particularly effective resources to control. They make you more valuable to the organization and therefore more likely to gain security, advancement, and a receptive audience for your ideas.

4. Make yourself appear indispensable. Since we're dealing with appearances rather than objective facts, you can enhance your power by appearing to be indispensable. That is, you don't have to really be indispensable as long as key people in the organization believe that you are. If the prime decision makers believe there is no ready substitute for what you are giving the organization, they are likely to go to great lengths to ensure that your desires are satisfied. How do you make yourself appear indispensable? The most effective means is to develop expertise through experience, contacts, secret techniques, natural talents, and the like—that is, perceived as critical to the organization's operations and that key decision makers believe no one else possesses to the extent that you do.

It also helps for others in your organization to perceive you as mobile and to believe you have employment options available at other organizations. Combining perceived mobility with perceived indispensability lessens the likelihood that your rise in your present organization will be stalled by the excuse that "we can't promote you right now because your current unit can't afford to lose your expertise."

5. Be visible. Since the evaluation of managerial effectiveness has a substantial subjective component, it is important that your boss and those in power in the organization be made aware of your contribution. If you are fortunate enough to have a job that brings your accomplishments to the attention of others, it may not be necessary to take direct measures to increase your visibility. But your job may require you to handle activities that are low in visibility, or your specific contribution may be indistinguishable because you're part of a group endeavor. In such cases—without creating the image of a braggart—you'll want to call attention to yourself by giving progress reports to your boss and others, being seen at social functions, being active in your professional associations, developing powerful allies who speak positively about your accomplishments, and similar tactics. Of course, the skilled politician actively and successfully lobbies to get those projects that will increase his or her visibility.

6. Get a mentor. A mentor is an individual, typically higher up in the organization, who takes on a protégé as ally and sponsor. A mentor is someone from whom you can learn and who can encourage and help you. When you have a mentor, that person can be expected to stand up for you at meetings and relay inside information that you otherwise wouldn't have access to. Additionally, just the fact that you have a mentor provides a signal to others in the organization that you have the resources of a powerful higher-up behind you.

But how do you get a mentor? Typically, mentors do the choosing. They spot someone lower in the organization with whom they identify and take that person on as a protégé. The more contacts you make with higher-ups—both formally and informally—the greater chance you have of being singled out as someone's protégé. Participating in company golf tournaments, going out for drinks with colleagues after work, and taking on visible projects are examples of activities that are likely to bring you to the attention of a potential mentor.

7. Develop powerful allies. It helps to have powerful people in your camp. In addition to a mentor, you can cultivate contacts with potentially influential people above you, at your level, and in the lower ranks. They can provide you with important information that may not be available through normal channels. Additionally, there will be times when decisions will be made by those with the greatest support. Sometimes—though not always—there is strength in numbers. Having powerful allies can provide you with a coalition of support if and when you need it.

8. Avoid "tainted" members. In almost every organization, there are fringe members whose status is questionable. Their performance and/or loyalty is under close scrutiny. Such individuals, while they are under the microscope, are "tainted." Carefully keep your distance from them. We all tend to judge others by the company they keep. Given the reality that effectiveness has a large subjective component, your own effectiveness might be called into question if you are perceived as being too closely associated with "tainted" people.

9. Support your boss. Your immediate future is in the hands of your current boss. Since he or she evaluates your performance, you will typically want to do whatever is necessary to have your boss on your side.

You should make every effort to help your boss succeed, make her look good, support her if she is under siege, and spend the time to find out what criteria she will be using to assess your effectiveness. Don't undermine your boss. Don't speak negatively of her to others. If she is competent, visible, and in possession of a power base, she is likely to be on the way up in the organization. By being perceived as supportive, you increase the likelihood of being pulled along too. At the worst, you'll have established an ally higher up in the organization. But what should you do if your boss' performance is poor and her power low?

Politically, it's better to switch than fight. Your credibility will be challenged if your boss is perceived as weak. Your performance evaluations—even if highly positive—are not likely to carry much weight. You'll suffer from guilt by association. It is extremely difficult to distance yourself from your immediate boss without your boss perceiving you as a traitor. The most effective solution in such a situation—and the one that carries the least risk—is to quietly lobby for a transfer. If you have a mentor, use that person to lobby for you. Of course, consistent with what we said earlier, couch your request for a transfer in terms of the organization's best interests (i.e., a transfer will increase your experience, prepare you to assume greater responsibilities, and allow you to make bigger contributions to the organization).

Specific Strategies

What specific strategies can you use to influence others and get them to support your objectives? When is one strategy preferable to another? Research has identified seven widely used options (Kipnis et al., 1984).

1. Reasoning is the use of facts and data to make a logical or rational presentation of ideas. This strategy is most likely to be effective in a culture characterized by trust, openness, and logic; and where the vested interests of other parties in your request are low.

2. Friendliness is using flattery, creating goodwill, acting humble, and being friendly prior to making a request. It is more effective for obtaining favors than for selling ideas. It also requires that you be well liked and that your interpersonal relations with the target of influence be good.

3. Coalitions get the support of other people in the organization to back up your request. Since this strategy is complex and requires coordination, it tends to be used for important outcomes, and where the final decision relies more on the quantity than on the quality of support (as in committees that make their decisions by majority rule).

4. Bargaining is the use of negotiation through the exchange of benefits or favors. This strategy is applicable where there is interdependence between you and the target, and where the culture promotes give-and-take.

5. Higher authority relies on gaining the support of higher-ups in the organization to back your requests. This is an effective strategy only if the higher-ups are liked or feared. Also, while appropriate in bureaucratic cultures where there is great respect for authority, this strategy is inappropriate in less structured cultures.

6. Assertiveness is a direct and forceful approach such as demanding compliance with requests, issuing reminders, ordering individuals to do what you need done, and pointing out that rules require compliance. This strategy is effective where the balance of power is clearly in your favor: you have considerable ability to reward and punish others, while their power over you is low. The drawback is that the target is likely to feel resentful and look for later opportunities to retaliate.

7. Sanctions is the use of organizationally derived rewards and punishments such as preventing or promising a salary increase, threatening to give an unsatisfactory performance appraisal, or withholding a promotion. This strategy is similar to assertiveness, except the influence here depends solely on your position. Obviously, this is not an approach for influencing superiors; and even when used with subordinates, it may be perceived as manipulative or illegitimate.

Considering the Cost-Benefit Equation

Before you select a political strategy, be sure to assess any potential costs of using it against its potential benefits. The inexperienced politician needs to be reminded that all forms of power are not alike. Some are accepted more readily than others, and there are many instances when the costs of applying influence exceed the benefits derived from such action. While the benefits of power are quite obvious, the costs are often overlooked. As Lawless (1972, p. 243) has noted, "Power is effective when held in balance. As soon as power is *used*, it gets out of balance and the person *against whom* the power is used automatically resorts to some activities designed to correct the power imbalance."

In physics, we know that for every action there is a reaction. In the study of management, we know that for every use of power there is a corollary use of power. So your choice of a strategy should depend not only on whether it will allow you to achieve your short-term goal. You should also try to minimize resentment and to use up the least possible amount of future credits. This would suggest a preference for reason, friendliness, and rewards to obtain compliance, and avoidance of coercive approaches whenever possible (French and Raven, 1960). Remember, whenever you use the "do this or else" approach, you run the risk that your bluff will be called. The result may not be very desirable in cost-benefit terms—you may win the battle but lose the war.

CONCEPT QUIZ

Do you understand the basic concepts in politicking? The following quiz will help answer that question. Remember, if you miss any, go back and find out why you got them wrong.

Circle the right answers:

True or False 1. Organizations are made up on individuals and groups with different values, goals, and interests.

True or False 2. Politics exists in organizations because decisions are made in a climate of ambiguity.

True or False 3. The existence of a formal performance appraisal system in an organization reduces the likelihood that politics will surface.

True or False 4. Because power tends to accrue to positions, all you need to know about a person's power in an organization is the position he or she holds.

True or False 5. For the control of a resource to convey power, the resource must be both scarce and important.

True or False 6. Your boss' support can be a negative as well as a positive.

True or False 7. Most middle- and upper-level managers are charismatic leaders.

True or False 8. All managerial positions come with some reward and coercive powers.

True or False 9. All other things being equal, you should try to avoid the use of coercive power.

True or False 10. "I did that for you, now you do this for me" is an example of a coalition strategy.

Answers: (1) True; (2) True; (3) False; (4) False; (5) True; (6) True; (7) False, (8) True; (9) True; (10) False.

```
┌────────────────────────────────────────────┐
│                 ATTENTION!                   │
│         Read all three of the following cases│
│            **before** coming to class.       │
└────────────────────────────────────────────┘
```

GROUP EXERCISES

In contrast to previous chapters, there are no specific political behaviors we can list that can be observed and evaluated in a role-play. The way to demonstrate that you can use the political skills described in this chapter is to apply them to a set of cases. The following cases can be discussed in groups or by the class as a whole.

Group Exercise 1*

When Chairman Franklin M. Jarman wrested control of Genesco, Inc. from his father, W. Maxey, to become chief executive officer four years ago [this was written in 1977], one of his primary goals was to impose a system of financial controls over the $1 billion retailing and apparel conglomerate. The 45-year-old Jarman did exactly that. His controls probably helped to save the company when it lost $52 million in 1973. But they were also chiefly responsible for his downfall last week.

Controls were an obsession with Jarman. According to insiders, he centralized management to the point of frustrating the company's executives and causing red tape and delay. Operations were virtually paralyzed by paperwork. One glaring example: Genesco's most recent annual report states that the company would spend $8 million this year to open 63 stores and renovate 124 others. Yet six months into the fiscal year, insiders report that little has been done because Jarman required more and more analysis for each project, postponing decisions.

Such delay and indecision can be particularly harmful in a company like Genesco, whose business is mostly in the fast-moving fields of apparel and retailing. Among its major product lines are Johnston & Murphy and Jarman Shoes, and its retail outlets include Bonwit Teller and S. H. Kress. "It was a classic case of the boss being in the way, and he had to go," explains one Genesco insider, who was among the more than two dozen executives participating in the palace revolt last week when Jarman was stripped of his authority.

---

*Source: "What Undid Jarman: Paperwork Paralysis," *Business Week* (January 24, 1977) pp. 67-68, by special permission, copyright 1977 by McGraw-Hill, Inc., New York, N.Y. 10029. All rights reserved.

The undoing.   Two of Genesco's inside directors, Vice Chairmen Ralph H. Bowles and Larry B. Shelton, had become alarmed by Genesco's inertia in October. At the same time many top managers complained to them that Jarman's management had been demoralizing. When Jarman seemed to be preparing to oust two key operating executives, Bowles and Shelton went to an outside director to explain how the company's fortunes were deteriorating. He in turn contacted other outside directors. Meanwhile, Bowles, Shelton, and several managers compiled for the directors a dossier of Jarman's managerial shortcomings.

Things all came together between Christmas and New Year's when Jarman was on vacation at Montego Bay. Bowles, Shelton, several managers, and four outside directors met in Washington. They called a special meeting of the board for the Monday after New Year's. With more than two dozen rank-and-file executives ready to quit if Jarman was not ousted—and waiting in the cafeteria next door on the second floor of the Genesco building in Nashville—the board did the next best thing. It took away Jarman's titles of president and chief executive officer and gave them to William M. Blackie, age 72, a retired executive vice president and former director, and told Jarman that he must take his orders from Blackie.

Jarman declined to be interviewed by *Business Week* for this article. But sources close to him and the company say that he was treated shabbily by the Genesco board and executives—many of whom owed their jobs to him. These sources say that Jarman was the victim of a conspiracy, which they say started after word got out that he was looking for a new president with marketing experience, a job for which he had hired the New York search firm of Knight & Zabriskie. According to this scenario, Bowles, age 46, and Shelton, age 42, feared that if a new president were brought in they would lose standing. Jarman came back from vacation and just before the board meeting issued a statement saying that it would be "inappropriate and contrary to the interests of the stockholders of Genesco to make any radical change in the company's management . . . With the approval of members of the board of directors, [Jarman has] been seeking to hire a new president." Bowles and Shelton maintain that they were not among those members and that all they knew was that Jarman was looking for a senior marketing executive.

The performance.   In any case, Genesco's performance under Jarman was erratic. Although he pared many losing operations and improved the balance sheet, Genesco lost money in two of his four years as CEO. For example, last year's earnings rebounded to $15.9 million, or about

$1 a share, after a loss of $14.4 million the year before, but in the first quarter of the this fiscal year ending October 31, earnings were off 61 percent, and Jarman had projected similarly disappointing results for the important second quarter, which includes Christmas.

Insiders are convinced there was a correlation between Genesco's earnings and the overcentralized and inflexible management style they say Jarman favored. Many criticisms of Jarman's management were chronicled by Genesco executives and by Bowles and Shelton in the form of internal memoranda. The memoranda were put in dossiers several inches thick and given to each director. The board took its action last week largely on the basis of this material.

One Genesco director thinks that this approach was amateurish and unnecessary, although he voted to oust Jarman. He says the material in the dossier consisted principally of "record memoranda—written to the files after conversations with Jarman—that were very self-serving." The memoranda, he adds, contained many inconsistencies, such as that Jarman was too involved in detail or that he was not involved enough.

An insider who has read the material says that there are inconsistencies because Jarman was an inconsistent manager. He cites the example of a new shoe store under consideration. Jarman demanded a seventy-five-page report on the $44,000 store dealing with such trifling details as whether it should have a water cooler and hot running water. On the other hand, this executive says that, if a division executive had an overwhelming personality, he could push through decisions with "no checks, no balances, not even pro forma financial statements"—as was done recently with a proposal for a new Bonwit Teller store.

As a matter of course, insiders say, Jarman got bogged down in minutiae. He delegated little real authority to his managers, even to the two vice chairmen.

"Better run it by Frank," was the company watchword for the most routine, everyday matters. He spent a great deal of time insisting that reports be bound properly in notebooks. Another criticism is that Jarman isolated himself and avoided contact with company executives. Typically, he dealt only with the four other members of the management committee, of which he was chairman and which included Bowles, Shelton, and two operating executives. Jarman, an engineer educated at the Massachusetts Institute of Technology, had come up through the financial side of Genesco and, as a director notes, "has never been good at handling people."

One executive says that, ever since Jarman had become CEO, top people in the company had been trying to get him to visit the company's many plants and offices. This executive says that Jarman did it just once. Moreover, Jarman canceled the customary annual management breakfast meetings that brought all the top executives together with the chairman. Without Jarman's isolation from other Genesco managers, it is doubtful that the revolt against him could have been carried out so smoothly.

Jarman's style was to work from computer printouts, checking them for aberrations. He reportedly used to say that managing a corporation was like flying an airplane—his avocation. "'You watched the dials to see if the plane deviated off course and when it did you nudged it back with the controls,' Jarman explained," the insider says. "At Genesco the computer printouts were the dials and Bowles and Shelton were the controls."

Sometimes, however, Jarman did not believe what the printouts said. He hired consultants to verify things, such as a division's overhead charges or the quality and pricing of its products. The footwear division, which has been consistently profitable, got this treatment several times.

Still, a surprise, Jarman's ouster, nevertheless, took many observers by surprise. To begin with, the board had recently granted him a $105,000 raise to $285,000 a year, even though Genesco pays no common stock dividend. (The board cut Jarman to $180,000 annually last week).

Equally surprising was the fact that Genesco's board has been structured to Jarman's specifications in recent years. Over a four-year period, it was reduced from eighteen to ten members, and many of the father's supporters were replaced by the son's choices, such as Bowles, Shelton, and Wilson, with whom Frank Jarman served on several corporate and civic boards.

To insiders, however, things were different. First, after news broke of Jarman's raise, Genesco employees signed petitions to protest. Moreover, there was overwhelming sentiment in middle management that Jarman had to go if Genesco was to survive. "You could count Jarman's supporters on the fingers of one hand," one executive said.

Last week the board started searching for an outsider to fill the presidency. Whoever lands the Genesco job will have a challenge not only to produce consistent earnings but also to gain the support of the managers, the vice chairmen, and the board of directors. "It's a slippery perch," says one corporate recruiter.

Questions:

1. If you were Franklin Jarman, looking back over what has happened, what might you have done differently to avoid being ousted?

2. If you were offered the presidency of Genesco, what would you do to gain the support of the company's management and board members?

Time: Not to exceed twenty-five minutes.

*Group Exercise 2**

The Savemore Corporation is a chain of 400 retail supermarkets located primarily in the northeastern section of the United States. Store 5116 employs more than 50 persons, all of whom live within suburban Portage, New York, where the store is located.

Wally Shultz served as general manager of store 5116 for six years. Last April he was transferred to another store in the chain. At that time the employees were told by the district manager, Mr. Finnie, that Wally Shultz was being promoted to manage a larger store in another township.

Most of the employees seemed unhappy to lose their old manager. Nearly everyone agreed with the opinion that Shultz was a "good guy to work for." As examples of his desirability as a boss, the employees told how Wally had frequently helped the arthritic black porter with his floor mopping, how he had shut the store five minutes early each night so that certain employees might catch their buses, of a Christmas party held each year for employees at his own expense, and his general willingness to pitch in. All employees had been on a first-name basis with the manager. About half of them had begun work with the Savemore Corporation when the Portage store was opened.

Wally Shultz was replaced by Clark Raymond. Raymond, about 25 years old, was a graduate of an Ivy League college and had been with Savemore a little over one year. After completion of his six-month training program, he served as manager of one of the chain's smaller stores, before being advanced to store 5116. In introducing Raymond to the employees, Mr. Finnie stressed his rapid advancement and the profit increase that occurred while Raymond had charge of his last store.

I began my employment in store 5116 early in June. Mr. Raymond was the first person I met in the store, and he impressed me as being more intelligent and efficient than the managers I had worked for in previous sum-

---

*Source: Reprinted by permission of John W. Hennessey, Jr., The University of Vermont. At the time of this case, the author, a college student, was employed for the summer as a checker and stockboy in store 5116.

mers at other stores. After a brief conversation concerning our respective colleges, he assigned me to a cash register, and I began my duties as a checker and bagger.

In the course of the next month I began to sense that relationships between Raymond and his employees were somewhat strained. This attitude was particularly evident among the older employees of the store, who had worked in store 5116 since its opening. As we all ate our sandwiches together in the cage (an area about 20-feet square in the cellar fenced in by chicken wire, to be used during coffee breaks and lunch hours), I began to question some of the older employees as to why they disliked Mr. Raymond. Laura Morgan, a fellow checker about 40 years of age and the mother of two grade-school boys, gave the most specific answers. Her complaints were:

1. Raymond had fired the arthritic black porter on the grounds that a porter who "can't mop is no good to the company."

2. Raymond had not employed new help to make up for normal attrition. Because of this, everybody's workload was much heavier than it ever had been before.

3. The new manager made everyone call him "mister . . . He's unfriendly."

4. Raymond didn't pitch in. Wally Schultz had, according to Laura, helped people when they were behind in their work. She said that Shultz had helped her bag on rushed Friday nights when a long line waited at her checkout booth, but "Raymond wouldn't lift a finger if you were dying."

5. Employees were no longer let out early to catch buses. Because of the relative infrequency of this means of transportation, some employees now arrived home up to an hour later.

6. "Young Mr. Know-it-all with his fancy degree . . . takes all the fun out of this place."

Other employees had similar complaints. Gloria, another checker, claimed that "he sends the company nurse to your home every time you call in sick." Margo, a meat wrapper, remarked, "Everyone knows how he's having an affair with that new bookkeeper he hired to replace Carol when she quit." Pops Devery, the head checker, who had been with the chain for over ten years, was perhaps the most vehement of the group. He expressed his views in the following manner: "That new guy's a real louse . . . got a mean streak a mile long. Always trying to cut corners. First it's not enough help, then no overtime, and now, come Saturday mornings, we have to use boxes for the orders 'til the truck arrives. If it wasn't just a year 'til retirement, I'd leave. Things just aren't what they used to be when Wally was around." The last statement was repeated in different forms by many of the other employees. Hearing all this praise of Wally, I was rather surprised when Mr. Finnie dropped the comment to me one morning that Wally had been demoted for inefficiency, and that no one at store 5116 had been told this. It was important that Mr. Schultz save face, Mr. Finnie told me.

A few days later, on Saturday of the busy weekend preceding the July 4 holiday, store 5116 again ran out of paper bags. However, the delivery truck did not arrive at ten o'clock, and by 10:30 the supply of cardboard cartons was also low. Mr. Raymond put in a hurried call to the warehouse. The men there did not know the whereabouts of the truck but promised to get an emergency supply of bags to us around noon. By eleven o'clock, there were no more containers of any type available, and the truck from the company warehouse bringing merchandise for sale and store supplies normally arrived at ten o'clock on Saturday morning. Frequently, the stock of large paper bags would be temporarily depleted. It was then necessary to pack orders in cardboard cartons until the truck was unloaded.

Mr. Raymond reluctantly locked the doors to all further customers. The twenty checkers and packers remained in their respective booths, chatting among themselves. After a few minutes, Mr. Raymond requested that they all retire to the cellar cage because he had a few words for them. As soon as the group was seated on the wooden benches in the chicken-wire enclosed area, Mr. Raymond began to speak, his back to the cellar stairs. In what appeared to be an angered tone, he began, "I'm out for myself first, Savemore second, the customer third, and you last. The inefficiency in this store has amazed me from the moment I arrived here. . . ."

At about this time I noticed Mr. Finnie, the district manager, standing at the head of the cellar stairs. It was not surprising to see him at this time because he usually made three or four unannounced visits to the store each week as part of his regular supervisory procedure. Mr. Raymond, his back turned, had not observed Finnie's entrance.

Mr. Raymond continued, "Contrary to what seems to be the opinion of many of you, the Savemore Corporation is not running a social club here. We're in business for just one thing . . . to make money. One way that we lose money is by closing the store on Saturday morning at eleven o'clock. Another way that we lose money is by using a 60-pound paper bag to do the job of a 20-pound bag. A 60-pound bag costs us over 2 cents apiece; a 20-pound bag costs less than a penny. So when you sell a couple of quarts of milk or a loaf of bread, don't use the big bags. Why do you think we have four different sizes anyway? There's no great intelligence or effort required to pick the right size. So do it. This store wouldn't be closed right now if you'd used your common sense. We started out this week with enough bags to last 'til Monday . . . and they would have lasted 'til Monday if you'd only used your brains. This kind of thing doesn't look good for the store, and it doesn't look good for me. Some of you have been bagging for over five years . . . you oughta be able to do it right by now . . ." Mr. Raymond paused and then said, "I trust I've made myself clear on this point."

The cage was silent for a moment, and then Pops Devery, the head checker, spoke up: "Just one thing, Mis-tuh Raymond. Things were running pretty well before you came around. When Wally was here we never ran outa bags. The customers never complained about overloaded bags or the bottoms falling out before you got here. What're you gonna tell somebody when they ask for a couple extra bags to use in garbage cans? What're you gonna tell somebody when they want their groceries in a bag, an' not a box? You gonna tell them the manager's too damn cheap to give 'em bags? Is that what you're gonna tell 'em? No sir, things were never like this when Wally Shultz was around. We never had to apologize for a cheap manager who didn't order enough then. Whatta you got to say to that, Mis-tuh Raymond?"

Mr. Raymond, his tone more emphatic, began again. "I've got just one thing to say to that, Mr. Devery, and that's this: store 5116 never did much better than break even when Shultz was in charge here. I've shown a profit better than the best he ever hit in six years every week since I've been here. You can check that fact in the book upstairs any time you want. If you don't like the way I'm running things around here, there's nobody begging you to stay. . ."

At this point, Pops Devery interrupted and, looking up the stairs at the district manager, asked, "What about that, Mr. Finnie? You've been around here as long as I have. You told us how Wally got promoted 'cause he was such a good boss. Supposin' you tell this young feller here what a good manager is really like? How about that, Mr. Finnie?"

A rather surprised Mr. Raymond turned around to look up the stairs at Mr. Finnie. The manager of store 5116 and his checkers and packers waited for Mr. Finnie's answer.

Question: If you're Mr. Finnie, what do you do?

Time: Not to exceed twenty minutes.

*Group Exercise 3**

When Boyd Denton was appointed superintendent of the Washington County School System in 1987 he was given the charge, by the school board, to improve the quality of student performance. His strategy for achieving this was to implement his philosophy of "competence and delegation." First, he would find very strong and very competent principals for each of the schools. Second, he would give each of them a great deal of autonomy. He allowed principals to make hiring decisions, to evaluate teachers, to make salary decisions and to decide how to spend the budget allocated to each school.

From 1987 to 1992, the school system made significant gains in student achievement. However, there was one school, Brewton, which was a problem for Denton. The principal at Brewton was David Starr. Starr was one of the first principals that Denton hired, but now Denton believed that he had made a mistake.

At Brewton, the teachers did not seem to care about the students. They were, by any measure, mediocre. However they were very loyal to Starr. He was well liked by them and they supported him. The reason is that Starr never put any pressure on them for performance and did not really hold them accountable.

When Denton became aware of this, he discussed it with Starr. Starr became angry and threatened to quit. He told Denton that the reason Brewton wasn't a good school was because Denton didn't give them enough resources to do the job right. Denton pointed out the opposite. In fact, by every budget measure, Starr and the Brewton School were well treated.

By 1992, Starr and Denton were on very bad terms. They argued often and all the other principals saw Starr as a prima donna and uncooperative. In one of their arguments, Starr threatened to resign. Denton told him, "Bring me the letter, now." Starr left the office and returned twenty minutes later with a letter of resignation. Denton didn't hesitate, "I'll take it," he said.

Denton searched for a replacement and found Joe Melcan, a bright young assistant superintendent in a nearby district. When he hired Melcan, Denton told him: "I want you to get Brewton straightened out and I'll help you. The teachers are well paid, and you've got good resources there, but the job does not get done. One of the main problems you will have is that most of the teachers are very loyal to Starr. They won't help you much, but I'll give you whatever help and support you need."

Source: Adapted from Henry Tosi, John Rizzo, and Stephen Carroll *Managing Organizational Behavior* (Boston: Ballinger Publishing Co. 1986). Reprinted with permission from Ballinger Publishing Company.

Melcan's approach was a straightforward one. He would let everyone know what was expected of them, make pay as contingent on performance as possible, and hire good new teachers. He thought that in three or four years, there would be enough turnover that with subsequent replacement, he could make Brewton into a high performing school.

Denton watched Melcan's progress and he was pleased. Three new young teachers were hired. Melcan instituted a different evaluation approach than Starr. He started to give substantial recognition to the good teachers and less to those who weren't so good. This was a major departure from the way Starr had managed and many of the Starr loyalists were angry. Some complained to Denton and some filed grievances. When Denton and the union investigated, they found that the charges were without foundation. It is true that things had changed, but now the school was not managed in the style of Starr, but in a performance-oriented style by Melcan.

This was exactly what Denton thought had to be done. Between 1992 and 1995, the student performance improved considerably. However, many of the teachers who were old Starr supporters were dissatisfied. They continued to complain and grumble. Each time, they came to Denton, however, he supported Melcan.

In 1995, Denton left Washington County to become an assistant to the State Superintendent of Schools. He was replaced by Mitchell Kraut. Kraut had been an assistant superintendent for Denton for several years. There were two things about Kraut that were of concern to Melcan. First, Kraut had been a teacher at Brewton during the first years of Starr's time as principal. They had, in fact, become close friends. Secondly, Kraut announced that he was going to centralize many activities which had been performed previously by the principals. No longer would the principals make budgeting decisions, evaluate personnel, or hire faculty. Joe Melcan was very worried.

Question: If you were Joe Melcan, what would you do?

Time: Not to exceed twenty minutes.

APPLICATION QUESTIONS

1. Why does politicking have a negative connotation in most organizations?

2. Can you be an effective manager in a large organization and avoid politics? Explain.

3. Is politicking dysfunctional to an organization's operations? Explain.

4. You have just joined a large organization as a first-line supervisor. Using your political skills, what can you do to increase the probability of succeeding in this job?

REINFORCEMENT EXERCISES

1. Review half a dozen recent issues of *Business Week* or *Fortune* magazines. Look for articles on reorganizations, promotions, and departures from upper management. Do these articles suggest political factors were involved in the management changes. Explain.

2. Interview three managers from three different organizations. Ask them to describe the role that they perceive politics plays in decision making in their organization. Ask for examples that they have participated in or been affected by.

3. Outline a specific action plan, based on the concepts in this chapter, that would improve your career progression in the organization where you currently work or an organization where you think you would like to be employed.

ACTION PLAN

1. Which behavior do I want to improve the most?

_____

_____

_____

2. Why? What will be my payoff?

_____

_____

_____

3. What potential obstacles stand in my way?

_____

_____

_____

4. What are the specific things I will do to improve? (For examples, see the Reinforcement Exercises.)

_____

_____

_____

5. When will I do them?

_____

_____

_____

6. How and when will I measure my success?

_____

_____

_____

Chapter 9

COACHING

SELF-ASSESSMENT EXERCISE

For each of the following statements, circle either True (T) or False (F).

AN EFFECTIVE COACH SHOULD

1.	Tell employees the right way to do a job.	T	F
2.	Suspend judgment and evaluation.	T	F
3.	Be a role model.	T	F
4.	Provide long-term career planning.	T	F
5.	Use a collaborative style.	T	F
6.	Apply active listening	T	F
7.	Respect an employee's individuality.	T	F
8.	Focus on getting each employee's performance up to a minimum standard.	T	F
9.	Dismiss mistakes.	T	F
10.	Delegate responsibility for coaching outcomes to the employee.	T	F

SKILL CONCEPTS

Coaching is a day-to-day, hands-on process of helping employees recognize opportunities to improve their work performance. A coach analyzes the employee's performance; provides insight as to how that performance can be improved; and offers the leadership, motivation, and supportive climate to help the employee achieve that improvement. As a coach, you provide instruction, guidance, advice, and encouragement to help employees improve their job performance.

Coaching requires you to suspend judgment and evaluation. Managers, in the normal routine of carrying out their jobs, regularly express judgments about performance against previously established goals. As a coach, you focus on accepting employees the way they are and help them to make continual improvement toward the goal of developing their full potential.

In this chapter we consider counseling as a subset of coaching. Counseling is similar but not synonymous with coaching. They both have the same objective: to improve the employee's performance, but *coaching* deals with ability issues while *counseling* deals with personal problems. Both apply essentially the same problem-solving process: listening and understanding, identifying the problem, clarifying alternatives, deciding on an action plan, and implementing the action plan. Both also require the same behavioral skills: establishing a supportive climate, active listening, being nonjudgmental and understanding, joint problem solving, and educating the employee to solve his or her own problems rather than assisting by doing it yourself. When an employee needs help mastering skills and figuring out how to apply instructions, coaching is required. When an employee has an attitude or emotional problem, your actions are more properly described as counseling.

Before we discuss specific procedures and skills, it should be pointed out that not all coaching is done by managers. In most work groups, buddy systems develop where more experienced employees informally help new members develop necessary skills and offer them guidance when they have problems. Organizations sometimes formalize buddy systems into *mentoring* programs where senior employees are assigned junior proteges to whom they lend the benefit of their experience. Mentors perform as both coaches and counselors as they guide their less experienced associates towards improved performance.

COACHING SKILLS AND BEHAVIORS

There are three general skills that managers can apply to help their employees generate breakthroughs in performance (Orth, Wilkinson, & Benfari, 1987). These general skills and the specific behaviors associated with each of them are:

1. Ability to analyze ways to improve an employee's performance and capabilities. A coach looks for opportunities for an employee to expand his or her capabilities and improve performance. To do this you need to observe your employee's behavior on a day-to-day basis. You can also *ask questions* of the employee: Why do you do a task this way? Can it be improved? What other approaches might be used? Then, *listen* to the employee. You need to understand the world from the employee's perspective. Finally, *show genuine interest* in the person as an individual, not merely as an employee. Respect his or her individuality. More important than any technical expertise you can provide about improving job performance is the insight you have into the employee's uniqueness.

2. Ability to create a supportive climate. It's the coach's responsibility to reduce barriers to development and facilitate a climate that encourages performance improvement.

Through *active listening* and *empowering* employees to implement appropriate ideas they suggest, you can create a climate that contributes to a free and open exchange of ideas. You can also *offer help* by being available for assistance, guidance, or advice if asked.

By being *positive and upbeat*, you can encourage your employees. Don't use threats because they create a climate of fear and inhibition. Focus on *mistakes as learning opportunities.* Change implies risk and employees must not feel that mistakes will be punished. When failure occurs, ask: "What did we learn that can help us in the future?"

Analyze the factors that you control and *reduce all obstacles* that you can to help the employee to improve his or her job performance. As a manager you must take personal responsibility for the outcome, but don't underplay employees' full responsibilities and contributions. *Validate employees' efforts* when they succeed, and point to what was missing when they fail but never blame employees for poor results. Express to the employee the value of his or her contribution to the department's goals.

3. Ability to influence employees to change their behavior. The ultimate test of coaching effectiveness is whether an employee's performance improves. But this is not a static concept. The *concern is for ongoing* *growth* and development. Consequently, you should help employees continually work toward improvement and encourage them by recognizing and *rewarding even small improvements.* Continual improvement, however, means that there are no absolute upper limits to an employee's job performance.

Your concern as a coach is to enable the receiver of your help to accomplish tasks independently at a high level of effectiveness when you are not there to assist. Although you could probably assist and help your subordinate to do a better job, that is like giving a vagrant money for a meal; it improves the immediate situation but does not enable the handling of reoccurrences more effectively. Your task is *education* or training so that the helpee can solve his or her own problems and perform effectively independently in the future (Kolb, Rubin, Osland, 1991, p. 325).

By using a *collaborative style* with appropriate *empowerment,* employees will be more responsive to accepting change as they participate in identifying and choosing among improvement ideas. When confronted with a difficult job that shakes employees' confidence, it can help to *break complex projects into a series of simpler tasks.* This way the seemingly overwhelming project which originally discouraged employees becomes a number of achievable ones where they are more likely to experience success. Achieving success on simpler tasks can encourage them to take on more difficult ones.

As a manager you need to do more than tell and encourage. *Model* the qualities that you expect from your employees. If, for example, you want openness, dedication, commitment, and responsibility from your employees, you must demonstrate these qualities yourself. Your employees will look to you as a role model so make sure your deeds match your words.

ADDITIONAL GUIDELINES WHEN COUNSELING IS REQUIRED

Counseling is the discussion of an emotional problem with an employee in order to resolve the problem or, at a minimum, help the employee to cope with it better. Examples of problems that might require you to counsel an employee include divorce, serious illness, personal financial problems, difficulty in getting along with a co-worker, a drinking problem affecting work performance, or frustration over a lack of career progress in the company.

When dealing with these emotional and personal problems to performance, an important additional principle is to maintain *confidentiality.* To really open up and share the reasons for many personal problems, employees must feel that they can trust you and that there is no threat to their self-esteem or their reputation with co-workers. So, as soon as you determine that counseling is what is called for, emphasize that everything the employee says regarding personal matters will be treated in confidence.

Although you are not a trained psychologist, there are several reasons why as a manager you should take on a counseling role before referring the employee to a professional therapist. Sometimes an employee just needs a sounding board for the *release of tension* which can become a prelude to clarifying the problem, identifying possible solutions, and taking corrective action. Emotions typically cloud rational thinking and counseling can help employees in the *clarification* of their thoughts into a more logical and coherent order.

Counseling can provide *reassurance* to employees that their problems have solutions and that they have the ability to improve. If this is not the case, counseling can *identify employee problems requiring professional treatment.* Severe depression, debilitating phobias, family disorders, and substance abuse are examples of employee problems that require professional help. Psychological counseling is now included in Employee Assistant Programs as part of most employee benefit health plans.

When successful, employee counseling can *circumvent the need for disciplinary actions* such as formal warnings, sanctions, or firing. In some instances it may be appropriate to advise an employee on what you think he or she should do to correct a problem or improve performance. As mentioned earlier, however, employees grow by learning to solve their own problems, not from looking to others to solve their problems for them. Also, if the advice you give proves to be wrong, you're likely to be blamed.

CONCEPT QUIZ

Do you understand the basic principles of coaching and counseling employees? Answer the following ten-question, true-false quiz. The answers are at the end of the quiz. If you miss any, go back and find out the correct answer.
    Circle the right answer:

True   or   False   1. Coaching is synonymous with counseling.

True   or   False.   2. You have to be judgmental with employees so they understand they need to improve.

True   or   False   3. A coach should look for opportunities for employees to improve their performance.

True   or   False   4. A coach focuses on mistakes as learning opportunities.

True   or   False   5. The test of coaching effectiveness is whether an employee's performance improves.

True   or   False   6. Threats are a good motivating tool.

True   or   False   7. Sometimes it is more beneficial for the employee's development just to do the task yourself

True   or   False   8. Once the employee has mastered the task satisfactorily your coaching job is done.

True   or   False   9. If you want your employees to behave in a certain way, model the behavior yourself.

True   or   False   10. Its preferable to let employees come up with their own ways to improve performance.

    Answers: (1) False; (2) False; (3) True; (4) True; (5) True; (6) False; (7) False; (8) False; (9) True; (10) True.

BEHAVIORAL CHECKLIST

Look for these specific behaviors when evaluating your coaching and counseling skills and those of others.

PROVIDING EFFECTIVE COACHING REQUIRES

- Asking questions to help the employee discover how to improve
- Actively listening to employees and showing genuine interest
- Offering help and assistance
- Being positive and upbeat rather than threatening
- Accepting mistakes and using them as learning opportunities
- Encouraging continual improvement
- Recognizing and rewarding even small improvements
- Modeling qualities you expect from employees

ATTENTION!

Don't read this or the following exercises until assigned to do so by your instructor.

MODELING EXERCISE

Actors: LORIN WILCOX (manager) and T.J. CORSETTI (broker).

Situation: Lorin Wilcox is the supervisor of the Napa Valley office of a large mortgage brokering company which has thirty offices in California. Lorin supervises seven mortgages brokers, an assistant, and a secretary. The business entails helping home buyers find mortgages and acting as a link between lenders and borrowers in getting loans approved and processed.

T.J. Corsetti is one of the brokers. T.J. has been in the Napa Valley office for two and a half years. Before that, he/she sold commercial real estate. Lorin Wilcox has been in the Napa Valley job for fourteen months, prior to supervising a smaller office for the same company.

LORIN WILCOX's role: You have not been pleased with T.J.'s job performance, so you decided to review his/her personnel file. T.J.'s first six-month review stated: "Enthusiastic. A bit disorganized but willing to learn. Seems to have good potential." After a year, T.J.'s previous supervisor had written, "T.J. seems to be losing interest. Seems frequently disorganized. Often rude to clients. Did not mention these problems to him previously. Hope T.J. will improve. Long-term potential now much more in question."

You have not spent much time with T.J. Your offices are far apart. But probably the real reason is that T.J.'s not a person who's easy to talk to and you have little in common. When you took the Napa Valley job, you decided that you'd wait some time before attacking any problems to make sure you had a good grasp of the people and the situation.

But T.J.'s problems have gotten too visible to ignore. He/she is consistently missing quarterly sales projections. Based on mortgages processed, T.J. is your lowest performer. In addition, T.J.'s reports are constantly late. After reviewing last month's performance reports, you made an appointment yesterday to meet him/her today at 9:00 A.M. But T.J. wasn't in his/her office when you arrived for that appointment. You waited fifteen minutes and gave up. Your secretary tells you that T.J. regularly comes in late for work in the morning and takes extra long coffee breaks.

Last week, Valerie Oletta, who has the office next to T.J.'s, complained to you that T.J.'s behavior was demoralizing her and some of the other brokers.

You don't want to fire T.J. It wouldn't be easy to find a replacement. Moreover, T.J. has a lot of contacts with new-home builders, which brings in a number of borrowers to your office. In fact, maybe 60 percent of the business generated by your entire office comes from builders who have personal ties to T.J. If T.J. were to leave your company and go to a competitor, he/she would probably be able to convince the builders to take their business somewhere else.

T.J. CORSETTI's role: The mortgage brokering business has been pretty good for you. From your previous job in commercial real estate you developed a lot of contacts with new-home builders, which bring in a number of borrowers to your office. In fact, maybe 60 percent of the business generated by your entire office comes from builders who have personal ties with you.

Although your old builder buddies supply you with plenty of business, you realized early in your first year that the brokering business required some word processing, mathematical, and computer skills that you never acquired ten years ago when you graduated from high school. Most of the other brokers have college degrees in business administration and one even has a M.B.A. You have been embarrassed to ask for help because you are older then most of the other brokers. Consequently, it takes you quite a bit longer than other brokers to process the mortgages which often makes your reports late because you have to type one key at a time.

To try a get up to speed, you have enrolled in an 8:00 A.M. extension course in typing and word processing at the community college, which makes you about an hour late for work three days a week, but you think it certainly is going to be worth it in the long run. You're hoping that the correspondence course in business mathematics you signed up for will have an equal payoff.

You are working on it in the evenings and during your breaks at work.

All this is a bit overwhelming at the moment, and you have fallen a little behind in your work. You overheard some of the other brokers discussing your lack of involvement with them a couple of weeks ago, but you're too busy to worry about that until you complete your courses. Then you will be right up with the best of them. Besides, you're still making a contribution in a way. It's your contacts with the builders that brings in a majority of the business for your office. In fact, you are also taking a broker course on weekends so you can take them with you and start your own company next year.

The broker in the next office mentioned that your boss, Lorin Wilcox, was at your office for an appointment that Lorin had scheduled for 9:00 A.M. yesterday. You went to your usual class and completely forgot about it. You decide to go up to T.J.'s office to see what the appointment was about.

TIME: Not to exceed ten minutes.

OBSERVER'S RATING SHEET

Evaluate the coaching skills of Lorin Wilcox on a 1 to 5 scale (5 being highest).

- Asks questions to help the employee
  discover how to improve   _____

- Actively listens to employees and shows
  genuine interest   _____

- Offers help and assistance   _____

- Is positive and upbeat versus threatening   _____

- Uses mistakes as learning opportunities   _____

- Encourages continual improvement   _____

- Recognizes and rewards even
  small improvements   _____

- Models qualities expected from employees   _____

Comments:

_____

_____

_____

_____

_____

_____

GROUP EXERCISES

Divide the class into groups of three. Each trio will conduct three coaching sessions, allowing every student the opportunity to share a school-related performance problem to get help with and to play the role of coach to help and counsel your colleague. If you do not have a school-related problem you want to share, you can role-play exercise 2 or 3 instead. Allocate approximately twenty minutes for the personal coaching session and fifteen minutes for each role play.

Group Exercise 1

Think of a school-related problem you are currently experiencing or have had in the past. Briefly share the nature of the problem and its consequences with your coach. Now the coach takes over and conducts the most appropriate type of coaching or counseling session. At the conclusion of the session the observer will provide the coach with feedback based on the following Observer's Rating Sheet. Group members can rotate roles and all share a problem to be coached on, or they can choose one of the following two exercises to role play.

Time: Not to exceed twenty minutes.

OBSERVER'S RATING SHEET

Evaluate the skills of the person on a 1 to 5 scale (5 being highest).

- Asks questions to help the employee
  discover how to improve   _____

- Actively listens to employees and shows
  genuine interest   _____

- Offers help and assistance   _____

- Is positive and upbeat versus threatening   _____

- Uses mistakes as learning opportunities   _____

- Encourages continual improvement   _____

- Recognizes and rewards even
  small improvements   _____

- Models qualities expected from employees   _____

Comments:

_____

_____

_____

_____

_____

_____

*Group Exercise 2**

ACTORS: LYNN BOSCO works in the blending department of a large pharmaceutical company. RICKY THOMAS is Lynn's supervisor.

SITUATION: Lynn works hard but can't concentrate very well on the task at hand recently. At age forty-five, Lynn was divorced after a fifteen-year marriage. Six months later, Lynn married a twenty-three-year-old aerobics instructor. In the last five years, Lynn has twice bid for a higher-paying job elsewhere in the company. In both cases Lynn was advised that he/she did not have the necessary educational qualifications for advancement into a skilled trade.

LYNN BOSCO's role: Your mind is continually wandering to your debts. With easy credit, you have become a chronic borrower. This borrowing is not due to illness, rent payments, or any of the other common reasons people go into debt. You borrow for luxuries like the new Acura you just bought and the jet-ski boat you bought last year. You realize that your work is falling off somewhat, but you are absolutely convinced you will get it straightened out soon.

RICKY THOMAS's role: You have noticed Lynn's work is beginning to deteriorate. The number of batches Lynn mixes per shift fell from fifteen to eleven in the last six months, and on several occasions Lynn has scorched a batch. The last time you talked to Lynn about this slump, Lynn responded, "Everything is all right, I'm just a little untracked right now, I'll get it going again." Despite this assurance, however, Lynn's work has continued to be poor. You know about Lynn's bids for other jobs in the company and suspect the problems may be financial. Lynn has always been a good worker who up to this point you want to keep if possible. You feel that Lynn is not going to get over these problems without some help. You decide to call Lynn in and see if you can help.

Observer: Use the previous Observer's Rating Sheet on page 161.

Time: Not to exceed fifteen minutes.

---

*Source: Adapted from William C. Donaghy, *The Interview: Skills and Applications* (Glenview, Ill.: Scott, Foresman, 1984), pp. 299–300.

Group Exercise 3

ACTORS: FRAN DELANO, a camera operator and ALEX MAHER, Fran's supervisor.

SITUATION: Alex has supervised the eleven camera operators at KSLC for more than five years. Fran has worked for Alex for over four of those years. Two years ago, Fran Delano was the number-one-rated camera operator at KSLC-TV in Salt Lake City. Of the eleven operators that the station employed, Fran was every producer's first choice. Fran had a choice of hours and shows. Fran was extremely competent, creative, and dependable. Fran's supervisor, Alex Maher, had even been a bit protective. As Alex said eighteen months ago, "Everyone knows Fran's the best we've got. Everyone wants Fran for their shows. I've got to make sure we don't burn out our best camera operator."

ALEX MAHER's role: You have become far less enthusiastic about Fran over the past four months. The problems began with Fran's coming in late for assigned shifts. First it was just ten or fifteen minutes late. Then it got to be thirty minutes. Last week, Fran was over an hour late for shifts twice, and fifteen to twenty minutes late each of the other three days. Yesterday, Fran called in sick just ten minutes before the show was to go "on the air." This morning, Fran came in forty minutes late.

In addition to the lateness, you have noticed two other disturbing signs. Fran is not nearly as talkative and outgoing as usual. And, several times last week, you are certain that you smelled alcohol on Fran's breath. Nick Randolph, another camera operator, told you two weeks ago that he was certain Fran had been drinking before coming to work, and again during the lunch break. Nick was particularly upset about the quality of Fran's work. Alex, of course, knew what he was talking about. Fran's mind seemed to be wandering during shows: missing director's instructions, and slow in getting the camera into new positions.

You don't know much about Fran's personal life. You've heard Fran lives with or is married to a graphic artist but that's about all you know.

Up to this point, you haven't said anything to Fran about this behavior. But now something has to be done. After today's work shift, you called Fran into your office. As Fran walks in, you can't help noticing the smell of alcohol.

FRAN DELANO's role: Becoming the number one-rated camera operator at KSLC-TV paid off in giving you your choice of hours and shows. The problem is you take every show you can possibly do. You feel that your place on the top rung is precarious because of the multitude of other talented camera operators jockeying to get some of your shows. It's very lucrative for you right now and you feel that you had better get all you can while the getting is good. Actually you don't have much choice if you are to maintain your house payments because your spouse has been unemployed as a graphic artist for the past two years and the prospects don't look good because there are hundreds of others in the same situation. In fact your spouse has quit looking recently and is quite depressed.

This is not an easy business and it requires all you've got to handle it: the intense concentration when everything depends on you during the show, the relentless hours from the early morning news broadcasts to late night variety shows, and the constant worry that someone else will show their stuff if you miss a show for any reason. As if this wasn't enough, you constantly worry about your spouse's deteriorating state of mind.

You are so exhausted when you get off work, often close to midnight, that you just go home and have a few drinks. That's what your spouse is doing anyway. You are usually happy when your spouse is already in bed because your relative success seems to cause hostile attacks or the silent treatment. You can't decide which is worse, but your relationship is definitely floundering.

Lately you noticed that it takes a whole bottle of wine or more than a six pack of beer to calm you down enough to get to sleep. You've discovered that a shot of brandy in your morning coffee seems to help the dull headaches you wake up with. Also, a couple of glasses of wine at lunch can make the stress seem much less severe, and a short nip from the flask of Wild Turkey you keep in your coat pocket helps you relax between shows.

You know you are probably drinking a little too much, but that seems to be the only way you can avoid worrying about your problems enough to focus on your work or even get a little sleep. You are sure that as soon as your spouse finds a job and you can cut back a little, you will be just fine.

Observer: Use the Observer's Rating Sheet on page 161.

Time: Not to exceed fifteen minutes.

SUMMARY CHECKLIST

Review your performance and look over others' ratings of your skill. Now assess yourself on each of the key learning behaviors. Make a check (✓) next to those behaviors on which you need improvement.

- I ask questions to help the employee
  discover how to improve.   _____

- I actively listen to employees and show
  genuine interest.   _____

- I offer help and assistance.   _____

- I am positive and upbeat versus threatening.   _____

- I use mistakes as learning opportunities.   _____

- I encourage continual improvement.   _____

- I recognize and reward even
  small improvements.   _____

- I model qualities I expect from employees.   _____

APPLICATION QUESTIONS

1. Think of a particularly effective coach you had in high school, college, or any other situation (e.g., sport, debate, music, etc.). Describe why he or she was so effective. How do this coach's qualities match up with those in the Behavioral Checklist on page 156 in this chapter.

2. How have your parents served as coaches for your development? What did they do that was particularly helpful? What could they have done better?

3. How is coaching similar to counseling? How are the two different?

4. Which of the interpersonal skills we have previously studied contribute to effective coaching? How do they relate?

5. How can a manager tell if he or she is being an effective coach? When and how does a manager know when the coaching job is completed?

6. What are three things you should never do in a coaching or counseling session and why?

REINFORCEMENT EXERCISES

1. Ask a coach of a local sports team (high school, college, club, or professional) for permission to observe the coach at work. Spend a few hours watching the coach do his/her job. How do this coach's qualities match up with those in the Summary Checklist on page 165 in this chapter.

2. Watch several episodes of the popular TV show "Coach." How does the "coach" on this sitcom portray the coaching behaviors described in this chapter. How do the situations developed on the show relate to the coaching skills you have read about?

3. Become a coach yourself. For example, coach a less able student through a class-related problem; help someone develop an athletic skill; or assist a friend in improving a difficult relationship.

ACTION PLAN

1. Which behavior do I want to improve the most?

_____

_____

_____

2. Why? What will be my payoff?

_____

_____

_____

3. What potential obstacles stand in my way?

_____

_____

_____

4. What are the specific things I will do to improve? (For examples, see the Reinforcement Exercises.)

_____

_____

_____

5. When will I do them?

_____

_____

_____

6. How and when will I measure my success?

_____

_____

_____

Chapter *10*

RUNNING A MEETING

SELF-ASSESSMENT EXERCISE

For each of the following questions, select the answer that best describes how you *have* or *would* behave in running a group meeting, not how you think you *should* behave.

WHEN RUNNING A GROUP MEETING, I:

	Usually	Sometimes	Seldom
1. Prepare an agenda beforehand.	☐	☐	☐
2. Ensure ahead of time that all participants are prepared for the meeting.	☐	☐	☐
3. Delay starting the meeting until everyone is present.	☐	☐	☐

4. Make sure that everyone knows the specific purpose(s) of the meeting. ☐ ☐ ☐

5. Keep disagreements over ideas to a minimum. ☐ ☐ ☐

6. Encourage participation by all members. ☐ ☐ ☐

7. Keep discussion focused on the issues. ☐ ☐ ☐

8. Extend the meeting past its stated finishing time if all items have not been covered. ☐ ☐ ☐

Scoring Key and Interpretation

For questions, 1, 2, 4, 6, and 7, give yourself 3 points for "Usually," 2 points for "Sometimes," and 1 point for "Seldom."

For questions 3, 5, and 8, give yourself 3 points for "Seldom," 2 points for "Sometimes," and 1 point for "Usually."

Sum up your total points. A score of 22 or higher indicates excellent skills at running a group meeting. Scores in the 16 to 21 range imply some deficiencies in this skill. Scores below 16 denote that you have considerable room for improvement.

SKILL CONCEPTS

If you're a typical manager, you'll spend a large part of your day in meetings. Studies have found that most managers spend between 25 to 30 percent of their time in meetings (Wakin, 1991; Michaels, 1989). And the higher up the the corporate ladder managers climb, the more meetings they attend. Chief executives have been found to spend 59 percent of their time in scheduled meetings and another 10 percent in unscheduled meetings (Mintzberg, 1980).

Many of the hours you'll spend in these meetings will be in a nonleadership role. You'll participate, but it won't be your responsibility to run the meeting. Preparing and contributing appropriately will be your resposibilities. Other times you'll be the person in charge. You'll choose who will attend. You'll set and control the agenda. Most importantly, what you do or don't do will largely influence the meeting's effectiveness. In this chapter, we'll look at group meetings to determine how those in a leadership role can make them as effective as possible.

The Importance of Meetings

It's been calculated that eleven million meetings take place every day in the United States (Jay, 1976, p. 46). Handled properly, these person-to-person encounters are probably the single most efficient mechanism for passing word down and, equally important, up the ranks (Kiechel, 1986). But group meetings are not only devices for disseminating information. They're also effective tools for decision making, introducing change, and developing a spirit of teamwork. When run *ineffectively*, however, meetings can be costly, time-consuming, and demoralizing to participants. If the dollar cost of a manager's time, including salary and benefits, is $100 an hour (which is fairly typical), ten managers meeting for a couple of hours and accomplishing nothing is a waste of several thousand dollars, plus the time lost from other tasks thay could have accomplished in that time!

The increasing use of telecommunication applications such as teleconferences, and audio, computer-based, and video conferences can save some of these costs by allowing a large number of meetings to take place among members who are physically separated but electronically linked. But telecommunications is not going to eliminate the traditional face-to-face meeting. Such meetings are currently alive and well in almost all organizations and are likely to be thriving for many years to come. Most of the concepts pertaining to the dynamics of group behavior apply to groups' members who are physically together or electronically linked.

*HOW TO RUN A MEETING**

Meetings are among the most overused and underutilized of all management tools. We have just seen that most managers spend from one-fourth to over two-thirds of their time in scheduled meetings, and the most important

---

Source: This section was prepared by James P. Ware. Copyright © 1977 by the President and Fellows of Harvard College. By permission of the Harvard Business School.

organizational decisions are almost always reached in meetings, or as a result of one or more meetings. Given their importance, and the amount of management time they consume, it is indeed a tragedy that so many meetings are so inefficient and, worse, ineffective. When unproductive meetings occur regularly, managers with demanding schedules begin to believe that their primary goal is to get out of the meeting rather than to get the most out of it (Michaels, 1989).

Yet planning and conducting a meeting are not difficult tasks. While there are no magic formulas to guarantee success, there are a number of simple procedures that effective managers employ to improve the quality of their meetings.

There are, of course, many different kinds of meetings, ranging from two-person interchanges all the way up to industry wide conventions with thousands of participants. Most management meetings, however, involve relatively small groups of people in a single organization. This section will concentrate on a number of techniques for running these kinds of management meetings more effectively. For further simplicity, we will focus primarily on scheduled meetings of managers who are at approximately the same level in the organization, and who have known each other and worked together before.

The suggestions that follow are divided into planning activities to carry out before the meeting and leadership activities to engage in during the meeting. Both kinds of work are essential: The most thorough preparation in the world will be wasted if you are careless during the meeting, while even outstanding meeting leadership rarely overcomes poor planning.

Preparing for the Meeting

Perhaps the most useful way to begin is simply to sit down with a blank sheet of paper and think through what the meeting will be like. Write down all the issues that are likely to come up, what decisions need to be made, what you want to happen after the meeting, and what things have to happen before the meeting can take place. Although the circumstances surrounding each meeting are unique, your planning should include the following activities:

Setting objectives. Most management meetings are called either to exchange information or to solve organizational problems. Generally, your reasons for calling the meeting are fairly obvious, especially to you. It is worth being very explicit about your purposes, however, because they have major implications for who should attend, which items belong on the agenda, when and where you hold the meeting, and what kinds of decision-making procedures you should use.

An information-exchange meeting can be an efficient mechanism if the information to be shared is complex or controversial, if it has major implications for the meeting participants, or if there is symbolic value in conveying the information personally. If none of these conditions is present, it may be more efficient, and just as effective, to write a memo or make several telephone calls.

Problem-solving meetings provide an opportunity to combine the knowledge and skills of several people at once. The ideas that evolve out of an open-ended discussion are usually richer and more creative than what the same people could produce working individually.

These two different objectives call for very different kinds of meetings. Thus, you should be very explicit about what you are trying to accomplish, both to yourself and to the other meeting participants.

Selecting participants.   Invite people to the meeting who will either contribute to, or be affected by, its outcome. Select individuals who have knowledge or skills relevant to the problem, or who command organizational resources (time, budgets, other people, power, and influence) that you need access to.

As you build your participant list, you should also give thought to the overall composition of the group. Identify the likely concerns and interests of the individual managers, and the feelings they have about each other. Try to obtain a rough balance of power and status among subgroups or probable coalitions (unless you have clear reasons for wanting one group to be more powerful).

Do everything you can to keep the size of the group appropriate to your objectives. While an information-exchange meeting can be almost any size, a problem-solving group should not exceed eight to ten people if at all possible.

Planning the agenda.   Even if you are planning an informal, exploratory meeting, an agenda can be a valuable means of controlling the discussion and of giving the participants a sense of direction. The agenda defines the meeting's purpose for participants and places boundaries between relevant and irrelevant discussion topics. Furthermore, the agenda can serve as an important vehicle for premeeting discussions with participants.

Some important principles of building an agenda are listed below:

- Sequence items so they build on one another if possible.
- Sequence topics from easiest to most difficult and/or controversial.
- Keep the number of topics within reasonable limits.
- Avoid topics that can be better handled by subgroups or individuals.
- Separate information exchange from problem solving.
- Define a finishing time as well as a starting time.
- Depending on meeting length, schedule breaks at specific times where they will not disrupt important discussions.

Not every meeting requires a formal, written agenda. Often you simply cannot predict where a discussion will lead, or how long it will take. However, focusing your attention on these issues can help you anticipate controversy and be prepared to influence it in a productive manner. Even if you do not prepare a public, written agenda, you should not begin the meeting without having a tentative, private one.

Doing your homework. Your major objective in preparing for the meeting is to collect all the relevant information you can, and to consider its implications. Some of these data may be in written documents, but much of them will probably be in other people's heads. The more important and the more controversial the subject, the more contact you should have with other participants before the actual meeting.

These contacts will help you anticipate issues and disagreements that may arise during the meeting. As you talk with the other participants, try to learn all you can about their personal opinions and objectives concerning the meeting topic. These personal objectives—often called "hidden" agendas—can have as big an impact on what happens during the meeting as your formal, explicit agenda. Thus, the more you can discover about the other participants' goals for the meeting, the better prepared you will be to lead an effective discussion.

These premeeting contacts also give you an opportunity to encourage the other participants to do their homework as well. If there is enough time before the meeting to collect and circulate relevant data or background materials, the meeting itself can proceed much more quickly. Few events are as frustrating as a meeting of people who are unprepared to discuss or decide the issues on the agenda.

As part of your preparation, you may want to brief your boss and other executives who will not be at the meeting, but who have an interest in its outcomes.

Finally, circulate the agenda and relevant background papers a day or two before the meeting if you can. These documents help to clarify your purposes and expectations, and they further encourage the other participants to come to the meeting well prepared. Keep your demands on their time reasonable, however. People are more likely to read and think about brief memos than long, comprehensive reports.

Setting a time and place.   The timing and location of your meeting can have a subtle but significant impact on the quality of the discussion. These choices communicate a surprising number of messages about the meeting's importance, style, and possible outcomes.

What time of day is best for your meeting? Often the work flow in the organization will constrain your freedom of choice. For example, you could not meet simultaneously with all of a bank's tellers during the regular business hours, or with all the entry clerks just as the mail arrives. Within these kinds of constraints, however, you often have a wide choice of meeting times. How should you decide?

Early in the day, participants will usually be fresher and will have fewer other problems on their minds. In contrast, late-afternoon meetings can be more leisurely, since there will usually be nothing else on anyone's schedule following your meeting. Perhaps the best question to ask is what the participants will be doing after the meeting. Will they be eager to end the meeting so they can proceed to other commitments, or will they be inclined to prolong the discussion? Which attitude best suits your purposes? There is no "best" time for a meeting, but you should consider explicitly what times would be most suitable for your particular objectives.

Two other factors may also influence when you schedule the meeting. First, try to be sure the time is sheltered so there will be an absolute minimum of interruptions. Second, gear your starting time to the meeting's probable, or desirable, length. For example, if you want the meeting to last only an hour, a good time to schedule it is at 11 A.M.

Try not to plan meetings that last more than ninety minutes. Most people's endurance—or at least their creative capacity—will not last much longer than that. If the subject is so complex or lengthy that it will take longer, be sure to build in coffee and stretching breaks at least every ninety minutes.

Another key decision is where to hold the meeting. The setting in which a discussion takes place can have a marked influence on its tone and content. Just consider the difference between calling three subordinates to your office and meeting them for lunch in a restaurant. Each setting implies a particular level of formality and signals what kind of discussion you expect to have. Similarly, if you are meeting with several peers, a "neutral" conference room creates a very different climate than would any one of your offices. In each case, the appropriate setting depends on your purposes, and you should choose your location accordingly.

The discussion climate will also be affected by the arrangement of the furniture in the meeting room. In your office, you can choose to stay behind your desk and thereby be more authoritative, or to use a chair that puts you on a more equal basis with the other participants. In a conference room, you can choose to sit at the head of the table to symbolize your control, or in the center to be "one of the group."

You should also be certain that you have arranged for any necessary mechanical equipment, such as an overhead or slide projector, an easel, or a blackboard. These vital aids can facilitate both information exchange and problem-solving discussions.

Summary. Each of these suggestions has been intended to help you convene a meeting of people who have a common understanding of why they have come together and are prepared to contribute to the discussion. Of course, this kind of thorough preparation is often simply impossible. Nevertheless, the more preparation you can do, the more smoothly the meeting will go. While you can never anticipate all the issues and hidden agendas, you can clearly identify the major sources of potential disagreement. That anticipation enables you to control the meeting, rather than being caught off guard. Even if you have to schedule a meeting only an hour in advance, you can still benefit from systematic attention to these kinds of details.

Conducting the Meeting

If you have done your homework, you probably have a good idea of where you want the group to be at the end of the meeting. But remember that you called the meeting because you need something from the other participants—either information relevant to the problem, or agreement and commitment to a decision. Your success in achieving those goals now depends not so much on what you know about the problem as on what you and the others can learn during the discussion. Thus, the primary concern as you begin the meeting should be with creating a healthy, problem-solving atmosphere in which participants openly confront their differences and work toward a joint solution.

The following suggestions and meeting leadership techniques should help you achieve that goal.

Beginning the meeting. If you are well prepared, the chances are that no one else has thought as much about the meeting as you have. Thus, the most productive way to begin is with an explicit review of the agenda and your objectives. This discussion gives everyone an opportunity to ask questions, offer suggestions, and express opinions about why they are there. Beginning with a review of the agenda also signals its importance and gets the meeting going in a task-oriented direction.

Be careful not to simply impose the agenda on the group; others may have useful suggestions that will speed up the meeting or bring the problem into sharper focus. They may even disagree with some of your plans, but you will not learn about that disagreement unless you clearly signal that you consider the agenda open to revision. The more the others participate in defining the meeting, the more committed they will be to fulfilling that definition.

This initial discussion also permits the meeting participants to work out a shared understanding of the problem that brought them together, and of what topics are and are not appropriate to discuss in this meeting.

Encouraging problem solving. As the formal leader of the meeting, you can employ a wide variety of techniques to keep the group in a problem-solving mode. Your formal authority as chairman gives you a great deal of power to influence the group's actions. Often a simple comment, a pointed look, or even just a lifted eyebrow is all you need to indicate approval or disapproval of someone's behavior.

Perhaps your best weapon is simply your own style of inquiry; if you focus on facts and on understanding points of disagreement, to the exclusion of personalities, others will generally do the same. As the discussion progresses, try to keep differing points of view in rough balance. Do not let a few individuals dominate; when you sense that participation has become unbalanced, openly ask the quieter members for their opinions and ideas. Never assume that silence means agreement; more often it signals some level of difference with the dominant theme of the discussion.

Effective problem-solving meetings generally pass through several phases. Early in the discussion that group will be seeking to understand the *nature* of the problem. At that point you need to encourage factual, nonevaluative discussion that emphasizes describing symptoms and searching for all possible causes. As understanding is gained, the focus will shift to a search for solutions. Again, you must discourage evaluative comments until all potential alternatives have been throughly explored. Only then should the discussion become evaluative, as the group moves toward a decision.

If you can develop a sensitivity to these stages of problem solving (describing symptoms, searching for alternatives, evaluating alternatives, selecting a solution), you can vary your leadership style to fit the current needs of the group. At all times, however, you want to keep the discussion focused on the problem, not on personalities or on unrelated issues, no matter how important they may be. Make your priorities clear and hold the group to them. Finally, maintain a climate of honest inquiry in which anyone's assumption (including yours) may be questioned and tested.

Keeping the discussion on track. When the meeting topic is controversial, with important consequences for the group members, you will have to work hard to keep the discussion focused on the issues.

Controversy makes most of us uncomfortable, and groups often avoid confronting the main issue by finding less important or irrelevant topics to talk about. If the discussion wanders too far from the agenda, you must be willing to exercise your leadership responsibility to swing the group back to the major topic.

Use your judgment in making these interventions, however. If the group is on the verge of splitting up in anger or frustration, a digression to a "safe" topic may be a highly functional way of reuniting. Generally, such digressions are most beneficial when they follow open controversy rather than precede it. If you think the group has reached a decision on the main issue, even if it is only an implicit one, then you may want to let the digression go on for a while. On the other hand, if the discussion is clearly delaying a necessary confrontation, then you will have to intervene to get the discussion back on the main issue.

If you began the meeting with an explicit discussion of the agenda, you will find this focusing task easier to carry out. Often a simple reminder to the group, with a glance at the clock, is enough. Another useful technique for marking progress is to periodically summarize where you think the group has been, and then ask the group to confirm your assessments.

If the discussion seems to bog down, or to wander too far afield, perhaps the group needs to take a short break. Even two minutes of standing and stretching can revitalize people's willingness to concentrate on the problem. And the break also serves to cut off old conversations, making it easier to begin new ones.

Do everything you can to keep the discussion moving on schedule, so you can end on time. The clock can be a very useful taskmaster, and busy managers rarely have the luxury of ignoring it. If you have set a specific ending time, and everyone knows you mean it, there will be far less tendency for the discussion to wander.

Controlling the discussion. How authoritatively should you exercise control over the discussion? The answer to that question depends so much on specific circumstances that a general response is almost impossible. The level of formality that is appropriate depends on the discussion topic, on which phase of the problem-solving cycle you are in, and on your formal and informal relationships with the other participants. You will normally want to exercise greater control when

- The meeting is oriented more toward information exchange.
- The topic generates strong, potentially disruptive feelings.
- The group is moving toward a decision.
- Time pressures are significant.

There is a whole range of techniques you can use to exert more formal control. For example, if you permit participants to speak only when you call on them, or if you comment on or summarize each statement, there will be very few direct confrontations between other individuals. If you use a flip chart or blackboard to summarize ideas, you will also increase the level of formality and reduce the number of direct exchanges. In some circumstances, you may even want to employ formal parliamentary procedures, such as requiring motions, limiting debate, taking notes, and so on. These procedures might be appropriate, for example, in meetings of a board of directors, in union-management contract negotiations, or in policy-setting sessions involving managers from several different parts of the organization.

Many of these techniques are clearly inappropriate for, and rarely used in, smaller management meetings. Although these techniques can give you a high degree of control, they cannot prevent participants from developing strong feelings about the issues—feelings that often become strong precisely because you have not permitted them to be openly expressed.

Thus, it is entirely possible to control a meeting in a fashion that minimizes conflict within the meeting itself. However, one result of that control may be increased tension and even hostility among the participants, leading to more serious future problems. On the other hand, if tension levels are already so high that a rational discussion will not evolve on its own, then some of these controlling techniques may be absolutely essential.

Reaching a decision. Many management groups will fall into decision-making habits without thinking carefully about the consequences of those habits. The two major approaches to reaching a group decision are voting and reaching a consensus. Each strategy has its advantages and disadvantages.

Voting is often resorted to when the decision is important and the group seems deadlocked. The major benefit of taking a vote is that you are guaranteed of getting a decision. However, voting requires public commitment to a position, and it creates a win-lose situation for the group members. Some individuals will be clearly identified as having favored a minority position. Losers on one issue often try to balance their account on the next decision, or they may withdraw their commitment to the total group. Either way, you may have won the battle but lost the war.

Reaching a group consensus is generally a much more effective decision-making procedure. It is often more difficult, however, and is almost always more time-consuming. Working toward a genuine consensus means hearing all points of view and usually results in a better decision—a condition that is especially important when the group members will be responsible for implementing the decision. Even when individuals do not fully agree with the group decision, they are more likely to support it (or less likely to sabotage it) when they believe their positions have had a complete hearing.

Ending the meeting.   The most important thing to do at the end of the meeting is to clarify what happens next. If the group has made a major decision, be certain you agree on whom is responsible for its implementation, and on when the work will be completed.

If the group has to meet again, you can save a lot of time by scheduling your next meeting then and there. Having everyone check their calendars and mark down the date and time of the next meeting will save you an unbelievable number of telephone calls.

Depending on the discussion topic and the decisions that have been made, either you or someone else should follow the meeting with a brief memo summarizing the discussion, the decisions, and the follow-up commitments that each participant has made. This kind of document serves not only as a record of the meeting, but also as a next-day reminder to the participants of what they decided and what they are committed to doing.

If you can, spend the last five minutes or so of the meeting talking about how well the meeting went. Although most managers are not accustomed to self-critiques, this practice is a useful habit that can contribute significantly to improved group problem-solving. The best time to share your reactions to the meeting is right after it has ended. You evaluate the effectiveness of other management techniques all the time; why not apply the same criteria to your meetings?

Summary

Management meetings occur so frequently that most of us fail to recognize how significant an impact they have on organizational productivity. Improving the effectiveness of your meetings is not a difficult task. Apply these simple techniques carefully, with sensitivity to the combination of people and problems you have brought together, and your meetings should become both more effective and more interesting. The important point, however, is that the techniqsues *are* simple. They require little more than systematic preparation before the meeting and sensitive observation and intervention while it is in progress.

Conclusions: Identifying the Desirable Behaviors

This knowledge about running group meetings can be translated into specific behaviors that a manager should demonstrate.

1. Prepare a meeting agenda. A large part of the chairperson's contribution occurs before the meeting begins. You will need to have a clear understanding of what is to be done at the meeting and what, if any, decisions are to be made. You'll have to determine who should attend and the right number of attendees to optimize the group's effectiveness. You'll also need to draw up the planning document that will guide the meeting—the agenda.

As a general rule, keep the number of participants as low as possible. It is unusual for more than a dozen people to do anything important at a meeting. When you get beyond ten or twelve participants, meetings typically get unwieldly. In fact, a meeting of more than a dozen probably exceeds a chairperson's span of control. Evidence indicates that decision-making committees of five are highly effective when all five members possess adequate skills and knowledge (Filley, 1970). As one author noted in assessing the effectiveness of group meetings whose purpose is to make a specific decision, "decision-making is not a spectator sport; onlookers get in the way of what needs to be done" (Grove, 1983, p. 137). So when you're preparing a meeting, include only people who either have the skills and knowledge to contribute or who are important links in the communication network. And keep in mind that effective interaction is less likely when the number of participants exceeds a dozen or so.

The agenda is the planning document that guides what you hope to accomplish at the meeting. This agenda should state the meeting's purpose. Is it only to exchange information or is it to make decisions? Will all relevant parties in the organization be included or merely their representatives? And if decisions are to be made, how are they to be arrived at? Will consensus be sought? If decisions are to be made by voting, what constitutes approval: a simple majority, a two-thirds majority, or . . . ? These issues should be clarified ahead of time in the agenda.

The agenda should also identify who will be in attendance; what, if any, preparation is required of each participant; a detailed list of items to be covered; the specific time and location of the meeting; and a specific finishing time.

2. Distribute the agenda in advance.   If you want specific people to attend your meeting, and particularly if participants need to do some homework beforehand, get your agenda out well in advance of the meeting. What's an adequate lead time? That depends on such factors as the amount of preparation necessary, the importance of the meeting, and whether the meeting will be recurring (i.e., every Monday at 8:30 A.M.) or is being called once to deal with an issue that has arisen and will be repeated only under similar circumstances.

3. Consult with participants before the meeting. An unprepared participant can't contribute to his or her full potential. It is your responsibility to ensure that members are prepared. What data will they need ahead of time? Do they have those data? If not, what can you do to help them get them?

4. Get participants to go over the agenda. The first thing you should do at the meeting is to get participants to review the agenda. Do modifications need to be made? If so, make them. Clarify the issues that you plan to discuss. After this review, get participants to approve the final agenda.

5. Establish specific time parameters. Meetings should begin on time and have a specific time for completion (Stoffman, 1986). It is your responsibility to specify these time parameters and to hold to them.

6. Maintain focused discussion. It is the chairperson's responsibility to give direction to the discussion; to keep it focused on the issues; and to minimize interruptions, disruptions, and irrelevant comments (Stoffman, 1986). If participants begin to stray from the issue under consideration, the chairperson should intercede quickly to redirect the discussion. Similarly, one or a few members cannot be allowed to monopolize the discussion or to dominate others. Appropriate preventive action ranges from a subtle stare, a raised eyebrow, or other nonverbal communication, on up to an authoritative command such as ruling someone "out of order" or withdrawing someone's right to continue speaking.

7. Encourage and support participation by all members. Participants were not selected randomly. Each is there for a purpose. To maximize the effectiveness of problem-oriented meetings, each participant must be encouraged to contribute. Quiet or reserved personalities must be drawn out so their ideas can be heard.

8. Maintain an appropriate level of control. The style of leadership can range from authoritative domination to laissez-faire. The effective leader pushes when necessary and is passive when need be.

9. Encourage the clash of ideas. You need to encourage different points of view, critical thinking, and constructive disagreement. Your goals should be to stimulate participants' creativity and to counter the group members' desire to reach an early consensus.

10. Discourage the clash of personalities. An effective meeting is characterized by the critical assessment of ideas, not attacks on people. When running a meeting, you must quickly intercede to stop personal attacks or other forms of verbal insult.

11. Exhibit effective listening skills. If your group meeting is to achieve its objectives, you need to demonstrate the listening skills discussed in Chapter 3. Effective listening reduces misunderstandings, improves the focus of discussion, and encourages the critical assessment of ideas. Even if other group members don't exhibit good listening skills, if you do, you can keep the discussion focused on the issues and facilitate critical thinking.

12. Bring proper closure. You should close a meeting by summarizing the group's accomplishments; clarifying what actions, if any, need to follow the meeting; and allocating follow-up assignments (Stoffman, 1986). If any decisions have been made, who will be responsible for communicating and implementing them?

CONCEPT QUIZ

After answering the following questions, remember to go back and check your understanding of any questions you missed.

Circle the right answer:

True or **False**   1. The benefits of meetings always exceed their costs.

True or **False**   2. Most management meetings are called either to exchange information or to solve organizational problems.

True or **False**   3. The more participants included in a meeting, the more effective that meeting is likely to be.

True or **False**   4. Topics on a meeting's agenda should be sequenced from most difficult to easiest.

True or **False**   5. Meetings should usually not be planned to exceed ninety minutes in length.

True or **False**   6. The most productive way to begin a meeting is to review the agenda.

True or **False**   7. For a meeting to be effective, the chairperson should avoid taking an authoritative role.

True or **False**   8. To maximize flexibility, meetings should not begin until everyone is present, even if that entails a significant delay.

True or **False**   9. Effective meetings are characterized by little or no disagreement

True or **False**   10. Reaching a group consensus is generally a more effective decision-making procedure than voting.

Answers: (1) False; (2) True; (3) False; (4) False; (5) True; (6) True; (7) False; (8) False; (9) False; (10) True.

BEHAVIORAL CHECKLIST

Look for these specific behaviors when evaluating your skills at running a group meeting and the skills of others.

RUNNING A GROUP MEETING EFFECTIVELY REQUIRES

- Preparing and distributing an agenda well in advance of the meeting
- Consulting with participants before the meeting to ensure proper preparation
- Establishing specific time parameters
- Maintaining focused discussion
- Encouraging and supporting participation by all members
- Encouraging the clash of ideas
- Discouraging the clash of personalities
- Bringing closure by summarizing accomplishments and allocating follow-up assignments

---

ATTENTION!

Don't read this or the following exercises until assigned to do so by your instructor.

MODELING EXERCISE

Actors: JAN FORBES, TERRY JAMES, LEE DARREN, BLAIR ROKEACH, and WHITNEY McFARLIN.

Situation: Jan Forbes is plant superintendent for a microchip manufacturer. Jan is responsbile for all production operations at the plant (the company also operates five other production facilities around the country). Jan has called a meeting to discuss a $3 million plant modernization program recently approved by the company's top management. The agenda for the meeting was sent to participants five days ago. The meeting is scheduled for today at 10 A.M. Participants in the meeting, in addition to Jan, are

- Terry James—supervisor for production control
- Lee Darren—supervisor for quality control
- Blair Rokeach—senior shift supervisor
- Whitney McFarlin—supervisor for maintenance

Time: Since this is a simulated meeting, it should last for only twenty minutes.

MEMO

To: Terry James, Lee Darren, Blair Rokeach,
      & Whitney McFarlin
From: Jan Forbes

I have scheduled a meeting for next Monday at 10 A.M. in the Production Conference Room to discuss the recent approval of a plant modernization program.

AGENDA

1. Top management's mandate
2. Time frame
3. Implications for manufacturing personnel
4. Implications for day-to-day operations

IMPORTANT-READ THIS!

Individuals chosen to play one of the
five roles are to read *only* their role.

JAN FORBES's role: You are chairing the meeting. You've worked with each of these people for many years and are aware that they have diverse personalities.

Top management has committed $3 million to modernizing the current plant. It's ten years old and is not nearly as cost-efficient as many of the company's other plants or those of competitors. The program will take three months to complete and will begin in about thirty days. Because of the construction work, production will be disrupted. However, your boss has told you that productivity levels must be maintained at least at the 70 percent level. Because of reduced operations, some operative personnel will have to be laid off during the three-month period. The purposes of this meeting are to inform key production people of what's going on, to identify potential problems, and to agree on solutions to those problems. Attempt to complete the agenda items in the allotted time.

TERRY JAMES's role: You're responsible for scheduling production operations. You see the modernization program as a tremendous headache. Because different parts of the plant will be torn apart during construction, scheduling the work flow will be very difficult. You don't think it's possible to achieve anything more than 40 percent of current productivity during construction. From your perspective, top management should close the plant completely during the three-month renovation.

LEE DARREN's role: You're responsible for ensuring that all finished microchips meet the company's quality standards. You see some problems—for example, quality may suffer as a result of staffing changes, a reduction in cleanliness standards, and the need to adapt to the new equipment. However, because you're essentially a reserved person who respects top management's authority, you play a passive role at this meeting. You speak only when spoken to.

BLAIR ROKEACH's role: You oversee the three shift supervisors. You've heard rumors about the modernization program but still think management should build a completely new plant adjacent to the current facility and then close the old one. You don't want to talk about implementing the modernization program. Rather, you want to discuss the logic of management's decision. Be assertive. Additionally, you hate to go to meetings at which Whitney McFarlin is present. You think Whitney is a wimp and you enjoy making personal attacks on him/her.

WHITNEY MCFARLIN's Role: You're responsible for the maintenance of the plant's equipment. You're a team player and value cooperation. You strongly dislike conflict and disagreement. You like to smooth over differences and know that some of your colleagues call you "Peace-at-any-price-McFarlin" behind your back. While the modernization program will create some problems for you—most specifically, your employees will have to be retrained to work on the new machines—you think everyone should do whatever is necessary to make the program a success.

OBSERVER'S RATING SHEET

Evaluate the skills of Jan Forbes on a 1 to 5 scale (5 being highest).

- Prepares and distributes agenda in advance   _____
- Consults with participants before meeting   _____
- Establishes time parameters   _____
- Maintains focused discussion   _____
- Encourages participation by all   _____
- Encourages clash of ideas   _____
- Discourages clash of personalities   _____
- Makes a proper closure   _____

Comments:

_____

_____

_____

_____

_____

GROUP EXERCISES

Form groups of six members each. Each group member is to state the first three digits in his or her Social Security number (or social insurance I.D. number used in your country). The person whose three digits sum to the highest total becomes the chairperson, for example, in the first exercise Fran Meltzer.

Group Exercise 1*

Directions: Assign roles from the roster below. Read the following description of the situation and your assigned role. Do not read the roles for the other actors.

ACTORS: **Fran Meltzer**, section head of the group. The engineers who report to Fran and their assistants are listed below:

Lee Clark:	Senior design engineer—21 years with the company, has two technicians
Chris Manos:	Senior design engineer—16 years with the company, has one technician
B.J. Pelter:	Senior design engineer—15 years with the company, has two technicians
Pat Rosen:	Design Engineer—8 years with the company, has one technician
Sandy Solas:	Design engineer—3 years with the company, has one technician

SITUATION: Five electronics engineers design new products for the Alta Electronics Company, a medium-sized firm manufacturing a variety of electronics products. The engineers work individually on projects aided by technicians and, when needed, drafters. All of the engineers in the design group are proud of the products that they have designed, both for the technical developments they incorporate and their reliable performance in use. Fran Meltzer is in charge of the group and has called a meeting to discuss some changes in the company travel policy.

---

*Source: Adapted from Roy J. Lewicki and Joseph A Litterer, *Negotiation: Readings, Exercises, and Cases*, (Homewood, Ill.: Richard D. Irwin, 1985), pp. 423–25, 565, 568, 572, 606, 627.

For the last several years the company has been experiencing financial difficulties. While these have not resulted in layoffs, there has been a severe restriction on wage increases and an absolute freeze on building alterations, travel to professional meetings, magazine subscriptions, and similar expenditures. While most of these have been of a minor nature, some (such as not attending professional meetings) have made it difficult for you and other engineers to keep abreast of technical developments and to maintain your professional contacts. Recently you have heard that the company has begun to see a modest economic upturn.

Company policy dictates that engineers are responsible for a project not only through the design phase but also to see it through production startup to the point where acceptable products are regularly being produced. On many projects the amount of time spent on handling problems in production is minor. On others, especially those with particularly difficult standards, the time spent in handling production problems can be considerable.

FRAN MELTZER's role: You are the section head of the design engineering group and have reporting to you a competent group of engineers who individually handle design products. Because of financial difficulties, the company has not allocated funds to send engineers to professional meetings for the last several years. You have just heard from your superior that enough money has been appropriated to send one engineer from each group to the national meetings of your professional society next month. He also stated that the vice president of engineering thought it would be best if the limited travel funds were allocated to engineers rather than to managerial personnel which includes section heads like yourself.

You are quite sure that all of your engineers will want to go and know that there is the possibility of hurt feelings and resentment developing over this matter unless it is handled properly. Therefore, you have decided that rather than make the decision yourself, you will call a meeting of your group and turn the matter over to them and let them make the decision. You will tell them of the funds available for travel and that you want them to make the decision as to who will go in the way they feel most fair. Your superior has also reminded you that these funds can only be used to send someone to the professional meetings. Do not take a position yourself as to who should be selected to go to the meetings.

SANDY SOLAS' role: You feel like the low person on the totem pole in this group. A lot of your equipment is old and frequently breaks down.

You don't think Fran has been particularly concerned about the inconvenience this has caused you. Further, ever since you have graduated from college you have not been able to attend a professional meeting because of the freeze the company has had on travel of this sort. You feel that this has kept you from making the contacts you need to develop professionally. You hope that the recent upturn in the company's business will finally make some money available to go to professional meetings.

CHRIS MANOS' role: You have been feeling a strong need to get to some professional meetings. Through no fault of your own, you missed attending meetings for several years before the freeze on travel was imposed. For two years there were crash projects that kept you tied to the plant. The year before that your daughter had gotten married. An unplanned chain of events, but one that has kept you from building new professional contacts or even maintaining old ones. As a result you feel you are in serious danger of slipping professionally and getting stale.

PAT ROSEN's role: Lately you have been swamped with making numerous lengthy tests on some new equipment you have designed. The work has completely swamped your technician and you have had to work along with him to keep the job moving. Even with your effort, however, it looks as if you may be on this a long time. You would like very much to get to the professional meetings next month to see the new testing equipment that will be on display in the hope that some manufacturer may have come out with an item that would ease your testing problem. You are thinking seriously of making a strong pitch for this to Fran even though you know there has been no money for such trips for the last several years. Additional technician help would be an alternative but you doubt there is any possibility of hiring a new technician.

B. J. PELTER's role: The line of work you are now in is taking you in exciting new directions not only for yourself and the company but also for your professional area. You feel a real need to talk to other engineers doing similar work both to confirm what you have been doing and also to get ideas on some problems you have been facing. You know that several will be giving papers on topics in the new area at the professional meeting next month. Fortunately you recently finished debugging the production problems on the last product you designed and now have more time to travel.

LEE CLARK:'s role: If funds become available for sending people to professional meetings and there are not enough to send everyone, you feel that you should be the person to go because you have the most seniority. You feel strongly that in professional work seniority should count. In addition, you have a wide array of contacts developed over the years through which you can pick up much information useful to the company.

TIME: This meeting should last for twenty-five minutes or less.

OBSERVER'S RATING SHEET

Evaluate the skills of Jan Forbes on a 1 to 5 scale (5 being highest).

- Prepares and distributes agenda in advance   _____
- Consults with participants before meeting   _____
- Establishes time parameters   _____
- Maintains focused discussion   _____
- Encourages participation by all   _____
- Encourages clash of ideas   _____
- Discourages clash of personalities   _____
- Makes a proper closure   _____

Comments:

_____

_____

_____

_____

Group Exercise 2*

Use the same six-person groups developed in Group Exercise 1—only this time, the person whose three-digit Social Security (insurance) number sums up to the *lowest* total becomes the chairperson. He or she has twenty-five minutes to lead the group members who are playing the other five roles in a decision-making meeting.

Before conducting the meeting all group members should read the "Situation" and "Roles" described in the following case. Each member should then individually fill out the "Personal Preference" part of the worksheet that follows from the perspective of his or her assigned role.

Actors: Supervisor, the crew chief, a seasoned manager, a union representative, a member of the human resources department, and a member of the company's affirmative action office.

Situation: Jimmy Lincoln has a grim personal background. He is the third child in an inner-city minority family. He has not seen his parents for several years. He recalls that his father used to come home drunk and beat up family members; everyone ran when he came staggering home.

His mother, according to Jimmy, wasn't much better. She was irritable and unhappy, and she always predicted that Jimmy would come to no good end. Yet she worked, when her health allowed, to keep the family in food and clothing. She frequently decried the fact that she was not able to be the kind of mother she would like to be.

Jimmy quit school in the seventh grade. He had great difficulty conforming to the school routine—misbehaving often, playing a truant frequently, and getting into fights with schoolmates. On several occasions he was picked up by the police and, along with other members of his group, questioned during investigations into cases of both petty and grand larceny. The police regarded him as a "high-potential troublemaker."

The juvenile officer of the court saw in Jimmy some good qualities that no one else seemed to sense. This man, Mr. O'Brien, took it on himself to act as a father figure to Jimmy. He had several long conversations with Jimmy, during which he manage to penetrate to some

---

*Source: Adapted from David A. Whetten and Kim S. Cameron, *Developing Management Skills: Applied Communication Skills* (New York: HarperCollins College Publishers, 1993), pp. 45–47, 111.

192   **T**raining in **I**nter**P**ersonal **S**kills

degree Jimmy's defensive shell. He represented to Jimmy the first semblance of a personal, caring influence in his life. Through Mr. O'Brien's efforts, Jimmy returned to school and obtained a high school diploma. Afterward, Mr. O'Brien helped him obtain his first job.

Now at age twenty-two, Jimmy is a stockroom clerk at Costello Pharmaceutical Laboratory. On the whole, his performance has been acceptable, but there have been glaring exceptions. One involved a clear act of insubordination, though the issue was fairly unimportant. On another occasion, Jimmy was accused by a co-worker, on circumstantial grounds, of destroying some expensive equipment. Though the investigation is still open, it appears that the destruction was accidental. He also appears to have lost an extremely important requisition (although he claims to have never seen it). In addition, his laid-back attitude and wisecracking ways tend to irritate his co-workers.

It is also important to note that Jimmy's appearance is disheveled. Researchers in the lab have commented that his appearance doesn't fit in with the company's image. Others have wondered aloud (half jokingly, half seriously) whether he is counting or taking drugs in the stockroom.

ATTENTION!

Read only your assigned role below.

Role for Jimmy's supervisor: You are fairly new to management and are not sure how to handle this situation. You see merit in giving Jimmy the benefit of the doubt and helping him out, but you frankly wonder if it's worth the hassle. Seeking advice, you organize a committee of individuals close to the situation. These include the *crew chief* (who has expressed frustration about the effects of Jimmy's performance and reputation on the morale of the work group, a *seasoned manager* (who has a reputation for being even-handed), a *union representative* (who tends to view most acts of employee discipline as an infringement on employee rights), a *member of the human resources department* (who is concerned about following proper company procedures), and a *member of the company's affirmative action office* (who is concerned that managers at Costello do not fully understand the handicap workers like Jimmy bring with them to the workplace).

Role for the crew chief: You are frustrated about the effects of Jimmy's performance and reputation on the morale of the work group. Something has to be done to stop these problems.

Role for the seasoned manager: You understand the situation from all points of view. Your main concern is that the problem is solved in an even-handed way.

Role for the union representative: You tend to view most acts of employee discipline as an infringement on employee rights, so you are very concerned about the possiblity of unfair discipline of an individual who is probably doing the best he can under the circumstances.

Role for the member of the human resources department: You have just lost a case regarding a firing for insufficient cause. You are primarily concerned about following proper company procedures. As long as it is done right, you don't particularly care what the outcome is.

Role for the member of the company's affirmative action office: You are concerned that managers at Costello do not fully understand the handicap workers like Jimmy bring with them to the workplace. Consequently, you plan to give them special assistance and direction.

Meeting Directions: When individuals have completed their personal preferences on the worksheet, the supervisor should act as chair of the committee and begin the discussion. The group's assignment is to reach consensus on the rank-ordered options (from this list). Group members should stay in role during the meeting. They should not use any statistical process to reach a rank-order, or show their worksheets to anyone else.

Time: Take no longer than twenty-five minutes to reach your decision.

WORKSHEET: Jimmy Lincoln Decision

Directions: Each group member should rank order his or her preferred solutions from the perspective of the role character being played after reading the case and before the group meeting in the Personal Preference column. Do not show anyone else your rankings.

    After the meeting, list the group's consensus rank ordering in the Group Decision column.

Personal   *Group*
Preference   *Decision*

____	____	1. Give Jimmy a warning that at the next sign of trouble a formal reprimand will be placed in his file.
____	____	2. Do nothing, as it is unclear that Jimmy has done anything seriously wrong. Back off and give him a chance to prove himself.
____	____	3. Create strict controls (do's and don'ts) for Jimmy with immediate discipline for any misbehavior.
____	____	4. Give Jimmy a great deal of warmth and personal attention (overlooking his annoying mannerisms) so he will feel accepted.
____	____	5. Fire him. It's not worth the time and effort spent for such a low-level position.
____	____	6. Treat Jimmy the same as everyone else, but provide an orderly routine so he can develop proper work habits.
____	____	7. Call Jimmy in and logically discuss the problem with him and ask what you can do to help.
____	____	8. Do nothing now, but watch him so you can reward him the next time he does something good.

SUMMARY CHECKLIST

Because of the time involved in conducting a meeting, not everyone in the class got the chance to practice all the behaviors identified in this chapter for running a meeting effectively. On the basis of your experiences and observations in the meetings you have participated in, try now to assess yourself on each of the key learning behaviors. Make a check (✓) next to those behaviors on which you think you need improvement.

I prepare and distribute the agenda well in advance of a meeting. I consult with participants before a meeting to ensure they are properly prepared. _____

I establish specific time parameters for a meeting. _____

I maintain focused discussion. _____

I encourage and support participation by all members. _____

I encourage the clash of ideas. _____

I discourage the clash of personalities. _____

I bring closure by summarizing accomplishments and allocating follow-up assignments. _____

APPLICATION QUESTIONS

1. It has been estimated that from one- third to one- half of time spent in meetings is a waste. Why would intelligent, task-oriented managers allow this inefficiency to develop and continue?

2. "Meetings are often effective but rarely efficient." Do you agree or disagree? Discuss.

3. One way to avoid conflicts at meetings is to avoid having the meeting in the first place. How would you suggest managing potential conflicts that might occur in meetings?

4. How do the formal meetings that you've participated in compare with the guidelines for effective meetings presented in this chapter? What were the main differences and consequences?

REINFORCEMENT EXERCISES

1. The next time you're in a meeting—at work, a social or professional club, at school, and so forth—pay close attention to the behavior of the chairperson. What did he or she do right in running the meeting? What could he or she have done to be more effective?

2. Volunteer to chair a committee at one of the clubs or associations to which you belong. Specifically practice the behaviors identified with effectively running a group meeting. You could do the same thing for a class-sponsored group project.

ACTION PLAN

1. Which behavior do I want to improve the most?

_____

_____

_____

2. Why? What will be my payoff?

_____

_____

_____

3. What potential obstacles stand in my way?

_____

_____

_____

4. What are the specific things I will do to improve? (For examples, see the Reinforcement Exercises.)

_____

_____

_____

5. When will I do them?

_____

_____

_____

6. How and when will I measure my success?

_____

_____

_____

Chapter 11

BUILDING TEAMS

SELF-ASSESSMENT EXERCISE

For each of the following questions, select the answer that best describes your behavior as a team member.

	Usually	Sometimes	Seldom
1. I seek agreement on a common purpose.	☐	☐	☐
2. I let other members worry about their specific goals.	☐	☐	☐
3. I clarify what each member is accountable for individually and collectively.	☐	☐	☐
4. I focus on home runs versus small wins.	☐	☐	☐
5. I keep my problems and limitations to myself.	☐	☐	☐

6. I respectfully listen to others' ideas.	☐	☐	☐
7. I'm dependable and honest.	☐	☐	☐
8. I don't bug others for feedback on how well I am doing.	☐	☐	☐
9. I offer advice on how group processes can be improved.	☐	☐	☐
10. I give others feedback on their contributions.	☐	☐	☐

SCORING KEY

For questions 1, 3, 6, 7, 9, and 10, give yourself 3 points for "Usually," 2 points for "Sometimes," and 1 point for "Seldom."

For questions 2, 4, 5, and 8, give yourself 3 points for "Seldom," 2 points for "Sometimes," and 1 point for "Usually."

Sum up your total points. A score of 27 or higher means you're a good team player. A score of 22 to 26 suggests you have some deficiencies as a team member. A score below 22 indicates that you have considerable room for improvement.

SKILL CONCEPTS

Groups and teams are not necessarily the same thing. A *group* is two or more individuals who interact primarily to share information and to make decisions to help each other perform within a given area of responsibility. Members of a group have no need to engage in collective work that requires joint efforts so their performance is merely the summation of each group member's individual contribution. There is no positive synergy that would create an overall level of performance that is greater than the sum of the inputs.

But it could be worse. If a group is plagued by factors such as poor communication, antagonistic conflicts, and avoidance of responsibilities, the product of these problems produces negative synergy and a *pseudoteam* where the sum of the whole is less than the potential of the individual parts Even though members may call themselves a team, they're not. Because it doesn't focus on collective performance and because members have no interest in shaping a common purpose, a pseudoteam actually underperforms a working group.

What differentiates a *team* from a group is that members are committed to a common purpose, have a set of specific performance goals, and hold themselves mutually accountable for the team's results. Teams can produce outputs that are something greater than the sum of their parts. The primary force that moves a work group toward a real high-performing team is its emphasis on performance.

"Going in the right direction but not there yet" is the best way to describe a *potential* team. It recognizes the need for, and is really trying hard to achieve, higher performance, but some roadblocks are in the way. Its purpose and goals may need greater clarity or the team may need better coordination. The result is that is has not yet established a sense of collective accountability. Its goal is to become a *real* team with a set of common characteristics that lead to consistently high performance. We can identify six characteristics of real teams.

BUILDING REAL TEAMS

Studies of effective teams have found that they contain a small number of people with complementary skills who are equally committed to a common purpose, goals, and working approach for which they hold themselves mutually accountable (Katzenback & Douglas, 1993, pp. 43–64).

Small Size

The best teams tend to be small. When they have more than about ten members, it becomes difficult for them to get much done. They have trouble interacting constructively and agreeing on much. Large numbers of people usually cannot develop the common purpose, goals, approach, and mutual accountability of a real team. They tend merely to go through the motions. So in designing effective teams, keep them to ten or less. If the natural working unit is larger, and you want a team effort, break the group into subteams. Federal Express, for instance, has divided the 1000 clerical workers at its headquarters into teams of five to ten members each.

Complimentary Skills

To perform effectively, a team requires three types of skills. First, it needs people with *technical expertise*. Second, it needs people with the *problem-solving* and *decision-making skills* to identify problems, generate alternatives, evaluate those alternatives, and make competent choices. Finally, teams need people with good *interpersonal skills*.

No team can achieve its performance potential without developing all three types of skills. The right mix is crucial. Too much of one at the expense of others will result in lower team performance.

Incidentally, teams don't need to have all the complementary skills at the beginning. Where team members value personal growth and development, one or more members often take responsibility to learn the skills in which the group is deficient, as long as the skill potential exists. Additionally, personal compatibility among members is not critical to the team's success if the technical, decision-making, and interpersonal skills are in place.

Common Purpose

Does the team have a meaningful purpose that all members aspire to? This purpose is a vision. It's broader than any specific goals. High-performing teams have a common and meaningful purpose that provides direction, momentum, and commitment for members.

The development team at Apple Computer that designed the Macintosh, for example, was almost religiously committed to creating a user-friendly machine that would revolutionize the way people used computers. Production teams at Saturn Corp. are united by the common purpose of building an American automobile that can successfully compete in terms of quality and price with the best of Japanese cars.

Members of successful teams put a tremendous amount of time and effort into discussing, shaping, and agreeing upon a purpose that belongs to them collectively and individually. This common purpose, when accepted by the team, becomes the equivalent of what celestial navigation is to a ship captain—it provides direction and guidance under any and all conditions.

Specific Goals

Successful teams translate their common purpose into specific, measurable, and realistic performance goals. Just as goals lead individuals to higher performance (see Chapter 4), they also energize teams. Specific goals facilitate clear communication and help teams maintain their focus on getting results. Examples of specific team goals might be responding to all customers within twenty-four hours, cutting production-cycle time by 30 percent over the next six months, or maintaining equipment at a level of zero downtime every month.

Common Approach

Goals are the ends a team strives to attain. Defining and agreeing upon a common approach ensures that the team is unified on the *means* for achieving those ends.

Team members must contribute equally in sharing the work load and agree on who is to do what. Additionally, the team needs to determine how schedules will be set, what skills need to be developed, how conflicts will be resolved, and how decisions will be made and modified. The recent implementation of work teams at Olin Chemicals' Macintosh, Alabama plant included having teams complete questionnaires on how they would organize themselves and share specific responsibilities. Integrating individual skills to further the team's performance is the essence of shaping a common approach.

Mutual Accountability

The final characteristic of high-performing teams is accountability at both the individual and group level.

Successful teams make members individually and jointly accountable for the team's purpose, goals, and approach. Members understand what they are individually responsible for and what they are jointly responsible for.

Studies have shown that when teams focus only on group-level performance targets and ignore individual contributions and responsibilities, team members often engage in *social loafing* (Sheppard, 1993, pp. 67–81). They reduce their efforts because their individual contributions can't be identified. They, in effect, become "free riders" and coast on the group's effort. The result is that the team's overall performance suffers. This reaffirms the importance of measuring both individual contributions to the team as well as the team's overall performance. And successful teams have members who collectively feel responsible for their team's performance.

OBSTACLES TO EFFECTIVE TEAMS

Teams have long been popular in Japan. When they were introduced into the United States in the late 1980s, critics warned that they were destined to fail: "Japan is a collectivist society. American culture is based on the values of individualism. American workers won't sublimate their needs for individual responsibility and recognition to be anonymous parts of a team." While the introduction of work teams in some organizations has met with resistance and disappointment, the overall picture has been encouraging. When teams are properly used in organizations and when the organization's internal climate is one that is consistent with a team approach, the results have been largely positive.

There are, of course, a number of obstacles to creating effective teams. Fortunately, there are also many effective techniques for overcoming those obstacles. The following critical obstacles can prevent teams from becoming high performers.

A Weak Sense of Direction

Teams perform poorly when members are not sure of their purpose, goals, and approach. Add weak leadership and you have the recipe for failure. Nothing will undermine enthusiasm for the team concept as quickly as the frustration of being an involuntary member of a team that has no focus.

Infighting

When team members are spending time bickering and undermining their colleagues, energy is being misdirected. Effective teams are not necessarily composed of people who all like each other; however, members must respect each other and be willing to put aside petty differences in order to facilitate goal achievement.

Shirking of Responsibilities

A team is in trouble if members exhibit lack of commitment to the team, maneuver to have others do part of their job, or blame colleagues or management for personal or team failures. The result is a pseudoteam—a team in name only and one that consistently underperforms even what the members could accomplish independently.

Lack of Trust

When there is *trust*, team members believe in the integrity, character, and ability of each other. When trust is lacking, members are unable to depend on each other. Teams that lack trust tend to be short-lived.

Critical Skills Gaps

When skill gaps occur, and the team doesn't fill these gaps, the team flounders. Members have trouble communicating with each other, destructive conflicts aren't resolved, decisions are never made, or technical problems overwhelm the team.

Lack of External Support

Teams exist within the larger organization. They rely on that larger organization for a variety of resources—money, people, equipment—and if those resources aren't there, it's difficult for teams to reach their potential. For example, teams must live with the organization's employee selection process, formal rules and regulations, budgeting procedures, and compensation system. If these are inconsistent with the team's needs and goals, the team suffers.

OVERCOMING THE OBSTACLES

There are a number of things that can be done to overcome obstacles and help teams reach their full potential.

Create Clear Goals

Members of high-performance teams have a clear understanding of their goals and believe that their goals embody a worthwhile or important result. Moreover, the importance of these goals encourages individuals to sublimate personal concerns to these team goals. In effective teams, members are committed to the team's goals, know what they are expected to accomplish, and understand how they will work together to achieve these goals.

Encourage Teams To Go
For Small Wins

The building of real teams takes time. Team members have to learn to think and work as a team. New teams can't be expected to hit home runs, right at the beginning, every time they come to bat. Team members should begin by trying to hit singles.

This can be facilitated by identifying and setting attainable goals. The eventual goal of cutting overall costs by 30 percent, for instance, can be dissected into five or ten smaller and more easily attainable goals. As the smaller goals are attained, the team's success is reinforced. Cohesiveness is increased and morale improves. Confidence builds. Success breeds success, but it's a lot easier for young teams to reach their goals if they start with small wins.

Build Mutual Trust

Trust is fragile. It takes a long time to build and can be easily destroyed. Several things can be done to create a climate of mutual trust (Bartolome, 1989, pp. 135–142).

Keep team members informed by explaining upper-management decisions and policies and by providing accurate feedback. Create a climate of openness where employees are free to discuss problems without fear of retaliation. Be candid about your own problems and limitations. Make sure you're available and approachable when others need support. Be respectful and listen to team members' ideas. Develop a reputation for being fair, objective, and impartial in your treatment of team members. Show consistency in your actions and avoid erratic and unpredictable behavior. Finally, be dependable and honest. Make sure you follow through on all explicit and implied promises.

Appraise Both Group
and Individual Performance

Team members should all share in the glory when their team succeeds, and they should share in the blame when it fails. So a large measure of each member's performance appraisal should be based on the overall team's performance. But members need to know that they can't ride on the backs of others. Therefore, each member's individual contribution should also be identified and made a part of his or her overall performance appraisal.

Provide the Necessary External Support

Managers are the link between the teams and upper management. It's their responsibility to make sure that teams have the necessary organizational resources to accomplish their goals. They should be prepared to make the case to key decision makers in the organization for tools, equipment, training, personnel, physical space, or other resources that the teams may require.

Offer Team-Building Training

Teams, especially in their early stages of formation, will need training to build their skills. Typically, these would include problem-solving, communication, negotiation, conflict-resolution, and group-processing skills. If you can't personally provide this kind of skill training for your team members, look to specialists in your organization who can or secure the funds to bring in outside facilitators who specialize in this kind of training.

Change the Team's Membership

When teams get bogged down in their own inertia or internal fighting, allow them to rotate members. To manage this change, consider how certain personalities will mesh and reform teams in ways that will better complement skills. If lack of leadership is the problem, use your knowledge of the people involved to create teams where there will be a high probability that a leader will emerge.

CONCEPT QUIZ

The answers to the following ten-question, true-false quiz are at the end of the quiz. If you miss any of these questions, go back and find out why you got them wrong.

Circle the right answer:

True or False   1. Groups produce synergy that creates performance that is greater than the sum of individual inputs.

True or False   2. The best teams tend to be small.

True or False   3. A team will perform effectively if all members have technical expertise.

True or False   4. High-performing teams have a common purpose.

True or False   5. Successful teams translate their vision into measurable performance goals.

True or False   6. Team members must contribute equally in sharing the work load.

True or False   7. Successful teams encourage social loafing by free riders.

True or False   8. If trust is lacking, team members are unable to depend on each other.

True or False   9. Teams should begin by trying to hit singles rather than home runs.

True or False   10. Members should all share the blame when the team fails.

Answers: (1) False; (2) True; (3) False; (4) True; (5) True; (6) True; (7) False; (8) True; (9) True; (10) True.

BEHAVIORAL CHECKLIST

Look for the following behaviors when evaluating your effectiveness in team building.

EFFECTIVE TEAM BUILDING REQUIRES

- Establishing a common purpose

- Assessing team strengths and weaknesses

- Developing specific individual goals

- Getting agreement on a common approach for achieving goals

- Encouraging acceptance of accountability for both individual and team performance

- Building mutual trust among members

- Maintaining an appropriate mix of team member skills and personalities

- Providing needed training and resources

- Creating opportunities for small achievements

MODELING EXERCISE

The entire class should read the following case. Five volunteers form a circle and reach a consensus for the answers to the questions following the case (twenty-five minutes). The remainder of the class observes the problem-solving team and rates its effectiveness for both (a) its case solution and (b) its own team process during the exercise. When the task team has completed its solution to the case, observers provide feedback on the team's case solution, how well it performed as a team, and for how it could be even more effective in the future (twenty minutes).

Time: Total time required for setup, exercise, and feedback is about fifty minutes. Do not exceed twenty-five minutes for the case analysis, ten minutes for the case solution feedback, or ten minutes for the team process feedback.

Case: Team Building After Mergers*

The MDI Conglomerate recognized that the Numero Company and Uno Incorporated possessed complementary technical and market attributes making them prime candidates for acquisition and merger which MDI completed. The newly merged companies were placed under tremendous pressure from their "parent" company to streamline operations and improve productivity which they did to the tune of a 10 percent improvement in productivity. Further improvement was mandated through the integration of functions and elimination of duplicate facilities.

The prescribed strategic plan for the newly merged Numero-Uno Company was to withdraw from mature industrial businesses and to concentrate on aerospace, defense, and selected industrial products by developing new technologies and streamlining operations to improve productivity. These ambitious goals and overwhelming changes put tremendous pressure on Numero-Uno's President and Chief Executive Officer, who was overwhelmed in picking up and restructuring the pieces of the newly merged company, and developing a team from the chaos which could persevere and accomplish its assigned mission.

The Numero-Uno merger had created a multitude of significant structural and interpersonal changes that the financial engineers of the merger had not even contemplated. These included: 1) considerable increase and redundancy in management personnel and structure; 2) a new CEO with ambiguous power and goals; 3) changing operating procedures and responsibilities; and 4) uncertain reward systems and career paths. These externally initiated changes led to a multitude of internal changes in organizational culture, interpersonal relationships, structural uncertainty, and career opportunities.

The executive staffs were extremely competent in their areas of expertise, but they were dependent on each other to make the organization function effectively. The different styles of staff members, coupled with the anxiety and resentment which rapidly developed regarding the ambiguity of careers and power bases, led to minimal communication and distrust of others' intentions, disorganization, and low productivity. The merger had transformed two effectively functioning teams into a group of disorganized and competing individuals who were threatening to reverse previous progress and possibly destroy the new company and everyone in it.

This was especially true of the executive staff, which was made up of the president, vice president, subsidiary company presidents, financial and legal

---

*Source: Adapted from Michael J. Driver, Kenneth R. Brousseau, and Philip L. Hunsaker, *The Dynamic Decision Maker* (San Francisco: Jossey-Bass Publishers, 1990), pp. 215–216.

division directors, and their immediate staffs. The need to streamline and increase productivity meant that all of the current group, which represented officers of both the previous Numero and Uno companies, would not remain at the end of the year because of considerable redundancies. The politics, lack of trust and openness, fear and hostility, and considerable differences in previous corporate cultures and behavioral styles created a group of territorial infighters. Clearly the Numero-Uno corporate staff was not a team.

Questions for Action

1. Why wasn't the Numero-Uno corporate staff a team?

2. What does it need to do to become a team?

3. What team-building suggestions would you recommend? Why?

OBSERVER'S RATING SHEET

Did the problem-solving team you just observed address the following team-building considerations in its *solution* to the Numero-Uno merger case?

Question 1. Was Numero-Uno's executive team

  a. Committed to a common purpose?
  b. Have a set of specific performance goals?
  c. Hold themselves mutually accountable for the team's results?
  d. Have complementary or competing/redundant skills?
  e. Have a common approach for achieving ends?

    If the answers to these questions are yes, Numero-Uno is a team. If the answers are no, it is not.

Questions 2 and 3. To become a team, suggestions for Numero-Uno should have included

  a. Establish a common purpose for the executive team
  b. Assess Numero-Uno's team strengths and weaknesses
  c. Develop specific goals for individual team members
  d. Obtain agreement to a common approach for achieving goals
  e. Get acceptance of accountability for both individual and team performance
  f. Build mutual trust among members
  g. Maintain an appropriate mix of team member skills and personalities
  h. Provide needed training and resources
  i. Create opportunities for small achievements

OBSERVER'S RATING SHEET

Evaluate the problem-solving *team's own application* of the following team-building skills while it worked to reach a solution to the merger case. Use a 1 to 5 scale (5 being highest).

- Establishes its common purpose   _____

- Assesses team-member strengths
  and weaknesses   _____

- Develops specific individual goals   _____

- Agrees to a common approach for
  achieving goals   _____

- Members accept accountability for
  both individual and team performance   _____

- Builds mutual trust among members   _____

- Accommodates its mix of team member
  skills and personalities   _____

- Asks questions and provides guidelines
  regarding case information and team process   _____

- Creates opportunities for small achievements   _____

GROUP EXERCISES

Break into an even number of five- or six-member groups. One-half of the groups will work on an assigned task while the other groups observe them. At the completion of the task, observing groups provide task groups with feedback according to the observer's rating sheet below. Then groups switch roles; the observer groups now work on Task 2, and the former task groups observe and provide feedback to them.

Task 1: Create a list of ten desirable team *member* characteristics. Rank order these characteristics according to their importance.

Task 2: Create a list of ten desirable team *leader* characteristics. Rank order these characteristics according to their importance.

Time: Do not exceed twenty-five minutes for task completion or fifteen minutes for feedback.

OBSERVER'S RATING SHEET

Evaluate the problem-solving team's own application of the following team-building skills while it worked to reach a solution to the merger case. Use a 1 to 5 scale (5 being highest).

- Establishes its common purpose   _____
- Assesses team-member strengths and weaknesses   _____
- Develops specific individual goals   _____
- Agrees to a common approach for achieving goals   _____
- Members accept accountability for both individual and team performance   _____
- Builds mutual trust among members   _____
- Accommodates its mix of team member skills and personalities   _____
- Asks questions and provides guidelines regarding case information and team process   _____
- Creates opportunities for small achievements   _____

SUMMARY CHECKLIST

Think about your own performance and review others' ratings of your skill. Assess yourself on each of the following key team-building behaviors. Make a check (✓) next to those behaviors on which you need improvement.

I make sure the team establishes a
common purpose. _____

I assess my teams strengths and weaknesses. _____

I ensure the development of specific
individual goals. _____

I get agreement to a common approach
for achieving goals. _____

I accept accountability for both individual
and team performance. _____

I try to build mutual trust with all members. _____

I push for an appropriate mix of team
member skills and personalities. _____

I seek training and resources needed for
the team I emphasize achieving small goals. _____

APPLICATION QUESTIONS

1. Think of a work group, club, or team you currently are in or have been a member of. Was this set of individuals a real team, a pseudoteam, or group? How do you know?

2. Have you ever been a member of a team that has social loafers going along for a free ride? How did this condition develop? What were the consequences? Was anything done to rectify the situation? If so what? If not, what should have been done?

3. Contrast a group you have been in where members trusted each other versus another group where members did not trust each other. How did these conditions develop? What were the consequences in terms of interaction patterns and performance?

REINFORCEMENT EXERCISES

1. Interview a coach of a sports team about the characteristics of an effective team.

2. Interview a team member of a sports team about what constitutes an effective team.

3. Watch a T.V. show or movie about a team and determine the team characteristics present. Examples are *Star Trek*, *The God Father*, "NYPD Blue," "Law and Order," "Coach", or reruns of "M.A.S.H." and the "Mary Tyler Moore Show."

4. Apply your team-building skills to a team you are currently a member of, for example, a sports team, a class project team. See what difference you can make in improving your team's effectiveness.

ACTION PLAN

1. Which behavior do I want to improve the most?

_____

_____

_____

2. Why? What will be my payoff?

_____

_____

_____

3. What potential obstacles stand in my way?

_____

_____

_____

4. What are the specific things I will do to improve? (For examples, see the Reinforcement Exercises.)

_____

_____

_____

5. When will I do them?

_____

_____

_____

6. How and when will I measure my success?

_____

_____

_____

Chapter *12*

RESOLVING CONFLICTS

SELF-ASSESSMENT EXERCISE

Indicate how often you do the following when you differ with someone.

WHEN I DIFFER WITH SOMEONE:

	Usually	Sometimes	Seldom
1. I explore our differences, not backing down, but not imposing my view either.	☐	☐	☐
2. I disagree openly, then invite more discussion about our differences.	☐	☐	☐
3. I look for a mutually satisfactory solution.	☐	☐	☐
4. Rather than let the other person make a decision without my input, I make sure I am heard and also that I hear the other out.	☐	☐	☐

5. I agree to a middle ground rather than look for a completely satisfying solution. ☐ ☐ ☐

6. I admit I am half wrong rather than explore our differences ☐ ☐ ☐

7. I have a reputation for meeting a person halfway. ☐ ☐ ☐

8. I expect to get out about half of what I really want to say. ☐ ☐ ☐

9. I give in totally rather than try to change another's opinion. ☐ ☐ ☐

10. I put aside any controversial aspects of an issue. ☐ ☐ ☐

11. I agree early on, rather than argue about a point. ☐ ☐ ☐

12. I give in as soon as the other party gets emotional about an issue. ☐ ☐ ☐

13. I try to win the other person over. ☐ ☐ ☐

14. I work to come out victorious, no matter what. ☐ ☐ ☐

15. I never back away from a good argument. ☐ ☐ ☐

16. I would rather win than end up compromising. ☐ ☐ ☐

Total your choices as follows: Give yourself 5 points for "Usually"; 3 points for "Sometimes"; and 1 point for "Seldom." Then total them for each set of statements, grouped as follows:

Set A: items 13–16	Set C: items 5–8
Set B: items 9–12	Set D: items 1–4

Treat each set separately.

A score of 17 or above on any set is considered high;
Scores of 8 to 16 are moderate;
Scores of 7 or less are considered low.

Sets A, B, C, and D represent different conflict-resolution strategies:

A = Forcing/domination. I win, you lose.
B = Accommodation. I lose, you win.
C = Compromise. Both win some, lose some.
D = Collaboration. I win, you win.

Everyone has a basic or underlying conflict-handling style. Your scores on this exercise indicate the strategies you rely upon most.

Source: Reprinted with permission of Macmillan Publishing Co. from *Supervision: Managerial Skills for a New Era* by Thomas J. Von der Embse. Copyright ©1987 by Macmillan Publishing Co.

SKILL CONCEPTS

Conflict is a natural phenomenon of organizational life. Why? Because organizational members have different goals and because organizations are made up of scarce resources. The forces that make politics endemic to organizations also act to create conflict. In addition, contemporary management practices increase the potential for conflict by emphasizing interdependence, coordination, and "we versus them" situations. Examples include matrix structures, task teams, participatory decision making, two-tier pay systems, and the restructuring of units to cut costs and increase efficiency. It's not surprising, then, that Tjosvold and Johnson (1983, p. 10) have found that "no skill is more important for organizational effectiveness than the constructive management and resolution of conflict."

Because conflict is natural to organizations, it can never be completely eliminated. That, of course, isn't necessarily bad. Conflict has some positive properties. It stimulates creativity, innovation, and change (Robbins, 1978).

If organizations were completely devoid of conflict, they would become apathetic, stagnant, and unresponsive to change. Yet all conflicts are clearly not functional or constructive. When managers typically talk about conflict problems, they are usually referring to conflict's dysfunctional effects and how they can be resolved. Given this reality, even though conflict management encompasses both conflict-stimulation and conflict-resolution techniques (Robbins, 1978), we'll limit our discussion in this chapter to conflict-resolution approaches and skills.

Resolving Conflicts and Other Interpersonal Skills

Few interpersonal skills draw upon other interpersonal skills the way conflict resolution does. Specifically, resolving conflicts uses goal setting, listening, feedback, and persuasion skills.

We know that formal goals guide and motivate employees and provide standards against which job performances can be compared. But they also prevent conflict. How? By reducing ambiguity and sublimating personal interests to the larger goals of the organization. Goal setting establishes specific job performance standards. These, in turn, make self-serving behaviors and dysfunctional conflicts more visible. Like politics, conflicts are more likely to grow and flourish in a climate of ambiguity. So goal setting lessens the need to use conflict-resolution skills.

Both listening and feedback skills are central to effective communication. As we'll show, distortions in communication are a frequent source of interpersonal conflict. The use of listening skills to improve communication clarity and the use of feedback skills to improve accuracy of understanding both act to reduce distortions in the communication process.

Finally, persuasion is an interpersonal skill closely tied to resolving conflicts. It's a means to get others to do what you desire when you don't have, or don't want to use, formal authority. When two or more parties in an organization disagree, you can use your persuasion skills to resolve their differences. In addition, effective negotiation depends on your ability to persuade others to reduce their demands and to see the merit in your offer.

Key Conflict Skills

To manage conflict effectively, you need to know yourself, as well as the conflicting parties; to understand the situation that has created the conflict; and to be aware of your options.

1. What's your underlying conflict-handling style? As we previously pointed out, particularly in Chapter 2, success in interpersonal relations begins with self-awareness. This appears to be especially true of conflict management. While most of us have the ability to vary our conflict response according to the situation, each of us has a preferred style for handling conflicts (Kilmann and Thomas, 1977). The questionnaire you completed at the opening of this chapter was designed to identify your basic conflict-handling style. Take another look at your results. You may be able to change your preferred style to suit the context in which a certain conflict occurs; however, your basic style tells you how you're *most* likely to behave and the conflict-handling approaches on which you *most often* rely.

2. Be judicious in selecting the conflicts that you want to handle. Every conflict doesn't justify your attention. Some may not be worth the effort; others may be unmanageable. Every conflict isn't worth your time and effort to resolve. While avoidance may appear to be a "copout," it can sometimes be the most appropriate response. You can improve your overall management effectiveness, and your conflict-management skills in particular, by avoiding trivial conflicts. Choose your battles judiciously, saving your efforts for the ones that count.

Regardless of our desires, reality tells us that some conflicts are unmanageable (Greenhalgh, 1986). When antagonisms are deeply rooted, when one or both parties wish to prolong a conflict, or when emotions run so high that constructive interaction is impossible, your efforts are unlikely to meet with much success.

So don't be naively lured into believing that a good manager can effectively resolve every conflict. Some aren't worth the effort. Some are outside your realm of influence. Still others may be constructive, and as such, are best left alone.

3. Evaluate the conflict players. If you choose to manage a conflict situation, it's important that you take the time to get to know the players. Who is involved in the conflict? What interests does each party represent? What are each player's values, personality, feelings, and resources? Your chances of success in managing a conflict will be greatly enhanced if you're able to view the conflict situation through the eyes of the conflicting parties.

4. Assess the source of the conflict. Conflicts don't pop out of thin air. They have causes. Since your approach to resolving a conflict is likely to be largely determined by its causes, you need to determine the source of the conflict. Research indicates that while conflicts have varying causes, they can generally be separated into three categories: communication differences, structural differences, and personal differences (Robbins, 1974). *Communication differences* are those disagreements arising from semantic difficulties, misunderstandings, and noise in the communication channels. People are often quick to assume that most conflicts are caused by lack of communication. As one author has noted, there is usually plenty of communication going on in most conflicts. The mistake many people make is equating good communication with having others agree with their views (Kursh, 1971). That is, people assume that if others don't accept their position, there must be a communication problem. What may, at first appearance, look like an interpersonal conflict based on poor communication is usually found, upon closer analysis, to be a disagreement due to different role requirements, unit goals, personalities, value systems, or similar factors. As a source of conflict for managers, poor communication probably gets more attention than it deserves.

Organizations, by their very nature, are horizontally and vertically differentiated (Robbins, 1987). Management divides tasks up, groups common tasks into departments, sets up a hierarchy of authority to coordinate departments, and establishes rules and regulations to facilitate standardized practices between departments. This *structural differentiation* creates problems of integration. The frequent result is conflicts. Individuals disagree over goals, decision alternatives, performance criteria, and resource allocations. These conflicts, however, are not due to poor communication or personal animosities. Rather, they are rooted in the structure of the organization itself. The "goodies" that people want—budgets, promotions, pay increases, additions to staff, office space, influence over decisions, and the like—are scarce resources that must be divvied up. The creation of horizontal units (departments) and vertical levels (the management hierarchy) brings about efficiencies through specialization and coordination but at the same time produces the potential for structural conflicts.

The third conflict source is *personal differences*. Conflicts can evolve out of individual idiosyncrasies and personal value systems. The chemistry between some people makes it hard for them to work together. Factors like background, behavioral styles, education, experience, and training mold each individual into a unique personality with a particular set of values. The result is people who may be perceived by others as abrasive, untrustworthy, or strange. These personal differences can create conflict.

5. Know your options. Thomas (1976) identified five conflict-resolution strategies: avoidance, accommodation, forcing, compromise, and collaboration. Each has particular strengths and weaknesses, and no one strategy is ideal for every situation. You should consider each strategy as a "tool" in your conflict-management "tool chest." While you may be better at using some tools than others, the skilled manager knows what each tool can do and when it is likely to be most effective.

As we noted earlier, every conflict doesn't require an assertive action. Sometimes *avoidance* is the best solution—just withdrawing from the conflict or ignoring its existence. When is avoidance a desirable strategy? When the conflict issue is trivial, when emotions are running high and time is needed to cool them down, or when the potential disruption from a more assertive action outweighs the benefits of resolution.

The goal of *accommodation* is to maintain harmonious relationships by placing another's needs and concerns above your own. You might, for example, yield to another person's position on an issue. This strategy is most viable when the issue under dispute isn't that important to you or when you want to build up credits for later issues.

In *forcing*, you attempt to satisfy your own needs at the expense of the other party. In organizations, this is most often illustrated by a manager using his or her formal authority to resolve a dispute. Forcing works well when you need a quick resolution, on important issues where unpopular actions must be taken, and where commitment by others to your solution is not critical.

A *compromise* strategy requires each party to give up something of value. This is typically the approach taken by management and labor in negotiating a new labor contract. Compromising can be an optimum strategy when conflicting parties are about equal in power, when it is desirable to achieve a temporary solution to a complex issue, or when time pressures demand an expedient solution.

Collaboration is the ultimate win-win solution. All parties to the conflict seek to satisfy their interests. It is typically characterized by open and honest discussion among the parties, intensive listening to understand differences, and careful deliberation over a full range of alternatives to find a solution that is advantageous to all. When is collaboration the best conflict strategy? When time pressures are minimal, when all parties seriously want a win-win solution, and when the issue is too important to be compromised.

6. Select the "best" option. Given that you're familiar with the options, how should you proceed? Start by looking at your preferred conflict-handling style (see the Self-Assessment exercise on page 219 of this chapter). This makes you aware of the styles with which you feel most comfortable. However, there is one problem with the self-awareness exercise at the beginning of this chapter: It overlooks avoidance. Some people seek to avoid conflicts at any price. They believe that no problem is so big that it can't be run away from! If you're such a person—and you'll know it if you are—you need to guard against this tendency.

The next thing you should look at is your goals. The *best* solution is closely intertwined with your definition of "best." Three goals seemed to dominate our discussion of strategies: the importance of the conflict issue, concern over maintaining long-term *interpersonal relations*, and the *speed* with which you need to resolve the conflict. All other things held constant, if the issue is critical to the organization's or the unit's success, collaboration is preferred. If sustaining supportive relationships is important, the best strategies, in order of preference, are accommodation, collaboration, compromise, and avoidance. If it's crucial to resolve the conflict as quickly as possible, forcing, accommodation, and compromise— in that order— are preferred.

Lastly, you need to consider the source of the conflict. What works best depends, to a large degree, on the cause of the conflict (Robbins, 1974). Communication-based conflicts revolve around misinformation and misunderstandings. Such conflicts lend themselves to collaboration. In contrast, conflicts based on personal differences arise out of disparities between the parties' values and personalities. Such conflicts are most susceptible to avoidance because these differences are often deeply entrenched. When managers have to resolve conflicts rooted in personal differences, they frequently rely on forcing—not so much because it placates the parties, but because it works! The third category—structural conflicts—seems to be amenable to most of the conflict strategies.

This process of blending your personal style, your goals, and the source of the conflict should result in identifying the strategy or set of strategies most likely to be effective for you in any specific conflict situation.

CONCEPT QUIZ

The following ten-question, true-false quiz is based on the previous material. If you miss any of these questions, be sure to go back and find out why you got them wrong.

True or False   1. All conflicts hinder organizational effectiveness.

True or False   2. Most people have the ability to vary their conflict response according to the situation.

True or False   3. Every conflict doesn't justify a manager's attention.

True or False   4. Some conflicts are unmanageable.

True or False   5. Most conflicts are caused by a lack of communication.

True or False   6. Research indicates that paying senior executives high salaries is a major source of conflict.

True or False   7. Accommodation requires each party to give up something of value.

True or False   8. Forcing is an effective strategy for resolving important issues where unpopular actions need implementing.

True or False   9. Collaboration is an effective strategy for arriving at an expedient solution under time pressures.

True or False   10. Collaboration has been consistently shown to be the most effective resolution strategy.

Answers: (1) False; (2) True; (3) True; (4) True; (5) False; (6) False; (7) False; (8) True; (9) False; (10) False.

BEHAVIORAL CHECKLIST

Look for these behaviors when evaluating your own or others' skills at resolving conflicts.

EFFECTIVE CONFLICT RESOLUTION REQUIRES

- Dealing directly with the conflict
- Ascertaining the conflict's source
- Empathizing with the conflicting parties
- Using the appropriate conflict-handling style
- Selection of the most appropriate conflict-resolution option

---

ATTENTION!

Don't read this or the following exercises until assigned to do so by your instructor.

MODELING EXERCISE

Actors: LEE LATTONI and B. J. O'MALLEY.

Situation: LEE LATTONI supervises an eight-member cost accounting department in a large metals fabricating plant in Albuquerque, New Mexico. Lee was promoted about six months ago to this supervisory position after only a year as an accountant. It was no secret that Lee got the promotion predominantly because of education—Lee has an M.B.A., whereas no one else in the department has a college degree.

LEE LATTONI's role: Your transition to supervisor has gone smoothly; you've encountered little in the way of problems until now.

Business has been prospering at the plant for some time, and it has become apparent that you need an additional cost accountant in the department to handle the increased workload. In fact, it has been on your mind for over a month. Department members have been complaining about the heavy workload. Overtime has become commonplace, and the large amount of overtime is adversely affecting your department's efficiency statistics. You don't think you'll have any trouble supporting your request for a new, full-time position with your boss.

The search for a new employee should be relatively hassle-free. The reason is that you have already spotted someone you think can fill the slot nicely. The person you have in mind is currently working in the production control department of the plant.

Unofficially, you have talked with the production control supervisor and the plant's personnel director about moving Regina Simpson, a young clerk in production, into your department. Regina has been with the company for eight months, has shown above average potential, and is only six units shy of her bachelor's degree (with a major in accounting), which she has been earning at night at the state university. You're aware that the department currently is made up of older male employees. None of them has a college degree and the attitude of most members is that advanced education is just a frivolous waste of time. They are a macho, raucous group who tell a lot of chauvinistic jokes but always get the job done well. You know through the grapevine that they get together every Tuesday night for their weekly poker game. You are aware that Regina may have a problem gaining acceptance in this group but she is certainly a qualified candidate and deserving of the promotion.

You met with Regina earlier in the week and discussed the possibility that cost accounting will have a vacancy. Regina told you that she was very interested in the position. After further discussion over lunch—all unofficially—you said that although you couldn't make any promises, you were prepared to recommend Regina for the job. However, you emphasized that it would be a week to ten days before a final decision and an official announcement were made.

You are in your office when B. J. O'Malley comes in. B. J. works for you as a cost accountant and has been at the plant for twenty-six years. You like B. J. but consider him closed-minded and the most extreme of the chauvinistic old-timers. If Regina were to join the department, you would expect B. J. to be the least receptive. Why? B. J. was raised in a conservative working-class family and you've heard him speak disparagingly about "college girls."

B. J. O'MALLEY's role: You are a cost accountant in the plant, working for Lee. You're fifty-eight years old, were raised in a conservative working-class family, and have been working at the Albuquerque plant since it opened twenty-six years ago. You have heard rumors that Lee is planning to bring Regina Simpson, a young inexperienced college student into the department. You understand the need to hire another cost accountant—the workload has gotten too heavy and the department's overtime budget has gotten out of hand. But the department is made up of an established group of male employees. None of them has a college degree and the attitude of most members is that advanced education is just a frivolous waste of time. They're a close-knit group—you've all worked together for years and even socialize together. For instance, the entire group has been getting together every Tuesday night for poker for more than six years. Your work group has a lot of fun, you tell a lot of chauvinistic jokes, take breaks throwing darts at each month's Playboy centerfold, but always get the job done properly and on time. You're concerned that Regina will cause problems for your group and you believe there must be equally qualified and experienced males who could do the job better.

You believe that Lee should be sensitive to your feelings. You're not prejudiced; you just don't want to disturb the camaraderie and efficiency of your department. You want Lee to talk with all department members before making an appointment. You view the department as a close-knit, homogeneous group and you don't want to add any newcomer who won't fit in. In the back of your mind, you know that if all the department members get to vote on who joins the department, a young, inexperienced, female college student who will probably need constant hand holding is unlikely to be hired. However, you also know that if you don't speak up, no one else will. You're quite upset and have decided to go to Lee's office and let Lee know that you have no intention of working with an uppity, know-it-all college girl who probably doesn't know the first thing about cost accounting.

Time: Not to exceed fifteen minutes.

OBSERVER'S RATING SHEET

Evaluate Lee Latoni's conflict-resolution skills on a 1 to 5 scale (5 being highest).

- Deals directly with the conflict   _____

- Ascertains the conflict's source   _____

- Empathizes with the conflicting
  parties   _____

- Uses the appropriate conflict-
  handling style   _____

- Selects the most appropriate
  conflict-resolution option   _____

Comments:

_____

_____

_____

_____

_____

GROUP EXERCISES

Group Exercise 1*

Actors: JAN and SUE.

Instructions: Divide into groups of three. One person is to play Jan, the manager. Another plays Sed, the secretary. The third observes. Everyone, including Sue, should read Jan's role; but Jan is not to read Sue's role.

JAN's role: You have been director of personnel for Beacon Lights for ten years. Just when you thought you had your job "down pat," the sky fell in. A strong labor union has been trying to organize your plant, the federal government recently filed a claim against your company for discriminatory hiring practices, the president and vice president of sales were forced to resign last month because of the company's poor performance, and on top of all that, your long-time secretary just died of a heart attack.

   A month ago you hired Sue to replace your secretary. She has two years of secretarial experience so you could save some salary money and you think that Sue should have no difficulty picking up the pieces. Sue asked for some temporary help recently, but you really can't afford it right now and told her you would keep her informed about the more urgent items you wanted her to concentrate on first. Your former secretary had no problems getting the job done and you don't expect that Sue will either.

   You have been asked to give a talk at a national convention on a new productivity program your company has pioneered, and you are looking forward to getting away from the office for a few days to catch your breath. You gave your talk to your new secretary, Sue, a couple of days ago so she would have plenty of time to get it typed and reproduced.

   This morning you have come into the office to proofread and rehearse your talk prior to catching a plane this evening and you are shocked to find a note saying your secretary called in ill this morning. You rush over to her desk and frantically begin searching for your paper. You find it mixed in with some material for the quarterly report

---

* *Source:* From *Developing Management Skills*, 2nd. ed. by David A. Whetton and Kim S. Cameron. Copyright 1991 by Harper Collins, pp. 438—39. Reprinted by permission.

that should have been sent in two weeks ago, a stack of overdue correspondence, and two days' unopened mail.

As you dial your secretary's home phone number, you realize that you are perspiring heavily and your face is flushed. This is the worst foul-up you can remember in years.

SUE's role: You hear the phone ring and it is all you can do to get out of bed and limp into the kitchen to answer it. You really feel rotten. On the way home last night, you slipped on your kid's skateboard in the driveway and sprained your knee. You can hardly move today and the pain is excruciating. You are also a bit hesitant to answer the phone because you figure it is probably your boss, Jan, calling to chew you out for getting behind in your work. You know you deserve some blame, but it wasn't all your fault. Since you began working for Jan a month ago, you have asked several times for a thorough job description. You feel you don't really understand Jan's priorities or your specific job responsibilities. You are replacing a woman who died suddenly after working for Jan for ten years. You were hired to pick up the pieces, but you have found working with Jan extremely frustrating. She has been too busy to train you properly and she assumes you know as much about the job as your predecessor. This is particularly a problem since you haven't worked as a secretary for three years, and you feel a bit "rusty."

Jan's talk is a good example of the difficulties you have experienced. She gave you the talk a couple of days ago and said it was urgent—but that was on top of a quarterly report that was already overdue and a backlog of correspondence, filing, and so forth. You never filled out a report like this before, and every time you asked Jan a question she said she'd discuss it with you later—as she ran off to a meeting. When you asked if it would be possible to get some additional help to catch up the overdue work, Jan said the company couldn't afford it because of poor sales. This irked you because you knew you were being paid far less than your predecessor. You knew Jan faced some urgent deadlines so you had planned to return to the office last night to type Jan's speech and try to complete the report, but two hours in the emergency room at the hospital put an end to that plan. You tried calling Jan to explain the problem, only to find out she has an unlisted number.

You sit down and prop up your leg, and wince with pain as you pick up the phone.

Time: Not to exceed fifteen minutes.

OBSERVER'S RATING SHEET

Evaluate Jan's conflict-resolution skills on a 1 to 5 scale (5 being highest).

- Deals directly with the conflict   _____

- Ascertains the conflict's source   _____

- Empathizes with the conflicting parties   _____

- Uses the appropriate conflict-handling style   _____

- Selects the most appropriate conflict-resolution option   _____

Comments:

_____

_____

_____

_____

_____

Group Exercise 2*

Actors: LARRY and ERIC.

Situation: The product marketing teams at Salvo, a designer of computer software programs, enjoy developing point-of-sale demo tapes of their new games or programs for use in dealer stores, and the dealers love them. They are filled with sound and color and clever graphics and are very successful as a sales tool. The sales staff uses them as demos when they make sales calls and then leave them with the store owners when they make the sale. The marketing people work up an outline for the tapes, based on the product content, and then submit them to a development team member in management information systems to work out displays and graphics before the sound is added and the videotapes are recorded.

It is a complex relationship, but the results have been highly successful. Larry, in marketing, submitted an outline of a new videotape to Eric for development. He received a highly technical memo from Eric in return, explaining why the project wouldn't work as presented. Larry is accustomed to working closely with his MIS counterparts, and he can't understand why he got a memo instead of a phone call. Furthermore, he can't understand the memo. He decides to go to Eric's office to straighten things out.

LARRY's role: Larry is energetic, has a good sense of humor, and has a demanding taste for excellence. He knows what a computer can do but he is not a programmer or technician. He is dependent on his MIS counterpart to translate his concepts and schedules into working and exciting displays and graphics.

ERIC's role: Eric is new at Salvo and has been assigned to Larry. He is one of the real experts on computer language and systems, having worked in all of them. His last two years were spent as a teacher at a university, and it has been hard for him to abandon his teacher image. He spends some of his time with the other programmers teaching them the history and usage of systems and computer language (even though they may not use this information at Salvo), and he delights in developing totally new programs to process already running assignments. He talks and writes in very technical language and has great difficulty commu-

---

*Source: From *An Executive's Coaching Handbook* by Mary Jean Parson. Copyright ©1986 by Mary Jean Parson. Reprinted with permission of Facts on File, Inc., New York.

nicating clearly with nonsystems people. His attitude, more often than not, comes off as condescending, because he seems incapable of speaking English to them, preferring to discuss a problem or project in "computerese."

Both employees' objective is the same: to carry out the tasks assigned by their managers without disruptive confrontation.

Larry appears at Eric's door.

Time: Not to exceed fifteen minutes.

OBSERVER'S RATING SHEET

Evaluate Larry's conflict-resolution skills on a 1 to 5 scale (5 being highest).

- Deals directly with the conflict   _____

- Ascertains the conflict's source   _____

- Empathizes with the conflicting parties   _____

- Uses the appropriate conflict-handling style   _____

- Selects the most appropriate conflict-resolution option   _____

Comments:

_____

_____

_____

_____

Group Exercise 3*

Form groups of three to five members. Each group member is to begin by independently ranking the five alternative courses of action in each of the following four incidents. You are to rank the responses from the most desirable or appropriate way of dealing with the conflict situation to the least desirable. Rank the most desirable course of action "1," the next most desirable "2," and so on, with the least desirable or least appropriate action as "5." Enter your rank for each item in the space next to each choice. Next, identify the conflict style being used with each of the possible courses of action (e.g., forcing, accommodation, avoidance, compromise, or collaboration).

After each person has done this for all four incidents, group members are to compare their answers. Begin with Incident 1. Do you all agree? If not, discuss. Be prepared to defend *why* you answered as you did. You may change your answers as a result of the discussion. After completion of Incident 1, do the same with Incident 2, and so on. Confine the analysis and discussion of each incident to ten minutes or less.

Incident 1: Pete is lead operator of a production molding machine. Recently, he has noticed that one of the men from another machine has been coming over to his machine and talking to one of his men (not on break time). The efficiency of Pete's operator seems to be falling off, and there have been some rejects because of his inattention. Pete thinks he detects some resentment among the rest of the crew. *If you were Pete, you would*

   a. Talk to your man and tell him to limit his conversations during on-the-job time.

   b. Ask the foreman to tell the lead operator of the other machine to keep his operators in line.

   c. Confront both men the next time you see them together (as well as the other lead operator, if necessary), find out what they are up to, and tell them what you expect of your operators.

   d. Say nothing now; it would be silly to make a big deal out of something so insignificant.

   e. Try to put the rest of the crew at ease; it is important that they all work well together.

---

*Source: Adapted from A. Zoll III, *Explorations in Managing*, 1974, ©Addison-Wesley Publishing Company, Inc. Based on a format suggested by Allen A. Zoll III. Reprinted with permission.

Incident 2: Sally is the senior quality control (QC) inspector and has been appointed group leader of the QC people on her crew. On separate occasions, two of her people have come to her with different suggestions for reporting test results to the machine operators. Paul wants to send the test results to the foreman and then to the machine operator, since the foreman is the person ultimately responsible for production output. Jim thinks the results should go directly to the lead operator on the machine in question, since he is the one who must take corrective action as soon as possible. Both ideas seem good, and Sally can find no ironclad procedures in the department on how to route the reports. *If you were Sally, you would*

a. Decide who is right and ask the other person to go along with the decision (perhaps establish it as a written procedure).

b. Wait and see; the best solution will become apparent.

c. Tell both Paul and Jim not to get uptight about their disagreement; it is not that important.

d. Get Paul and Jim together and examine both of their ideas closely.

e. Send the report to the foreman, with a copy to the lead operator (even though it might mean a little more copy work for QC).

Incident 3: Ralph is a module leader; his module consists of four very complex and expensive machines and five crewmen. The work is exacting, and inattention or improper procedures could cause a costly mistake or serious injury. Ralph suspects that one of his men is taking drugs on the job, or at least is showing up for work under the influence of drugs. Ralph feels he has some strong indications, but he knows he does not have a "case." *If you were Ralph, you would*

a. Confront the man outright, tell him what you suspect and why, and that you are concerned for him and for the safety of the rest of the crew.

b. Ask that the suspected offender keep his habit off the job; what he does on the job is part of your business.

c. Not confront the individual right now; it might either "turn him off" or drive him underground.

d. Give the man the "facts of life"; tell him it is illegal and unsafe to use drugs, and that if he gets caught, you will do everything you can to see that he is fired.

e. Keep a close eye on the man to see that he is not endangering others.

Incident 4: Gene is foreman of a production crew. From time to time in the past, the product development section tapped the production crews for operators to augment their own operator personnel to run test products on special machines. This put very little strain on the production crews, since the demands were small, temporary, and infrequent. Lately, however, there seems to be an almost constant demand for four production operators. The rest of the production crew must fill in for these missing people, usually by working harder and taking shorter breaks. *If you were Gene, you would*

    a. Let it go for now; the "crisis" will probably be over soon.

    b. Try to smooth things over with your own crew and with the development foreman; we all have jobs to do and cannot afford a conflict.

    c. Let development have two of the four operators they requested.

    d. Go to the development supervisor or his or her foreman and talk about how these demands for additional operators could best be met without placing production in a bind.

    e. Go to the supervisor of production (Gene's boss) and get him or her to "call off" the development people.

Time: Not to exceed ten minutes per incident.

SUMMARY CHECKLIST

On the basis of your experiences and observations, assess yourself on each of the key learning behaviors. Make a check (✓) next to those behaviors on which you think you need improvement.

- I deal directly with conflicts.   _____

- I ascertain the conflicts's source.   _____

- I try to empathize with the conflicting
  parties.   _____

- I try to apply the appropriate conflict-
  handling style.   _____

- I try to resolve the conflict most appropriately
  for the specific person and situation.   _____

APPLICATION QUESTIONS

1. Most people dislike conflict because it is dysfunctional. Do you agree or disagree? Why?

2. When is conflict likely to hinder an organization? When can it help?

3. Is conflict inevitable in organizations? Why?

4. What are the key steps in diagnosing a conflict situation?

REINFORCEMENT EXERCISES

1. Describe, in detail, three recent interpersonal conflicts you have experienced. How did your basic conflict-handling style influence your actions? To what degree do you believe your conflict style is flexible? The next time you find yourself in a conflict situation (a) be sure to recall your basic conflict style; (b) consider its appropriateness to this specific situation; and (c) if inappropriate, practice exhibiting more appropriate conflict resolution behavior.

2. Think of a recent conflict you had with a colleague, friend, or relative. What was the source of the conflict? What goals did you seek? How did you handle the conflict? Was it resolved consistently with your goals? Were there other ways of handling this conflict that might have been more effective?

3. Take the role of a third-party consultant for an individual or a group involved in a conflict. Advise the party/parties as to their options. Note how your advice works.

ACTION PLAN

1. Which behavior do I want to improve the most?

_____

_____

_____

2. Why? What will be my payoff?

_____

_____

_____

3. What potential obstacles stand in my way?

_____

_____

_____

4. What are the specific things I will do to improve? (For examples, see the Reinforcement Exercises.)

_____

_____

_____

5. When will I do them?

_____

_____

_____

6. How and when will I measure my success?

_____

_____

_____

Chapter *13*

NEGOTIATION

SELF-ASSESSMENT EXERCISE

For each of the following statements, indicate your degree of agreement or disagreement by circling one of the five responses.

SA	=	Strongly Agree
A	=	Agree
U	=	Undecided
D	=	Disagree
SD	=	Strongly Disagree

1. I believe everything is negotiable.   SA   A   U   D   SD

2. In every negotiation, someone
   wins and someone loses.   SA   A   U   D   SD

3. I try to get as much information
   as possible about the other party
   prior to negotiation.   SA   A   U   D   SD

4. The other party's initial offer
   shapes my negotiating strategy.   SA   A   U   D   SD

5. I try to open negotiations with a positive action such as offering a small concession.   SA   A   U   D   SD

6. I build an image of success by focusing on winning as much as possible in every bargaining situation. SA   A   U   D   SD

SCORING DIRECTIONS AND KEY

For questions 1, 3, and 5, give yourself 5 points for SA, 4 points for A, 3 points for U, 2 points for D, and 1 point for SD. For questions 2, 4, and 6, reverse the scoring; that is, give yourself 1 point for SA, 2 points for A, and so forth.

A score of 25 or above suggests you have a basic understanding of how to be an effective negotiator. Scores of 19–24 indicate you have room for improvement. Those who scored 18 or less should find the following discussion and exercise very valuable to improving their negotiating effectiveness.

SKILL CONCEPTS

What is *negotiation*? It's a process in which two or more parties exchange goods or services and attempt to agree upon the exchange rate for them. For our purposes, we'll also use the term interchangeably with *bargaining*.

We know that lawyers and car salespersons spend a lot of time negotiating, but so, too, do managers. They have to negotiate salaries for incoming employees, cut deals with superiors, bargain over budgets, work out differences with associates, and resolve conflicts with subordinates.

BARGAINING STRATEGIES

There are two general approaches to negotiation: *distributive bargaining* and *integrative bargaining*.

You see a used car advertised for sale in the newspaper. It appears to be just what you've been looking for. You go out to see the car. It's great and you want it. The owner tells you the asking price. You don't want to pay that much. The two of you then negotiate over the price. The negotiating process you are engaging in is called *distributive bargaining*. Its most identifying feature is that it operates under zero-sum conditions. That is, any gain I make is at your expense, and vice versa. Referring back to the used-car example, every dollar you can get the seller to cut from the car's price is a dollar you save. Conversely, every dollar more he or she can get from you comes at your expense. Thus the essence of distributive bargaining is negotiating over who gets what share of a fixed pie.

Figure 13.1 depicts the distributive bargaining strategy. Parties A and B represent the two negotiators. Each has a *target point* that defines what he or she would like to achieve. Each also has a *resistance point*, which marks the lowest outcome that is acceptable—the point below which he or she would break off negotiations rather than accept a less favorable settlement. The area between their resistance points is the settlement range. As long as there is some overlap in their aspiration ranges, there exists a settlement area where each one's aspirations can be met.

When engaged in distributive bargaining, your tactics should focus on trying to get your opponent to agree to your specific target point or to get as close to it as possible. Examples of such tactics are persuading your opponent of the impossibility of getting to his or her target point and the advisability of accepting a settlement near yours; arguing that your target is fair, while your opponent's isn't; and attempting to get your opponent to feel emotionally generous toward you and thus accept an outcome close to your target point.

Now let's look at integrative bargaining. Assume a sales representative for a women's sportswear manufacturer has just closed a $15,000 order from a small clothing retailer. The sales rep calls in the order to her firm's credit department. She is told that the firm can't approve credit to this customer because of a past slow-pay record. The next day, the sales rep and the firm's credit supervisor meet to discuss the problem. The sales rep doesn't want to lose the business. Neither does the credit supervisor, but he also doesn't want to get stuck with an uncollectible debt. The two openly review their options. After considerable discussion, they agree on a solution that meets both their needs: The credit supervisor will approve the sale, but the cloth-

FIGURE 13.1   Staking Out the Bargaining Zone

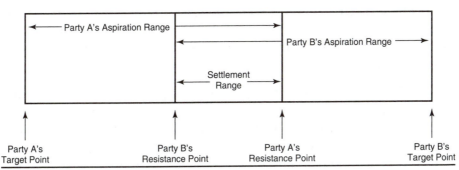

ing store's owner will provide a bank guarantee that will assure payment if the bill isn't paid within sixty days.

The sales-credit negotiation is an example of *integrative bargaining*. In contrast to distributive bargaining, integrative problem solving operates under the assumption that there is at least one settlement that can create a win-win solution.

In general, integrative bargaining is preferable to distributive bargaining. Why? Because the former builds long-term relationships and facilitates working together in the future. It bonds negotiators and allows each to leave the bargaining table feeling that he or she has achieved a victory. Distributive bargaining, on the other hand, leaves one party a loser. It tends to build animosities and deepen divisions between people who have to work together on an ongoing basis.

Why, then, don't we see more integrative bargaining in organizations? The answer lies in the conditions necessary for this type of negotiation to succeed. These conditions include openness with information and frankness between parties, sensitivity on the part of each party to the other's needs, the ability to trust one another, and a willingness by both parties to maintain flexibility. Because many organizational cultures and interpersonal relationships are not characterized by openness, trust, and flexibility, it isn't surprising that negotiations often take on a win-at-any-cost dynamic.

GUIDELINES FOR EFFECTIVE NEGOTIATING

The essence of effective negotiation can be summarized in the following eight guidelines.

1. Consider the other party's situation.   Acquire as much information as you can about your opponent's interests and goals. What are his or her real needs versus wants? What constituencies must he or she appease? What is his or her strategy?

This information will help you understand your opponent's behavior, predict his or her responses to your offers, and frame solutions in terms of his or her interests. Additionally, when you can anticipate your opponent's position, you are better equipped to counter his or her arguments with the facts and figures that support your position.

2. Have a concrete strategy.   Treat negotiation like a chess match. Expert chess players have a strategy. They know ahead of time how they will respond to any given situation. How strong is your situation and how important is the issue? Are you willing to split differences to achieve an early solution? If the issue is very important to you, is your position strong enough to let you play hardball and show little or no willingness to compromise? These are questions you should address before you begin bargaining.

3. Begin with a positive overture.   Establish rapport and mutual interests before starting the negotiation. Then begin bargaining with a positive overture—perhaps a small concession. Studies show that concessions tend to be reciprocated and lead to agreements. A positive climate can be further developed by reciprocating your opponent's concessions.

4. Address problems, not personalities.   Concentrate on the negotiation issues, not on the personal characteristics of your opponent. When negotiations get tough, avoid the tendency to attack your opponent. If other people feel threatened, they concentrate on defending their self-esteem, as opposed to solving the problem. It's your opponent's ideas or position that you disagree with, not him or her personally. Separate the people from the problem and don't personalize differences.

5. Maintain a rational, goal-oriented frame of mind.   Use the previous guideline in reverse if your opponent attacks or gets emotional with you. Don't get hooked by emotional outbursts. Let the other person blow off steam without taking it personally while you try to understand the problem or strategy behind the aggression.

6. Pay little attention to initial offers.   Treat an initial offer as merely a point of departure. Everyone has to have an initial position. These initial offers tend to be extreme and idealistic. Treat them as such. Focus on the other person's interests and your own goals and principles, while you generate other possibilities.

7. Emphasize win-win solutions.   Bargainers often assume that their gain must come at the expense of the other party. As noted with integrative bargaining, that needn't be the case. There are often win-win solutions. But assuming a zero-sum game means missed opportunities for trade-offs that could benefit both sides. So if conditions are supportive, look for an integrative solution. Create additional alternatives, especially low cost concessions you can make that have high value to the other party. Frame options in terms of your opponent's interests and look for solutions that can allow your opponent, as well as yourself, to declare a victory.

8. Insist on using objective criteria.   Make your negotiated decisions based on principles and results, not emotions or pressure (Fisher and Ury, 1986). Agree upon objective criteria that can aid both parties assess the reasonableness of an alternative. Don't succumb to emotional pleas, assertiveness, or stubbornness if their underlying rational does not meet these criteria.

CONCEPT QUIZ

The following ten-question, true-false quiz is based on the previous material in this chapter. The answers are at the end of the quiz. If you miss any of these questions, be sure to go back and find out why you got them wrong.
Circle the right answer:

True or False   1. Distributive bargaining is preferable to integrative bargaining.

True or False   2. Don't plan a bargaining strategy so that you can remain flexible during negotiation.

True or False   3. When negotiations get tough, the best defense is a good offense.

True or False   4. Begin negotiations with a tough stance so your opponent won't try to take advantage of you.

True or False   5. Don't take initial offers seriously.

True or False   6. Always try for a win-win solution if possible.

True or False   7. Emotional pleas are just as important as rational criteria in reaching an agreement.

True or False   8. Making minor concessions can help you achieve a beneficial outcome.

True or False   9. Don't be provoked by your opponent's attacks and emotional outbursts

True or False   10. Integrative bargaining requires openness, trust, and flexibility.

Answers: 1. False; 2. False; 3. False; 4. False; 5. True; 6. True; 7. False; 8. True; 9. True; 10. True.

BEHAVIORAL CHECKLIST

Look for these specific behaviors when evaluating your negotiating skills and those of others.

EFFECTIVE NEGOTIATING REQUIRES

- Considering the other party's situation
- Planning a concrete strategy before negotiating
- Beginning with a positive overture
- Addressing problems, not personalities
- Maintaining a rational, goal-oriented frame of mind
- Not taking initial offers very seriously
- Emphasizing win-win solutions
- Insisting on using objective criteria

MODELING EXERCISE

Actors: TERRY, the department supervisor, and DALE, Terry's boss.

Directions: The entire class class should read the following situation. The two people chosen to play the roles of Terry and Dale should not read each other's role. The remainder of the class may read everything including the observer's guide for evaluating the role-play.

SITUATION: Terry and Dale work for Nike in Portland, Oregon. Terry supervises a research laboratory. Dale is the manager of research and development. Terry and Dale are former college runners who have worked for Nike for more than six years. Dale has been Terry's boss for two years.

One of Terry's employees has greatly impressed Terry. This employee is Lisa Roland. Lisa was hired eleven months ago. She is twenty-four years-old and holds a master's degree in mechanical engineering. Her entry-level salary was $32,500 a year. She was told by Terry that, in accordance with corporate policy, she would receive an initial performance evaluation at six months and a comprehensive review after one year. Based on her performance record, Lisa was told she could expect a salary adjustment at the time of the one-year evaluation.

Terry's evaluation of Lisa after six months was very positive. Terry commented on the long hours Lisa was putting in, her cooperative spirit, the fact that others in the lab enjoyed working with her, and that she was making an immediate positive impact on the projects she had been assigned. Now that Lisa's first anniversary is coming up, Terry has again reviewed Lisa's performance. Terry thinks Lisa may be the best new person the R&D group has ever hired. After only a year, Terry has rated Lisa as the number-three ranked performer in a department of eleven.

Salaries in the department vary greatly. Terry, for instance, has a basic salary of $57,000, plus eligibility for a bonus that might add another $5,000 to $8,000 a year. The salary range of the eleven department members is $26,400 to $51,350. The lowest salary is a recent hire with a bachelor's degree in physics. The two people that Terry has rated above Lisa earn base salaries of $47,700 and $51,350. They're both twenty-seven years-old and have been at Nike for three and four years, respectively. The median salary in Terry's department is $42,660.

TERRY's role: You want to give Lisa a big raise. While she's young, she has proven to be an excellent addition to the department. You don't want to lose her. More importantly, she knows in general what other people in the department are earning and she thinks she's underpaid. The company typically gives one-year raises of 5 percent, although 10 percent is not unusual and 20 to 30 percent increases have been approved on occasion. You'd like to get Terry as large an increase as Dale will approve.

DALE's role: All your supervisors typically try to squeeze you for as much money as they can for their people. You understand this because you did the same thing when you were a supervisor. But your boss wants to keep a lid on costs.

He wants you to keep raises for recent hires generally in the 5 to 8 percent range. In fact, he's sent a memo to all managers and supervisors saying this. However, your boss is also very concerned with equity and paying people what they're worth. You feel assured that he will support any salary recommendation you make, as long as it can be justified. Your goal, consistent with cost reduction, is to keep salary increases as low as possible.

Terry has a meeting scheduled with Dale to discuss Lisa's performance review and salary adjustment.

Time: Fifteen minutes.

OBSERVER'S RATING SHEET

Evaluate the negotiating skills of Terry and Dale on a 1 to 5 scale (5 being highest).

	Terry	Dale
• Considers the other party's situation	_____	_____
• Plans a concrete strategy before negotiating	_____	_____
• Begins with a positive overture	_____	_____
• Addresses problems, not personalities	_____	_____
• Maintains a rational, goal-oriented frame of mind	_____	_____
• Doesn't take to initial offers very seriously	_____	_____
• Emphasizes win-win solutions	_____	_____
• Insists on using objective criteria	_____	_____

Comments:

_____

_____

_____

_____

_____

GROUP EXERCISES

Directions: Divide the class into trios. Two people play the roles and negotiate a settlement, while the third person observes and provides feedback according to the observer's rating sheet. Rotate observer roles for each of the three exercises. Do not read the other person's role when you are playing a role in an exercise.

Group Exercise 1*

Actors: CHRIS LODGE, Manager of Unit One in the Production Supply Department and LEE DEORE, Manager of Unit Two in the Production Supply Department.

Situation: Unit One has been working overtime for the past three months on a new project which has caused pressure on the workers, especially since it required a change in the vacation schedule. The project has expanded even more, but Unit Two has been assigned to help out and share the overtime requirements projected for the next two months any way the two managers mutually decide.

CHRIS LODGE's role: You manage ten people in Unit One in Production Supply. You've been with the department almost two years now and are quite pleased with your job. Three months ago your unit was assigned to a new project. It required your people to work a lot of overtime and change vacation plans. Now the project has been expanded and another unit, headed by Lee Deore, who has transferred recently from another branch office, has been brought in to help. Employees will still need to work overtime for at least two months.

The people in your unit are tired and are complaining that they haven't seen much of their families during the past three months. You feel Lee's people should assume the major portion of the overtime to give your employees a rest. Your people are burned out and morale is slipping. Lee's people, on the other hand, are fresh and could really give you a rest. You have heard, however, that Lee intends to have the new unit pick up only half the overtime.

---

*Source: Adapted from W.C. Morris and M. Saskin, *Organizational Behavior in Action* (St. Paul, MN: West Publishing Company, 1976), pp. 177–180.

Your manager has told you that he expects you and Lee to settle the overtime issue and then inform him of your joint decision. On the way to get a cup of coffee, you meet Lee Deore. You decide to bring up the issue.

LEE DEORE's role: You manage ten people in Unit Two in Production Supply. You've been with the agency just over one year and are generally happy with your job.

Your unit has been assigned to help Chris Lodge on a recently expanded project. The project has required and will continue to require people to work overtime. The project is expected to last at least two months.

Your manager has asked that you and Chris work out the distribution of overtime. You like Chris and look forward to working on this project. You feel the overtime should be evenly split between your two units. That way, there will be minimal disruptions in people's schedules as vacations near.

However, you have heard through the grapevine that Chris expects your unit to assume all the overtime. It is Chris's feeling that someone else has to take up the slack because Chris's people have done it for the past three months. You can sympathize, but you don't want your people to take on all the overtime. Your manager has told you that she expects the two of you to work out the details and inform her of your decision. On the way to get a cup of coffee, you meet Chris Lodge. You decide to bring up the issue.

Time: Not to exceed ten minutes

OBSERVER'S RATING SHEET

Evaluate the negotiating skills of Chris and Lee on a 1 to 5 scale (5 being highest).

	Chris	Lee
• Considers the other party's situation	_____	_____
• Plans a concrete strategy before negotiating	_____	_____
• Begins with a positive overture	_____	_____
• Addresses problems, not personalities	_____	_____
• Maintains a rational, goal-oriented frame of mind	_____	_____
• Doesn't take to initial offers very seriously	_____	_____
• Emphasizes win-win solutions	_____	_____
• Insists on using objective criteria	_____	_____

Comments:

_____

_____

_____

_____

_____

Group Exercise 2

Actors: BUYER and SELLER

Situation: You are going to negotiate the purchase/sale of a used car. Before advertising it in the local newspaper, the seller took the car to the local Volkswagen dealer, who has provided the following information:

Red with white interior and top.

AM/FM, (no cassette); 60,350 miles.

New tires and brakes.

No rust; small ding on passenger door.

Muffler is loud and will need replacing at some point (estimate at dealer is $225).

"Blue book" retail value is $5,500; wholesale is $4,200.

BUYER's role: You are a second semester college freshman who has just obtained a part time job at the Price Club located seven miles from campus. Since this is too far to walk and not located on any bus routes, you need an economical car that you can afford. It would be nice to have something a little fun also. The Cabriolet that was advertised looks like a good deal, and you would like to buy it right away if possible, so that you can stop begging your roommates for rides or to borrow their cars. You have $3,000 in savings and will be obtaining a $1,500 student loan within a week. You have another $500 in your checking account but you intended to spend most of that on a ski trip with an extremely attractive classmate.

You can't borrow any more money from your parents because they are already forking over the burdensome out-of-state tuition, plus room and board. You have a VISA card but that already has $324 outstanding at 23% on its $1,000 limit. The Cabriolet is the best deal you've seen, and the car is fun to drive. Your roommate's sister has a 1989 Ford Escort that you can immediately buy for $3,600 (the wholesale value). Its a boring brown, four-door model which has been pretty well trashed, but it would be reliable transportation and you could handle it as long as no one sees you in it.

The seller of the Cabriolet is a graduating senior who you have never meet before. The reason given for selling the car is that the seller has a good out of state job offer and wants to upgrade the car.

Before beginning this negotiation, set the following targets for yourself:

1. The price you would like to pay for the car.   _____
2. The price you will initially offer the seller.   _____
3. The highest price you will pay for the car.   _____

SELLER's role: You are a second semester college senior who has just put a deposit down on a perfect one year old BMW 325i convertible which was just traded in to the local dealer by a well-to-do client who trades up every year. The down payment is $4,700, with steep monthly payments, but you have been hired by an out-of-state firm at a good starting salary, so you think you can handle them in a few months. Besides, you want to celebrate your pending graduation and new job, after four tough years of study and deferred partying. Right now, however, you are low on cash and stretched on credit, so if you can't come up with the down payment, you will have to borrow at 18 percent. You and your friends are going to pick up the Bemmer in two hours, so you want to sell your old VW convertible before you go.

You advertised the car (which is in particularly good condition) in the newspaper and have had several calls. Most prospective buyers are college students, however, who cannot come up with the cash and want you to take payments. Your only really good prospect right now is a freshman whom you have never meet before but says that if a deal can be reached, cash payment is no problem. You don't *have* to sell it to this person right now, but if you don't, you will have to pay high interest charges to cover the down payment until you do sell it.

The BMW dealer will only give you $4,200 for the Cabriolet because he will have to resell it to a Volkswagen dealer at the wholesale price. The local VW dealer will not give you any more for your car because he just received a shipment of new cars.

Before beginning this negotiation, set the following targets for yourself:

1. The price you would like to receive for the car   _____
2. The price you will initially request   _____
3. The lowest price you will accept for the car   _____

Time: Not to exceed 15 minutes.

OBSERVER'S RATING SHEET

Evaluate the negotiating skills of the Buyer and Seller on a 1 to 5 scale (5 being highest).

	Buyer	Seller
• Considers the other party's situation	_____	_____
• Plans a concrete strategy before negotiating	_____	_____
• Begins with a positive overture	_____	_____
• Addresses problems, not personalities	_____	_____
• Maintains a rational, goal-oriented frame of mind	_____	_____
• Doesn't take to initial offers very seriously	_____	_____
• Emphasizes win-win solutions	_____	_____
• Insists on using objective criteria	_____	_____

Comments:

_____

_____

_____

_____

_____

Group Exercise 3*

Actors: RUSTY BUCHANAN, manager of client inquiries; MANNY CAPUTO, manager of documentation.

Situation: There is a problem with the use of the copying machine. In the last two weeks, members of two work units have been fighting for the use of the machine they share. Yesterday the conflict erupted into an argument with yelling and name calling between workers from each unit. Managers Rusty Buchanan and Manny Caputo have decided to meet and try to solve the problem. They have just entered the conference room which they reserved for the next fifteen minutes.

RUSTY BUCHANAN's role: Your unit has extensive contact with the public. You have ten workers who need to use the machine for routine documentation of their work. Most of the copies are photocopies of signed documents that must be returned to the signer. The original is filed.

    Your unit's work is regular, not sporadic, and in the past workers made their single copies throughout the day and returned to their workstation. Your workers need access to the machine throughout the day.

MANNY CAPUTO's role: Although your unit has less direct contact with the public, your unit is responsible for periodically mailing important documents to citizens throughout the state. You have three workers who use the machine for larger work orders.

    They need one to two hours at a time to complete the copying. Your unit's work flow is sporadic and not predictable, but you have tight deadlines when you do get work.

Time: Not to exceed fifteen minutes.

---

*Source: Adapted from Robert E. Quinn, Sue R. Faerman, Michael P. Thompson, and Michael R. McGrath, *Becoming a Master Manager* (New York: John Wiley & Sons, 1990), pp. 297–298.

OBSERVER'S RATING SHEET

Evaluate the negotiating skills of Rusty and Manny on a 1 to 5 scale (5 being highest).

	Rusty	Karry
• Considers the other party's situation	_____	_____
• Plans a concrete strategy before negotiating	_____	_____
• Begins with a positive overture	_____	_____
• Addresses problems, not personalities	_____	_____
• Maintains a rational, goal-oriented frame of mind	_____	_____
• Doesn't take to initial offers very seriously	_____	_____
• Emphasizes win-win solutions	_____	_____
• Insists on using objective criteria	_____	_____

Comments:

_____

_____

_____

_____

_____

SUMMARY CHECKLIST

Review your performance and look over others' ratings of your negotiating skills. Now assess yourself on each of the key learning behaviors. Make a check (✓) next to those behaviors on which you need improvement.

I consider the other party's situation. _____

I plan a concrete strategy before negotiating. _____

I begin with a positive overture. _____

I address problems, not personalities. _____

I maintain a rational, goal-oriented frame of mind. _____

I do not take to initial offers very seriously. _____

I emphasize win-win solutions. _____

I insist on using objective criteria. _____

APPLICATION QUESTIONS

1. Why is integrative bargaining preferable to distributive bargaining. Why don't we see more integrative bargaining in organizations?

2. Think of a recent negotiation you have participated in with your boss, significant other, parents, or roommate. Which of the negotiation behaviors did you successfully apply? How could those negotiation behaviors you did not use have helped?

3. How do you know when you are involved in distributive bargaining? What is your objective? What tactics would be most appropriate?

4. How do you know when you are involved in integrative bargaining? What is your objective? What tactics would be most appropriate?

5. You are representing your company in an important negotiation. After being stuck in a stalemate for several hours, your counterpart misquotes and misrepresents you on a number of earlier statements. After you correct the record, your opponent loses his temper and aggressively slanders your character in front of others on your negotiating team. What should you do? Why?

REINFORCEMENT EXERCISES

1. Negotiate with a professor to raise the grade on an exam or paper on which you think you should have received a higher grade.

2. The next time you purchase a relatively expensive item (e.g., automobile, apartment lease, appliance, jewelry), negotiate a better price and gain some concessions such as an extended warranty, smaller down payment, or maintenance services, and so forth.

3. Negotiate a more favorable set of task assignments for yourself with your roommates or significant other.

4. Research collective bargaining negotiations in the news media when they occur, for example, baseball player strikes, union strikes, individual sports celebrity salary negotiations, plea bargains. What type of negotiation is going on? What skills and tactics are being applied?

5. Research international crisis negotiations in the news media when they occur, for example, trade negotiations, military or hostage crises, political party bargaining. What type of negotiation is going on? What skills and tactics are being applied?

ACTION PLAN

1. Which behavior do I want to improve the most?

_____

_____

_____

2. Why? What will be my payoff?

_____

_____

_____

3. What potential obstacles stand in my way?

_____

_____

_____

4. What are the specific things I will do to improve? (For examples, see the Reinforcement Exercises.)

_____

_____

_____

5. When will I do them?

_____

_____

_____

6. How and when will I measure my success?

_____

_____

_____

Chapter *14*

INTERVIEWING

SELF-ASSESSMENT EXERCISE

Are the following questions true (T) or false (F)? Circle what you believe is the right answer.

1. An important part of an effective interview begins before you ask the interviewee your first question. T F

2. It's illegal to ask an applicant about his or her past work experience. T F

3. A problem-solving approach to interviewing is most desirable. T F

4. Interviewing requires both good questioning and listening skills. T F

5. It's a good idea to tape record or take notes during an interview. T F

6. A good interviewer takes control
   of an interview and does most of
   the talking.   T   F

7. Avoid asking questions that can
   be answered with a simple yes or no.   T   F

8. Early in the interview, you should
   provide the interviewee with
   information about the purpose and
   process of the interview.   T   F

SCORING INSTRUCTIONS

Questions 1, 3, 4, 5, 7, and 8 are true. Questions 2, and 6 are false. If you got seven or eight correct, you already have some understanding of how to conduct an effective selection interview.

SKILL CONCEPTS

An *interview* is a structured form of communication conducted to accomplish a specific task-related purpose (Downs, Smeyak, & Martin, 1980). Three of the main reasons managers conduct interviews are for information gathering, employment selection and performance appraisal. Many interviews are ineffective because managers treat them too casually or have not prepared properly. There are general guidelines and skills that can help you properly plan and conduct an interview. After reading the previous chapters, you are already familiar with many of the behaviors necessary for effective communicating. We will review their application to interviewing, share some additional guidelines, and show how to apply them to employment and performance appraisal situations.

All effective interviews require both *advanced preparation* and the *application of appropriate interpersonal skills.* Keeping the purpose of the interview in mind, you need to consider what *information* you want to find out and what kind of *relationship* you want to develop or maintain with the interviewee. Based on these considerations, you can develop your agenda of topics and develop a game plan for how you will relate with the interviewee.

There is considerable overlap in the skills needed to effectively conduct the three types of interviews. First, we will elaborate on the skills used in the most general type of interview, information gathering, and then examine the more specific requirements of employment and appraisal interviews.

INFORMATION GATHERING

Information gathering is the most generic type of interview which actually includes employment-selection and performance-appraisal interviews. Information gathering interviews are conducted when you need to collect facts to solve a problem or make a decision. The previously learned skills of listening and persuading are applicable to this type of interview, as are the general guidelines which follow.

All interviews can be broken down into four stages. They begin with *preparation*, followed by the *opening*, a period of *questioning and discussion*, and a *conclusion.*

In the preparation stage, developing *appropriate questions* is a key to successful interviewing. Questions should be unambiguous and tailored to the specific characteristics of the interviewee, so that they will get you the information you need. Open questions that can't be answered with only a yes or no will allow the interviewee to share and elaborate on information that you may not have thought of yourself. They can also develop more rapport with the interviewee by making him or her feel some shared influence in how the interview progresses. Inquiries that begin with *how* or *why* tend to stimulate extended answers. At times, of course, you may want to ask *closed* questions for expediency or to determine specific information.

EMPLOYMENT INTERVIEW

In conducting an employment interview, you're trying to get answers to three questions: (1) Can the applicant do the job? (2) Is the applicant motivated to do the job? (3) Will the applicant fit into your work group and organization? Everything you do regarding the interview—from preparation to closure—should help you to answer these three questions.

Preparation

Prior to meeting the candidate, you should review his or her application form and resume. You should also review the job description and job specification for the position the applicant is interviewing. What skills will the job require? With whom does it entail working?

Next, structure the agenda for the interview. Specifically, prepare a set of questions you want to ask the applicant. Avoid leading questions that telegraph the desired response (such as "Would you say you have good interpersonal skills?") and bipolar questions that require the applicant to choose an answer from only two choices (such as "Do you prefer working with people or working alone?"). Figure 14.1, provides a list of some typical questions that are likely to provide insight into the candidate's education, work experience, abilities, and motivation. In most cases, questions relating to marital and family status, age, race, religion, sex, ethnic background, credit rating, and arrest record are prohibited by law in the United States unless you can demonstrate that they are in some way related to job performance. Questions such as "Are you married?" or "Do you have children?" are illegal in the United States. What you can ask, however, is "Are there any reasons why you might not be able to work overtime several times a month?" Of course, to avoid discrimination, you have to ask this question of both male and female candidates.

Opening

Job applicants are often tense and nervous. To get valid insights into what applicants are really like, you'll need to put them at ease. Introduce yourself. Be friendly. Begin with a few simple questions or statements that can break the ice, for example, "Did you run into much traffic coming over?" or "I see you went to school at the University of Minnesota. I grew up in Minnesota."

Once the applicant is fairly relaxed, provide a brief orientation. Preview what topics will be discussed, how long the interview will take, and explain if you'll be taking notes. Encourage the applicant to ask questions. Provide some basic information about your organization, department, and the job opening. Don't, however, tell the candidate too much about the job. That can lead to the applicant shaping answers to fit what you want to hear. After the brief orientation, ask an opening question which the candidate can answer fairly easily. Then move directly into the essential questioning and discussion part of the interview.

Figure 14.1

Sample of Questions to Ask Job Applicants

- What was your most rewarding experience in college?
- What were some of the courses you liked best in college? Why?
- What subjects were the most difficult for you to master? Why?
- How does your education prepare you for this job?
- What have you done in previous jobs that demonstrate your creativity? Your ability to demonstrate leadership?
- What personal characteristics do you possess that especially prepare you for this job?
- On your last job, what was it that you most wanted to accomplish but didn't? Why not?
- What was the best boss you ever had? Worst boss? Why?
- On your last job, what criticism of your work did you receive?
- What are your greatest strengths? Weaknesses?
- What are your plans for self-improvement during this year?
- Where would you like to be in five years? Ten years?
- Why should I hire you?

Questioning and Discussion

The questions you developed during the preparation stage will provide a general road map to guide you. But don't rely rigidly on these questions. They're a guide, not a straight jacket. Listen to the answers the candidate gives. Select follow-up questions that naturally flow from the answers given.

Follow-up questions should seek to probe deeper into what the applicant says. If you feel that the applicant's response is superficial or inadequate, seek elaboration. Ask a question such as "Tell me more about that issue." If you need to clarify information, say something like, "You said working overtime was okay *sometimes*. Can you tell me specifically when you'd be willing to work overtime?" If the applicant doesn't directly answer your question, follow up by repeating the question or paraphrasing it. Finally, never underestimate the power of silence in an interview. One of the biggest errors that inexperienced interviewers make is that they talk too much. You're not learning anything about the candidate when you're doing the talking. Pause for at least a few seconds after the applicant appears to have finished an answer. Your silence encourages the applicant to continue talking.

Concluding

Once you're through with the questions and discussion, you're ready to wrap up the interview. Let the applicant know this fact with a statement like, "Well, that covers all the questions I have. Is there anything about the job or our organization that I haven't answered for you?" Then, let the applicant know what's going to happen next. When can he or she expect to hear from you? Will you write or phone? Are there likely to be more follow-up interviews? Finish your interaction with the applicant by thanking him or her for taking time to meet with you.

Before you consider the interview complete, write your evaluation while it's fresh in your mind. Ideally, you kept notes or recorded the applicant's answers to your questions and made comments of your impressions. Now that the applicant has gone, take the time to assess the applicant's responses. How does the candidate stack up against the job criteria? Is the candidate qualified? What's your impression of his or her motivation? How well would he or she fit into your work group and the organization? What's your overall assessment of the candidate and how does he or she rate against other candidates?

PERFORMANCE-APPRAISAL INTERVIEWING

At least once a year, most managers undertake the formal ritual of appraising each of their employees' job performance. The performance appraisal provides much of the data on which key personnel decisions—salary increases, promotions, and other rewards—are made. The performance appraisal also identifies areas where employee growth and development are needed (Kavanagh, 1982).

The performance-appraisal process is typically described as encompassing five steps: (1) establishing performance standards; (2) communicating performance expectations to the employee; (3) gathering performance data; (4) rating performance; and (5) discussing the results in a formal performance-review interview. Note that not all of these steps involve interpersonal skills. For example, identifying specific performance criteria for each job and making accurate and consistent ratings are critical performance-appraisal skills, but they're *technical* skills, not *interpersonal* ones. For the most part, the interpersonal aspects of performance appraisal surface in the performance-review interview (Beer, 1987).

The performance-appraisal interview can be broken down into the same four stages as the selection interview. It begins with *preparation*, followed by the *opening*, a period of *questioning and discussion*, and a *conclusion*.

Most contemporary discussions of the performance-review interviews advocate the problem-solving approach where the manager acts as a partner and works jointly with the subordinate to develop the employee's performance (Maier, 1976). This requires the manager to practice both joint goal setting and effective listening

Preparation

Schedule the appraisal interview in advance and be prepared. If a performance-review interview is to be effective, planning must precede it (Beer, 1987). Review the employee's job description. Go over your rating sheet. Have you carefully considered the employee's strengths as well as weaknesses? Can you substantiate, with specific examples, all points of praise and criticism? Given your past experiences with the employee, what problems, if any, do you anticipate popping up in the review? How do you plan to react to these problems? Once you have worked out these kinds of issues, you should schedule a specific time and place for the review and give the employee ample advance notice. You should also do whatever is necessary to ensure there are no outside interruptions once the interview begins, for example, close your office door, and have your phone calls held.

Opening

Put the employee at ease. As in a selection interview, you are responsible for creating a supportive climate for the employee. The performance review can be a traumatic experience for the best of employees. People don't like to hear their work criticized. Add the fact that people tend to overrate themselves—approximately 60 percent place their own performance in the top 10 percent ("How Do I Love Me?" 1980)—and you have the ingredients for tension and confrontation. Since the employee is apt to be nervous at the very least, be supportive and understanding.

Be sure that the employee understands the purpose of the appraisal interview. Employees are often concerned whether the results of the appraisal interview will be used for personnel decisions or to promote their growth and development (Kirkpatrick, 1986). In the problem-solving approach, the interview provides recognition for things the employee is doing well and a opportunity to discuss any job-related problems. Any uncertainty the employee may have about what will transpire during the review and the resulting consequences should be clarified at the start (Beer, 1987).

Questioning and Discussion

Minimize threats. Create a helpful and constructive climate (Dorfman, Stephan, and Loveland, 1986). Try to maximize encouragement and support, while minimizing threats (Baker and Morgan, 1984).

Obtain employee participation. Let employees do the majority of the talking. The more employees talk, the more satisfied they will be with the appraisal (Baker and Morgan, 1984). Encourage the employee to engage in self-evaluation. If the climate is supportive, employees may openly acknowledge performance problems you've identified, thus eliminating your need to raise them. They may even offer viable solutions to these problems.

Criticize performance but not the person. If something needs to be criticized, direct the criticism at specific job-related behaviors that negatively affect the employee's performance (Fletcher, 1986). It's the person's performance that is unsatisfactory, not the person himself.

When criticizing, soften the tone but not the message. If criticism is necessary, don't water down the message, don't dance around the issue, and certainly don't avoid discussing a problem in the hope that it'll just go away. State your criticism thoughtfully and show concern for the employee's feelings, but don't soften the message. Criticism is criticism, even if it's constructive. When you try to sell it as something else, you're liable to create ambiguity and misunderstanding.

Don't exaggerate.   Don't make extreme statements in order to make a point. If an employee has been late for four out of five recent meetings, don't say "You are *always* late to meetings." Avoid absolutes like "always" or "never." Such terms encourage defensiveness and undermine your credibility. An employee only has to introduce one exception to your "always" or "never" statement to destroy the entire statement's validity.

Use specific examples to support your ratings.   Document your employee's performance ratings with specific examples (Beer, 1987). This adds credibility to your ratings and helps employees better understand what you mean by "good" and "bad" performance.

Give positive as well as negative feedback.   Avoid turning the performance review into a totally negative feedback session (Fletcher, 1986). Also, state what was done well and why it deserves recognition.

Conclusion

Have the employee sum up the appraisal interview.   As the review nears its conclusion, encourage the employee to summarize the discussion that has taken place (Brett and Fredian, 1981). This gives your subordinate an opportunity to put the entire review into perspective. It will also tell you whether you have succeeded in clearly communicating your evaluation.

Detail a future plan of action.   Where there are performance inadequacies, the final part of the review should be devoted to helping the employee draft a detailed, step-by-step plan to improve the situation (Beer, 1987). Your role should be supportive: "What can I do to provide assistance?" Do you need to make yourself more available to answer questions? Do you need to give the employee more freedom or responsibility? Would securing funds to send the employee to professional meetings, or training programs help (Dorfman, Stephan, and Loveland, 1986)?

CONCEPT QUIZ

Do you understand the basic concepts of interviewing for selection and performance appraisal? The following quiz will help answer that question. Remember, if you miss any answers, go back and find out why you got them wrong.

Circle the right answer:

True   or   False   1. One of the most important parts of an interview starts before it actually begins.

True   or   False   2. One of the biggest errors that inexperienced interviewers make is that they talk too much.

True   or   False   3. Closed-ended questions are usually most effective for both types of interviews.

True   or   False   4. Rating an employee on the degree to which she shows initiative is an example of evaluating employee behavior.

True   or   False   5. Most people overrate their own performance.

True   or   False   6. A manager should let the interviewee do most of the talking during an interview.

True   or   False   7. A manager should avoid criticizing an employee's job performance during the appraisal interview.

True   or   False   8. Don't exaggerate during a performance review.

True   or   False   9. Interviewees should sum up the interview themselves.

True   or   False   10. A detailed future plan of action will include commitments by both the employee and the manager.

Answers: (1) True; (2) True; (3) False; (4) False; (5) True; (6) True; (7) False; (8) True; (9) True; (10) True.

BEHAVIORAL CHECKLIST

Look for these specific behaviors when evaluating your interviewing skills and those of others.

EFFECTIVE INTERVIEWING REQUIRES

- Preparing in advance
- Putting the employee at ease
- Explaining the purpose of the interview
- Obtaining participation by the employee
- Indicating what will happen with the information
- Using appropriate questions
- Being silent when appropriate
- Having the employee sum up the interview
- Detailing a future plan of action

ATTENTION!

Don't read this or the following exercises until assigned to do so by your instructor.

MODELING EXERCISE*

Actors: DANA (Head of Personnel) and BLAIR (Employee Relations Manager).

DANA's role: You are Head of Personnel for a manufacturing firm. You are well thought of in the firm and have excellent rapport with your boss, the Vice President for Administration. Blair is your Employee Relations Manager. You know that Blair is reasonably good at his/her job. But you also know that Blair believes him/herself to be "outstand-

---

*Source: Based on Srinivasan Umapathy, "Teaching Behavioral Aspects of Performance Evaluation: An Experiential Approach," *The Accounting Review,* January 1985, pp. 107–108. With permission.

ing," which isn't true. Blair is scheduled to have a meeting with you in five minutes, and you would like to establish clearer communication, as well as to convince Blair to adopt a less grandiose self-image.

You believe that Blair is on the right track, but it will take him/her about two years to reach the stage at which he/she can be promoted. As to Blair's performance, you have received some good reports, as well as *three* letters of complaint. Blair prepared four research reports that you considered to be above average—but to keep him/her motivated and happy, you exaggerated and said they were "excellent." Maybe that was a mistake.

You are worried about the impact on other employees, whose performance is nearly as good as Blair's, if Blair is promoted. So you plan to set meaningful targets for Blair this year, evaluate his/her performance one or two years from now, and then give the promotion if it's deserved.

BLAIR's role: You are the Employee Relations Manager in a manufacturing firm. Dana is your boss and his/her title is Head of Personnel. You know that you are one of the best performers in your department, and may even be the best. However, you were not promoted last year, even though you expected to be. So you would like to be promoted this year.

You expect your boss to raise some obstacles to your promotion. Dana is bound to mention three letters of complaint against you, for instance. Dana seems to point out only your errors. Up front, you plan to remind Dana that you wrote four research reports that Dana him/herself said were *excellent*. If Dana tries to delay your promotion unnecessarily, you plan to confront him/her and, if necessary, take the issue to Dana's boss, the Vice President for Administration. You think there have been many instances in which you were rated better on performance than your colleagues in the department. You have decided that you will press your point of view firmly, but also rationally, in a professional manner.

Time: Not to exceed fifteen minutes.

OBSERVER'S RATING SHEET

Evaluate the key behaviors of the appraisal interviewer on a 1 to 5 scale (5 being highest).

- Puts employee at ease   _____

- Obtains employee participation   _____

- Gets employee to engage in self-evaluation   _____

- Criticizes performance, not person   _____

- Softens tone, not message   _____

- Uses specific examples for support   _____

- Gives positive as well as negative feedback   _____

- Has employee sum up review   _____

- Details future plans   _____

Comments:

_____

_____

_____

_____

_____

_____

GROUP EXERCISES

Break into groups of three and perform three role-plays so that everyone gets a chance to play the interviewer and receive feedback. Remember that observers are to evaluate interview skills using the behaviors identified on the Observer's Rating Sheet.

1. Spend up to ten minutes as a group to write up to five challenging job-interview questions that you think would be relevant in the hiring of new college graduates for a sales-management training program at Procter & Gamble. Each hiree will spend 18-24 months as a sales representative calling on retail grocers. After this training period, successful candidates can be expected to be promoted to the position of district sales supervisor.

2. Each individual should spend five minutes outlining a brief resume of his or her background and experience.

3. Groups exchange their five questions with another group.

4. Each group should allocate one of the following roles to their three members: interviewer, applicant, and observer. The person playing the applicant should give his or her resume to the interviewer.

5. Role-play a job interview. The interviewer should include, but not be limited to, the questions provided by the other group.

6. Provide the interviewer with feedback based on the following Observer's Rating Sheet.

7. Repeat the process two more times by exchanging questions with another group and switching roles so that all three members of your trio have acted as the interviewer and received feedback.

Time: Do not take more than ten minutes for each interview in this role play.

OBSERVER'S RATING SHEET

Evaluate the key behaviors of the appraisal interviewer on a 1 to 5 scale (5 being highest).

- Puts employee at ease   _____

- Obtains employee participation   _____

- Gets employee to engage in self-evaluation   _____

- Criticizes performance, not person   _____

- Softens tone, not message   _____

- Uses specific examples for support   _____

- Gives positive as well as negative feedback   _____

- Has employee sum up review   _____

- Details future plans   _____

Comments:

_____

_____

_____

_____

_____

_____

SUMMARY CHECKLIST

Review your performance and look over others' ratings of your skill. Now assess yourself on each of the key learning behaviors. Make a check (✔) next to those behaviors on which you need improvement.

- I put the employee at ease.   _____
- I explain the purpose of the interview.   _____
- I obtain employee participation.   _____
- I get the employee to engage in self evaluation.   _____
- I criticize performance, not the person.   _____
- I use specific examples for support.   _____
- I give positive as well as negative feedback.   _____
- I have the employee sum up the review.   _____
- I detail a future plan of action.   _____

APPLICATION QUESTIONS

1. What are some of the most common interview problems? How can they be prevented or overcome?

2. What are the common elements of the three types of interviews discussed in this chapter? How do they differ?

3. Which of the behavioral skills already studied in this book apply to interviewing? How should you adapt them?

4. Why are questions an important interviewing tool? What types are there? When should each be used?

5. What are the positive nonverbal behaviors that an effective interviewer should exhibit?

REINFORCEMENT EXERCISES

The following suggestions are activities you can do to practice and reinforce the interviewing techniques you learned in this chapter.

1. Using the techniques learned in this chapter, interview three managers about how they appraise their employees. What methods do they use? How often do they conduct appraisal interviews? What problems have they experienced?

2. Watch several television talk shows. Compare the hosts' interviewing techniques. Which hosts most clearly followed the guidelines in this chapter? What are the results when the guidelines were or were not followed?

3. Talk to friends who have recently experienced a job interview. Find out what kinds of questions they were asked, how they responded, and what, if anything they learned from the experience.

4. Make an appointment to interview a professional interviewer in a human resources department of a local company. Find out how the interviewer plans, conducts, and concludes selection interviews. Find out if the interviewer does other types of interviews (e.g., appraisal, exit, problem solving) and how they differ from each other.

ACTION PLAN

1. Which behavior do I want to improve the most?

_____

_____

_____

2. Why? What will be my payoff?

_____

_____

_____

3. What potential obstacles stand in my way?

_____

_____

_____

4. What are the specific things I will do to improve? (For examples, see
   the Reinforcement Exercises.)

_____

_____

_____

5. When will I do them?

_____

_____

_____

6. How and when will I measure my success?

_____

_____

_____

Chapter **15**

INTEGRATION

In this, the last chapter of the book, you won't be exposed to any new skills. The objectives here are to help you summarize those skill areas where you need to concentrate in the future and to give you an opportunity to try out a number of the skills you have learned.

SKILL ASSESSMENT REVIEW

You have undoubtedly done well on a number of the skills presented in this book. But if you're like most people, your skills have been deficient in some areas. It's now time to review those deficiencies in order to identify common patterns.

Look back through the Summary Checklists in Chapters 3 through 14. Make a list of all those skill techniques where you made a check mark. Do you see any patterns to your deficiencies? In a paragraph or two, summarize any insights you have drawn from reviewing those areas in which you have shown deficiencies:

_____

_____

_____

_____

_____

_____

Now review your Self-Awareness Profile (see Chapter 2). In a couple of sentences, summarize your interpersonal values, needs, assertiveness level, and behavioral style:

_____

_____

_____

_____

What insights into the sources of your deficiencies do these sentences give you?

_____

_____

_____

_____

INTEGRATIVE EXERCISE

In the real world, interpersonal activities don't come neatly separated and packaged into topics like goal setting, listening, and delegating. In practice, the interpersonal skills this book has introduced you to greatly overlap. For instance, goal setting and feedback go hand in hand. So, too, do running a group meeting and managing conflict. In the real world, a performance-appraisal review typically requires the skills of interviewing, listening, persuasion, feedback, coaching, and conflict management.

The following exercise* encompasses a number of the interpersonal skills you've previously practiced. It gives you the opportunity to see how well you've assimilated the skills and the degree to which you can move from directed and narrow skill development to applying the skills in less focused situations.

Actors: CHRIS AMON and LEE PETTY.

Instructions: Break into groups of two. One person will play the role of Chris Amon (the manager), while the other will play Lee Petty (the employee). Both individuals should read the following background information, and then their own role.

Time: Take fifteen minutes to read the background and role information. You then have up to thirty minutes to enact the role-play.

Background information: The Sloane Company, headquartered in New York, produces and markets four major brands of cosmetics. The marketing function is organized as shown in the figure below, with Product Managers reporting to Brand Managers. This exercise involves a meeting between Chris Amon, the Brand Manager, and Lee Petty, one of Chris' three Product Managers. Both came to the Sloane Company after receiving their M.B.A.'s from the Amos Tuck School of Business at Dartmouth College. Chris has been with Sloane for ten years, Lee for four.

An important event in the relationship between Brand Managers and Product Managers is the performance review, which is supposed to occur every three months. The fourth such meeting every year is also

---

Source: This exercise was developed by Leonard Greenhalgh, Jeanne Brett, and Roy Lewicki for The National Institute for Dispute Resolution. Copyright ©1985. Reprinted with permission.

the annual salary review. Because of Chris Amon's rather hectic travel schedule during the past few months, six months have elapsed since Lee Petty's last review, which was also the annual salary review session. Lee's salary was raised 14 percent.

The most recent review was a positive one, with no corrective action suggested. During the interview, Lee had asked Chris to see if it would be possible to trade weekend work for longer vacation time. Lee felt the company's vacation policy favored high-seniority employees too much (see the following table). After checking with the Vice President-Human Resources, Chris reported back to Lee that such a trade was impossible because it might set a precedent that would upset the vacation benefits structure. The Vice President-Human Resources did, however, assure Chris that the entire benefits structure at the Sloane Company would be reviewed.

Organization Chart Summarizing the Marketing Function at the Sloane Company

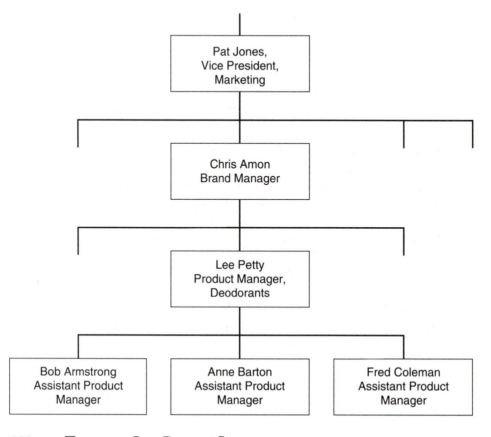

Vacation Policy of the Sloane Company

Number of Years of Service	Vacation
Less than 1 year	None
1–5 years	2 weeks
6–7 years	3 weeks
8–9 years	4 weeks
10–15 years	5 weeks
Over 15 years	6 weeks

The interview begins with Chris calling Lee to arrange a location for the meeting.

Now read your role. *Remember to read only your own role!* Lee's role follows; Chris's role begins on page 286.

LEE PETTY's role: Your immediate supervisor, Chris Amon, has returned from extended overseas travel and is now catching up on a backlog of administrative duties. Among these are long-overdue reviews of the Product Managers. Chris has been a good boss over the past two years since you were promoted from Assistant Product Manager and has been particularly supportive of you, but has a tendency to dump things in your lap and not be around to follow through.

During the past six months, for instance, Chris tried to pass two projects onto you and your group of three Assistant Product Managers. Each happened to come at a bad time for your group, but Chris was out of town at these times and didn't realize that your group was particularly busy while other groups were running slack. Chris was reasonable when you pointed this out and quickly reassigned the projects, but you felt a little bad because you always try to cooperate. If Chris had been in the office more, these projects—which weren't particularly interesting or challenging—would automatically have gone to less busy Product Managers.

You suspect that Chris tends to think of your group first because you have the best track record. On the one hand, this is flattering; but on the other hand, your group is, in effect, being penalized for being good by getting saddled with extra projects that are just "busywork." The other Product Managers seem a little jealous of what you've accomplished. One is a Harvard M.B.A. and the other a Wharton M.B.A., and there has always been some rivalry. But you feel that they have at times gone beyond kidding around and have actually tried to undermine you in the eyes of higher management. In addition, they are eager to ask for help from you and your group, but seldom give you credit or return the favor when you need help. This is an organization in which the rewards flow from producing, not from cooperating. When your rivals take the credit after you helped them out, you get hurt.

The other Product Managers have gone beyond exploiting you and your group and have actually tried to undermine you by making nit-picking complaints to higher management about your attempt to build a little flextime into an overly rigid organization. Your group always gets the job done, even if it means working evenings and weekends. Other groups miss deadlines because they like to keep to a nine-to-five schedule. You occasionally return the favor to your Assistant Product Managers by being flexible when they have something special to do outside the office. Such flexibility is inconsistent with company policy, which was developed for the hourly workers. Thus, when the Assistant Product Managers have received your approval to take time off, they leave an official message in the office saying they are "working at home," "visiting the agency," or something similar. You wish you didn't have to do things this way, but the company's inflexible policies on time off leave you little choice. The rules were written for secretaries and others who must consistently be available during the hours the office is open; you think they should not apply to professionals such as the Assistant Product Managers.

The animosity of the other Product Managers and their groups is particularly bothersome as you contemplate your upcoming performance review with Chris because of a strange occurrence in your office over the weekend. You came in to catch up with some work last Saturday and made a phone call to the home of an advertising agency executive. She was very busy when you called, and her husband said she would call back in fifteen minutes. While you were waiting, you wrote a quick letter to Leslie, with whom you have been romantically involved for the past six months, but who, unfortunately, lives in Boston.

When you had almost finished the second page of the letter, your fountain pen hemorrhaged and spoiled the page. You rewrote the page and had finished the letter by the time your call was returned. You had forgotten about this event until Monday morning.

Monday started off badly. You were menaced on the subway by two adolescent thugs. Then you had to wait forever for a new and obviously incompetent waitress to serve you breakfast. When it finally arrived, you found you had been given an onion bagel instead of your usual plain bagel, but you were already late, so you didn't dare send it back and wait for another one. Because you didn't want to taste your breakfast all day, you bought a pack of Dentyne (you were short-changed!) and chewed a piece as you walked to your office.

When you sat down at your desk and wanted to discard your gum, you looked in the wastebasket for a piece of paper to wrap the gum in. There was one crumpled piece of paper, the second page of your note to Leslie, which you remembered discarding the previous Saturday. You opened it up to place the used gum in it and saw the number "1990" written in ball-point pen on the back. This was puzzling. You were sure you began with a clean sheet, and the office had been locked from the time you left on Saturday until your arrival Monday morning.

You then reread the other side, and became concerned. If a rival Product Manager photocopied that page, in your very distinctive handwriting, the information could be used to discredit you. The text of what you wrote is shown in the following figure.

Text of One Page of Lee Petty's Letter

> . . . and it's probably OK with them.
>
> I'm delighted you can get the time off work to meet me in San Diego. We'll have a hotel to stay in, a rental car, and an expense account. All I have to do is register for the convention. We can skip out every day since it's a bullshit convention anyway. You'll love Black's Beach. And a friend of mine has an 18-foot Hobie Cat that we can take out whenever we want.
>
> I'll be calling you next week when I'm in Boston. I hope

[note-writing stopped at this point because of a large ink blot; the page was obviously crumpled before the ink had dried].

It was poor judgment on your part to express in writing a practice that is fairly common among junior-level marketing people at Sloane. The company's vacation policy is so unreasonable that people have to bend the rules a little to adapt. Product Managers do a lot of traveling. A key source of information about new developments by competitors is the components manufacturers. For instance, Sloane first found out its major competitor was planning to launch an aerosol antiperspirant from the aerosol-valve manufacturer. Thus, there is almost always someone from Sloane at trade meetings and conventions. Since these events are often held at vacation resorts, attendees often manage to budget a lot of leisure time during the event.

The convention in San Diego you referred to in your letter is put on by the Cosmetics Chemicals Manufacturers Association. You have little interest in or knowledge of chemistry, but a strong interest in San Diego, where your friends live. You wrote a routine memo to get the trip approved. The request was approved without question.

You don't feel at all guilty about asking to go to a convention that you're *not really* interested in. It's a standard perquisite of the job, and people informally told you of this benefit during your call-back interview. But you're a little worried that some rival Product Manager might have seen the page and mentioned it to Chris to make trouble for you.

You flushed both the paper and the gum down the toilet last Monday morning. You never did figure out why someone would write "1990" on your sheet of paper.

CHRIS AMON's role: You have been back in town for only a week after an extensive travel schedule to explore new overseas opportunities for the brand. You are now catching up on your backlog of administrative duties, which include the (now quite late) reviews of your three Product Managers.

Overall, Lee Petty has been doing a very good job. A creative, conscientious, and hard worker, Lee has consistently exceeded your expectations since being promoted by you from Assistant Product Manager two years ago. Lee's group is the best of the three; they take new problems in stride and have consistently improved their performance.

You have received some mild complaints about Lee's cooperation with other Product Managers. When other groups need help, for instance, Lee's group is seen as reluctant to provide it, despite their obvious wealth of talent and energy. On one occasion, another Product Manager made a mistake that was costly and a little embarrassing to the company. This mistake could easily have been avoided had Lee given him some key information.

During the past six months, Lee was reluctant to take on two general assignments that directly concerned the brand. Lee's complaint was that the assignments were routine and uninteresting, and would divert the group's energy from some more challenging tasks that needed to be tackled and were more directly concerned with the group's product. You didn't push the point, since one other group was slightly less busy during that period, but one of the other Product Managers made a joking comment about favoritism that has bothered you. The joke concerned the fact that you and Lee are the only two Tuck graduates in the company.

There has also been some resentment of Lee's group bending the rules on attendance. Lee has been an outspoken critic of the company's vacation policy. There are rumors that Lee compensates informally by allowing the Assistant Product Managers extra time off under the guise of "working at home," "working over at the agency," or "checking out point-of-purchase displays." You haven't yet said anything to Lee about this. The group always gets its work done and often works evenings and weekends when necessary. But you have been criticized by your own boss for your laxity in bringing Lee's group into line: There is resentment of Lee's group's privileges among employees who are made to conform to a nine-to-five schedule.

What bothers you most about your upcoming interview, however, is evidence you found that Lee has apparently arranged a de facto vacation in Southern California at the company's expense. In an atmosphere in which there is already talk of favoritism toward another Tuck graduate, there is some risk that this could blow up on you.

You were in the office last Sunday, catching up on your paperwork. You needed some market data for the past five years and didn't want to wait until the next day to ask Lee for them, so you used your master key and went into Lee's office and looked them up in a three-ring binder. You needed a piece of paper on which to copy down the numbers, but didn't want to go into Lee's desk; you already felt a little uncomfortable invading Lee's office when no one was around. You spotted a crumpled piece of paper in the wastebasket, so you uncrumpled it and started writing on it.

For some reason, you stopped writing and turned it over. You immediately recognized Lee's elegant handwriting on the Sloane Company stationery. It was obviously the second page of a letter. It had apparently been discarded after Lee's fountain pen had leaked. Absentmindedly, you read the page, even though something inside you told you that you should not. You threw the page back in the wastebasket and left the office. The text of that page is shown in the following figure.

Text of One Page of Lee Petty's Letter

> *. . . and it's probably OK with them.*
>
> *I'm delighted you can get the time off work to meet me in San Diego. We'll have a hotel to stay in, a rental car, and an expense account. All I have to do is register for the convention. We can skip out every day since it's a bullshit convention anyway. You'll love Black's Beach. And a friend of mine has an 18-foot Hobie Cat that we can take out whenever we want.*
>
> *I'll be calling you next week when I'm in Boston. I hope*
>
> [note-writing stopped at this point because of a large ink blot; the page was obviously crumpled before the ink had dried].

Reading that page made you very angry. Lee had asked to attend a cosmetics-chemicals convention in San Diego during May. The request seemed odd, because Lee knows nothing about chemistry and has never before shown any interest in the chemicals that go into the product line. However, you trusted Lee and approved the request, even though you were questioned by your boss about it. Now you are in a quandary. You don't want to admit to having snooped around a subordinate's office over the weekend, much less to having rummaged through a wastebasket and then read personal mail. On the other hand, you don't feel you can let Lee's duplicity go unchallenged.

Directions: After you have read the background and your role, advise your partner. Then begin the role-play: Chris calls Lee to arrange a location for the meeting.

Directions for Evaluation Feedback: After the exercise is completed, evaluate your own behavior and that of your partner on the evaluation forms included below. Then partner A shares his or her self-evaluations, one item at a time. Partner B responds with his or her rating of partner A to confirm or provide feedback about discrepancies to partner A. Then the process is reversed with partner B sharing self-ratings and partner A confirming or explaining why there are discrepancies.

EVALUATION SHEET FOR CHRIS AMON

Evaluate Christ Amon's Interpersonal Skills on a 1 to 5 scale (5 being highest)

Listening

Makes eye contact _____

Exhibits affirmative
   head nods and appropriate facial expressions _____

Avoids distracting actions or gestures that
   suggest boredom _____

Asks questions _____

Paraphrases using his or her own words _____

Avoids interrupting the speaker _____

Doesn't overtalk _____

Makes smooth transitions between role of
   speaker and listener _____

Providing Feedback

Supports negative feedback with hard data _____

Focuses on specific rather than general behaviors _____

Keeps comments impersonal and job-related _____

Ensures clear and full understanding by the recipient _____

Ensures negative feedback is directed toward
   behavior which is controllable by the recipient _____

Adjusts frequency, amount, and content of feedback
   to reflect the recipient's past performance and
   estimate of future potential _____

Resolving Conflicts

Evaluates the conflict players _____

Assesses source of the conflict _____

Knows options _____

Selects the best option _____

Interviewing

Explains the purpose of interview   _____

Obtains employee participation   _____

Uses appropriate questions   _____

Has employee sum up the interview   _____

Details a future plan of action   _____

Coaching

Asks questions to help employee discover
   how to improve   _____

Is positive rather then threatening   _____

Accepts mistakes and uses them to learn   _____

Models qualities expected from employees

Negotiating

Considers the other party's situation   _____

Addresses problems, not personalities   _____

Maintains a rational, goal-oriented frame of mind   _____

Insists on using objective criteria   _____

EVALUATION SHEET FOR LEE PETTY

Evaluate Lee Petty's interpersonal skills on a 1 to 5 scale (5 being highest).

Listening

Makes eye contact _____

Exhibits affirmative head nods and appropriate
  facial expressions _____

Avoids distracting actions or gestures that
  suggest boredom _____

Asks questions _____

Paraphrases using his or her own words _____

Avoids interrupting the speaker _____

Doesn't overtalk _____

Makes smooth transitions between role of
  speaker and listener _____

Persuasion

Uses a positive, tactful tone _____

Presents ideas one at a time _____

Presents strong evidence to support position _____

Tailors argument to the listener _____

Appeals to the subject's self-interest _____

Makes logical argument _____

Uses emotional appeals _____

Politicking

Frames arguments in terms of organizational goals _____

Projects right image _____

Gains control of organizational resources _____

Develops powerful allies _____

Supports boss _____

Negotiating

Considers the other party's situation	_____
Addresses problems, not personalities	_____
Maintains a rational, goal-oriented frame of mind	_____
Insists on using objective criteria	_____

QUESTIONS FOR DISCUSSION

1. What solution did your interview arrive at? How did each party feel as a consequence?

2. How many people role-playing Chris confronted Lee at the outset with the evidence? Why or why not?

3. How many of the Lees initiated the discussion by confessing their actions? Why?

4. How many of you were able to focus on the other person's interests? What facilitated this?

5. Does Chris have a responsibility to correct the ripoff? Explain.

6. For those playing Lee, how effective were your persuasion efforts?

7. Did Chris approach this situation as a coaching, conflict resolution, or team building dilemma?

8. What interviewing skills did Chris demonstrate?

9. How did the two parties negotiate?

FUTURE ACTION PLANS

As a result of the Skill Assessment Review at the beginning of this chapter, and the feedback you have just received after the integration role-play, are there behaviors that you still want to improve in the future?

1. Which behaviors do I want to improve in?

_____

_____

_____

2. Why? What will be my payoff?

_____

_____

_____

3. What potential obstacles stand in my way?

_____

_____

_____

4. What are the specific things I will do to improve?

_____

_____

_____

5. When will I do them?

_____

_____

_____

6. How and when will I measure my success?

_____

_____

_____

REFERENCES

AACSB, "Accreditation Research Project: Report on Phase I," *AACSB Bulletin*, Winter 1980, pp. 1-46.

AACSB, "Outcome Measurement Project of the Accreditation Research Committee, Phase II: An Interim Report," American Assembly of Collegiate Schools of Business, December 1984.

AACSB, "Outcome Measurement Project: Phase III Report, "American Assembly of Collegiate Schools of Business, May 1987.

AACSB, "The Cultivation of Tomorrow's Leaders: Industry's Fundamental Challenge to Management Education," *Newsline*, Vol. 23, No. 3, Spring 1993, pp. 1-3.

ALESSANDRA, TONY, and PHIL HUNSAKER, *Communicating at Work*, New York, Simon & Schuster, 1993, pp. 86-90.

ALESSANDRA, TONY, and MICHAEL J. O CONNOR, *Behavioral Profiles: Self-Assessment*, San Diego: Pfeiffer & Company, 1994.

ALLEN, ROBERT W., DANIEL L. MADISON, LYMAN W. PORTER, PATRICIA A. RENWICK, and BRONSTON T. MAYES, "Organizational Politics: Tactics and Characteristics of Its Actors," *California Management Review*, Fall 1979, pp. 77-83.

ARVEY, RICHARD D., and ALLEN P. JONES, "The Use of Discipline in Organizational Settings: A Framework for Future Research," in L. L. Cummings and B. M. Staw (eds.), *Research in Organizational Behavior*, Vol. 7. Greenwich, Conn.: JAI Press, 1985, pp. 367-408.

BAKER, H. KENT, and PHILIP L. MORGAN, "Two Goals in Every Performance Appraisal," *Personnel Journal*, September 1984, pp. 74-78.

BANDURA, ALBERT, *Social Learning Theory*. Englewood Cliffs, N.J.: Prentice Hall, 1977.

BARTOLOME, FERNANDO, "Nobody Trusts the Boss Completely—Now What?" *Harvard Business Review*, March-April 1989, pp. 135-42.

BARTOLOME, FERNANDO, "Teaching About Whether to Give Negative Feedback," *The Organizational Behavior Teaching Review*, Vol. XI, Issue 2, 1986-87, pp. 95-104.

BEER, MICHAEL, "Performance Appraisal," in J. W. Lorsch (ed.), *Handbook of Organizational Behavior*. Englewood Cliffs, N.J.: Prentice Hall, 1987, pp. 286-300.

BELOHLAV, JAMES A., *The Art of Disciplining Your Employees*. Englewood Cliffs, N.J.: Prentice Hall, 1985.

BERNARDIN, H. JOHN, and C. S. WALTER, "Effects of Rater Training and Diary-Keeping on Psychometric Error in Ratings," *Journal of Applied Psychology*, February 1977, pp. 64-69.

BOURNE, LYLE E., JR., and C. VICTOR BUNDERSON, "Effects of Delay of Information Feedback and Length of Post-Feedback Interval on Concept Identification," *Journal of Experimental Psychology*, January 1963, pp. 1-5.

BOWEN, DONALD D., "Toward a Viable Concept of Assertiveness," in D. T. Hall, D. D. Bowen, R. J. Lewicki, and F. S. Hall, (eds.), *Experiences in Management and Organizational Behavior*, 2nd ed. New York: John Wiley & Sons, 1982, pp. 414-417.

BOWEN, DONALD D., "Developing a Personal Theory of Experiential Learning," *Simulation & Games*, Vol. 18, No. 2, June 1987, pp. 192-206.

BOYATZIS, RICHARD E., *The Competent Manager: A Model for Effective Performance*. New York: John Wiley & Sons, 1982.

BRASS, DANIEL, "Being in the Right Place: A Structural Analysis of Individual Influence in an Organization," *Administrative Science Quarterly*, December 1984, pp. 518-539.

BRETT, RANDALL, and ALAN J. FREDIAN, "Performance Appraisal: The System Is Not the Solution," *Personnel Administrator*, December 1981, p. 62.

BUREAU OF NATIONAL AFFAIRS, *Employee Conduct and Discipline*, Personnel Policies Forum, Survey No. 102. Washington, D.C.: Bureau of National Affairs, August 1973.

BURKE, MICHAEL J., and RUSSELL R. DAY, "A Cumulative Study of the Effectiveness of Management Training," *Journal of Applied Psychology*, May 1986, pp. 232-245.

BURKE, RONALD J., R. J. WEITZEL, and T. WEIR, "Characteristics of Effective Employee Performance Review and Development Interviews: Replication and Extension," *Personnel Psychology*, Winter 1978, pp. 903-919.

Business Week, "The Battle of the B-Schools Is Getting Bloodier," March 24, 1986, pp. 61-70.

CAMERON, DAN, "The When, Why and How of Discipline," *Personnel Journal*, July 1984, pp. 37-39.

CASCIO, WAYNE F., *Applied Psychology in Personnel Management*, 3rd ed. Englewood Cliffs, N.J.: Prentice Hall, 1987.

CLARK, HEWITT B., RANDY WOOD, TIMOTHY KUCHNEL, STEPHEN FLANAGAN, MARK MOSK, and JAMES T. NORTHRUP, "Preliminary Validation and Training of Supervisory Interactional Skills," *Journal of Organizational Behavior Management*, Spring/Summer 1985, pp. 95-115.

COFFEY, ROBERT E., CURTIS W. COOK, and PHILLIP L. HUNSAKER, *Management and Organizational Behavior.* Burr Ridge, Ill.: Austin Press/Irwin, 1994.

COPLIN, WILLIAM D., MICHAEL K. O'LEARY, and CAROLE GOULD, *Power Persuasion: A Surefire Way to Get Ahead.* Boston: Addison-Wesley, 1985.

CROCKER, J. Paper presented at the Speech Communication Association meeting; Minneapolis, Minn., 1978. Reported in D. A. Whetten and K. S. Cameron, *Developing Management Skills.* Glenview, Ill.: Scott-Foresman, 1984, p. 218.

CUMMINGS, LARRY L., "Appraisal Purpose and the Nature, Amount, and Frequency of Feedback." Paper presented at the American Psychological Association meeting, Washington, D.C., September 1976.

CUMMINGS, LARRY L., "Reflections on Management Education and Development: Drift or Thrust Into the 21st Century?" *The Academy of Management Review*, Vol. 15, No. 4, October 1990, pp. 694-696.

DAVIS, KEITH, and JOHN W. NEWSTROM, *Human Behavior at Work: Organizational Behavior*, 7th ed. New York: McGraw-Hill, 1985.

DECENZO, DAVID A. and STEPHEN P. ROBBINS, *Personnel/Human Resource Management*, 3rd ed. Englewood Cliffs, N.J.: Prentice Hall, 1988.

DECKER, PHILIP J., "The Enhancement of Behavioral Modeling Training of Supervisory Skills by the Inclusion of Retention Processes," *Personnel Psychology*, Summer 1982, pp.323-332.

DECOTIIS, THOMAS, and ANDRE PETIT, "The Performance Appraisal Process: A Model and Some Testable Propositions," *Academy of Management Review*, July 1978, pp. 635-646.

DiMARCO, N. J., "Supervisor-Subordinate Life Style and Interpersonal Need Compatibilities as Determinants of Subordinate's Attitudes Toward the Supervisor," *Academy of Management Journal*, Vol. 17, 1974, pp. 575-578.

DORFMAN, PETER W., WALTER G. STEPHAN, and JOHN LOVELAND, "Performance Appraisal Behaviors: Supervisor Perceptions and Subordinate Reactions," *Personnel Psychology*, Autumn 1986, pp. 579-597.

DOWNS, C. W., G. P. SMEYAK, and E. MARTIN, *Professional Interviewing.* New York: Harper & Row, 1980.

DRIVER, MICHAEL J., KENNETH R. ROUSSEAU, and PHILLIP L. HUNSAKER, *The Dynamic Decision Maker.* San Francisco: Jossey-Bass Publishers, 1990, pp. 215-216.

DUNHAM, RANDALL B., *Organizational Behavior: People and Processes in Management.* Homewood, Ill.: Richard D. Irwin, 1984.

FARRELL, DAN, and JAMES C. PETERSEN, "Patterns of Political Behavior in Organizations," *Academy of Management Review*, July 1982, pp. 430-442.

FIEDLER, FRED E., "Engineering the Job to Fit the Manager," *Harvard Business Review*, September-October 1965, pp. 115-122.

FILLEY, ALAN C., "Committee Management: Guidelines from Social Science Research," *California Management Review*, Fall 1970, pp. 13-21.

FINNEY, MICHAEL, and CAREN SIEHL, "The Current MBA: Why Are We Failing?", *The Organizational Behavior Teaching Review*, Vol. X, No. 3, 1985-86, pp. 12-18.

FISHER, CYNTHIA, "Transmission of Positive and Negative Feedback to Subordinates: A Laboratory Investigation," *Journal of Applied Psychology*, October 1979, pp. 533-540.

FLETCHER, CLIVE, "The Effects of Performance Review in Appraisal: Evidence and Implications," *Journal of Management Development*, Vol. 5, No. 3, 1986, pp. 3-12.

FRENCH, JOHN R. P., Jr., and BERTRAM RAVEN, "The Bases of Social Power," in Dorwin Cartwright and A. F. Zander (eds.), *Group Dynamics: Research and Theory*. New York: Harper & Row, 1960, pp. 607-623.

GOFFMAN, ERVING, *The Presentation of Self in Everyday Life*. New York: Doubleday, 1959.

GOLDHABER, GERALD M., *Organizational Communication*, 4th ed. Dubuque, Iowa: William C. Brown, 1980, p. 189.

GREENHALGH, LEONARD, "Managing Conflict," *Sloan Management Review*, Summer 1986, pp. 45-51.

GROVE, ANDREW S., "How (and Why) to Run a Meeting," *Fortune*, July 11, 1983, pp. 132-139.

HALPERIN, KEITH, C. R. SNYDER, RANDEE J. SHENKEL, and B. KENT HOUSTON, "Effect of Source Status and Message Favorability on Acceptance of Personality Feedback," *Journal of Applied Psychology*, February 1976, pp. 85-88.

HILL, R. E. "Interpersonal Needs and Functional Areas of Management," *Journal of Vocational Behavior*, Vol. 4, 1974, pp. 15-24.

"How Do I Love Me? Let Me Count the Ways," *Psychology Today*, May 1980, p. 16.

HULTMAN, KENNETH E., "Gaining and Keeping Management Support," *Training and Development Journal*, April 1981, pp. 106-110.

HUNSAKER, PHILLIP L., and ANTHONY J. ALESSANDRA, *The Art of Managing People*. New York: Simon & Schuster, 1986.

ILGEN, DANIEL, CYNTHIA D. FISHER, and M. SUSAN TAYLOR, "Consequences of Individual Feedback on Behavior in Organizations," *Journal of Applied Psychology*, August 1979, pp. 349-371.

IVANCEVICH, JOHN M., and J. T. McMAHON, "The Effects of Goal Setting, External Feedback, and Self-Generated Feedback on Outcome Variables: A Field Experiment," *Academy of Management Journal*, June 1982, pp. 359-372.

JAY, ANTONY, "How to Run a Meeting," *Harvard Business Review*, March-April 1976, pp. 43-57.

JOHNSON, DAVID W., and FRANK P. JOHNSON, *Joining Together: Group Theory and Group Skills*. 5th Ed. Boston: Allyn and Bacon, 1994.

KANE, JEFFREY S., and EDWARD E. LAWLER III, "Performance Appraisal Effectiveness," in Barry M. Staw (ed.), *Research in Organizational Behavior*, Vol. 1. Greenwich, Conn.: JAI Press, 1979, pp. 425-478.

KARLINS, MARVIN, and HERBERT I. ABELSON, *Persuasion: How Opinions and Attitudes Are Changed*, 2nd ed. New York: Springer Publishing, 1970.

KATZ, ROBERT L., "Skills of an Effective Administrator," *Harvard Business Review*, September-October 1974, pp. 90-102.

KATZENBACK, JON R. and DOUGLAS K. SMITH, *The Wisdom of Teams*. Boston: Harvard Business School Press, 1993, pp. 43-64.

KAVANAGH, MICHAEL J., "Evaluating Performance," in Kendrith M. Rowland and Gerald R. Ferris (eds.), *Personnel Management*. Boston: Allyn & Bacon, 1982, pp. 187-226.

KHARBANDA, OM P., and ERNEST A. STALLWORTHY, "Listening—A Vital Negotiating Skill," *Journal of Managerial Psychology*, Vol. 6, No. 4 (1991), pp. 6-9, 49-52.

KIECHEL, WALTER III, "How to Take Part in a Meeting," *Fortune*, May 26, 1986, pp. 177-180.

KILMANN, RALPH H., and KENNETH W. THOMAS, "Developing a Forced-Choice Measure of Conflict Handling Behavior: The MODE Instrument," *Educational and Psychological Measurement*, Summer 1977, pp. 309-325.

KIPNIS, DAVID, STUART M. SCHMIDT, C. SWAFFIN-SMITH, and IAN WILKINSON, "Patterns of Managerial Influence: Shotgun Managers, Tacticians, and Bystanders," *Organizational Dynamics*, Winter 1984, pp. 58-67.

KIRKPATRICK, DONALD L., "Performance Appraisal: Your Questions Answered," *Training and Development Journal*, May 1986, pp. 68-71.

KOLB, DAVID A., *Experiential Learning: Experience as the Source of Learning and Development*. Englewood Cliffs, N.J.: Prentice Hall, 1984.

KOLB, DAVID A., IRWIN M. RUBIN, and JOYCE S. OSLAND, *Organizational Behavior: An Experiential Approach*. Englewood Cliffs, N.J.: Prentice Hall, 1991, p. 277.

KOMAKI, JUDITH L., ROBERT L. COLLINS, and PAT PENN, "The Role of Performance Antecedents and Consequences in Work Motivation," *Journal of Applied Psychology*, June 1982, pp. 334-340.

KURSH, CHARLOTTE O., "The Benefits of Poor Communication," *The Psychoanalytic Review*, Summer-Fall 1971, pp. 189-208.

LANDY, FRANK J., and JAMES L. FARR, "Performance Ratings," *Psychological Bulletin*, January 1980, pp. 72-107.

LATHAM, GARY P., and EDWIN A. LOCKE, "Goal Setting—A Motivational Technique That Works," *Organizational Dynamics*, Autumn 1979, pp. 68-80.

LATHAM, GARY P., TERENCE R. MITCHELL, and DENNIS L. DOSSETT, "Importance of Participative Goal Setting and Anticipated Rewards on Goal Difficulty and Job Performance," *Journal of Applied Psychology*, April 1978, pp. 163-171.

LATHAM, GARY P., and LISE M. SAARI, "The Effects of Holding Goal Difficulty Constant on Assigned and Participatively Set Goals," *Academy of Management Journal*, March 1979a, pp. 163-168.

LATHAM, GARY P., and LISE M. SAARI, "Application of Social Learning Theory to Training Supervisors Through Behavioral Modeling," *Journal of Applied Psychology*, June 1979b, pp. 239-246.

LATHAM, GARY P., and KENNETH N. WEXLEY, *Increasing Productivity Through Performance Appraisal.* Reading, Mass.: Addison-Wesley, 1981.

LATHAM, GARY P., and GARY A. YUKL, "A Review of Research on the Application of Goal Setting in Organizations," *Academy of Management Journal*, December 1975, pp. 824-845.

LAWLESS, DAVID J., *Effective Management.* Englewood Cliffs, N.J.: Prentice Hall, 1972.

LEANA, CARRIE R., "Predictors and Consequences of Delegation," *Academy of Management Journal*, December 1986, pp. 754-774.

LERBINGER, OTTO, *Designs for Persuasive Communication.* Englewood Cliffs, N.J.: Prentice Hall, 1972.

LEVINE, HERMAINE Z., "Supervisory Training," *Personnel*, November-December 1982, pp. 4-12.

LEWIS, BLAKE D., Jr., "The Supervisor in 1975," *Personnel Journal*, September 1973, pp. 815-818.

LIDDELL, W. W. and J. W. SLOCUM, Jr., "The Effects of Individual-Role Compatibility Upon Group Performance: An Extension of Schutz's FIRO Theory," *Academy of Management Journal*, Vol 19, 1976, pp. 413-426.

LOCKE, EDWIN A., and GARY P. LATHAM, *Goal-Setting: A Motivational Technique That Works!* Englewood Cliffs, N.J.: Prentice Hall, 1984.

LOCKE, EDWIN A., and DAVID M. SCHWEIGER, "Participation in Decision Making: One More Look," in B. M. Staw (ed.), *Research in Organizational Behavior*, Vol. 1. Greenwich, Conn.: JAI Press, 1979, pp. 265-339.

LOCKE, EDWIN A., KARYLL N. SHAW, LISE M. SAARI, and GARY P. LATHAM, "Goal Setting and Task Performance: 1969–1980," *Psychological Bulletin*, July 1981, pp. 125-152.

McCONKEY, DALE D., *No-Nonsense Delegation.* New York: AMACOM, 1974.

McGREGOR, DOUGLAS, *The Human Side of Enterprise.* New York: McGraw-Hill, 1960.

McGREGOR, DOUGLAS, "Hot Stove Rules of Discipline," in George Strauss and Leonard Sayles (eds.), *Personnel: The Human Problems of Management.* Englewood Cliffs, N.J.: Prentice Hall, 1967.

MAIER, NORMAN R. F., *The Appraisal Interview: Three Basic Approaches.* La Jolla, Cal.: University Associates, 1976.

MANZ, CHARLES C., and HENRY P. SIMS, Jr., "Vicarious Learning: The Influence of Modeling on Organizational Behavior," *Academy of Management Review*, January 1981, pp. 105-113.

MICHAELS, EDWARD A., "Business Meetings," S*mall Business Reports*, (February 1989), pp. 82-88.

MILL, CYRIL R., "Feedback: The Art of Giving and Receiving Help," in Larry Porter and Cyril R. Mill (eds.), *The Reading Book for Human Relations Training*. Bethel, Me.: NTL Institute for Applied Behavioral Science, 1976, pp. 18-19.

MILLER, GEORGE A., "The Magical Number Seven, Plus or Minus Two: Some Limits on Our Capacity for Processing Information," *The Psychological Review*, March 1956, pp. 81-97.

MINER, JOHN B., and NORMAN R. SMITH, "Decline and Stabilization of Managerial Motivation over a 20-Year Period," *Journal of Applied Psychology*, June 1982, pp. 297-305.

MINTZBERG, HENRY, *The Nature of Managerial Work*. Englewood Cliffs, N.J.: Prentice Hall, 1980.

MORSE, JOHN J., and FRANCIS R. WAGNER, "Measuring the Process of Managerial Effectiveness," *Academy of Management Journal*, March 1978, pp. 23-35.

MURPHY, KEVIN J., *Effective Listening*. New York: Bantam Books, 1987.

NICHOLS, RALPH G., and LEONARD A. STEVENS, *Are You Listening?* New York: McGraw-Hill, 1957.

ORTH, CHARLES D., HARRY E. WILKINSON, and ROBERT C. BENFARI, "The Manager's Role as Coach and Mentor," *Organizational Dynamics*, Spring 1987, p. 67.

PAVETT, CYNTHIA M., and ALAN W. LAU, "Managerial Work: The Influence of Hierarchical Level and Functional Specialty," *Academy of Management Journal*, March 1983, pp. 170-177.

PFEFFER, JEFFREY, *Power in Organizations*. Marshfield, Mass.: Pitman Publishing, 1981.

PFEFFER, JEFFREY, and GERALD R. SALANCIK, *The External Control of Organizations: A Resource Dependence Perspective*. New York: Harper & Row, 1978.

PORRAS, JERRY, and BRAD ANDERSON, "Improving Managerial Effectiveness Through Modeling-Based Training," *Organizational Dynamics*, Spring 1981, pp. 60-77.

PORTER, LYMAN W., "Teaching Managerial Competencies: An Overview," *Exchange: The Organizational Behavior Teaching Journal*, Vol. VIII, No. 2, 1983, pp. 8-9.

PORTER, LYMAN W., and LAWRENCE E. MCKIBBIN, *Future of Management Education and Development: Drift or Thrust into the 21st Century?* New York: McGraw-Hill, 1988.

PRINGLE, CHARLES D., "Seven Reasons Why Managers Don't Delegate," *Management Solutions*, November 1986, pp. 26-30.

ROBBINS, STEPHEN P., "'Conflict Management' and 'Conflict Resolution' Are Not Synonymous Terms," *California Management Review*, Winter 1978, pp. 67-75.

ROBBINS, STEPHEN P., *Managing Organizational Conflict: A Nontraditional Approach*. Englewood Cliffs, N.J.: Prentice Hall, 1974.

ROBBINS, STEPHEN P., "Reconciling Management Theory with Management Practice," *Business Horizons*, February 1977, pp. 38-47.

ROBBINS, STEPHEN P., *Organization Theory: Structure, Design, and Applications*, 2nd ed. Englewood Cliffs, N.J.: Prentice Hall, 1987.

ROBBINS, STEPHEN P., *Supervision Today*, Englewood Cliffs, N.J.: Prentice Hall 1994.

ROGERS, CARL R., *On Becoming a Person*. Boston: Houghton Mifflin, 1961.

ROGERS, CARL R., and RICHARD E. FARSON, *Active Listening*. Chicago: Industrial Relations Center of the University of Chicago, 1976.

SAPIENZA, ALICE M., "Believing Is Seeing: How Culture Influences the Decisions Top Managers Make," in R. H. Kilmann, M. J. Saxton, and R. Serpa (eds.), *Gaining Control of the Corporate Culture*. San Francisco: Jossey-Bass, 1985, pp. 66-83.

SCHNEIER, CRAIG ERIC, RICHARD W. BEATTY, and LLOYD S. BAIRD, "Creating a Performance Management System," *Training and Development Journal*, May 1986, pp. 74-79.

SCHNEIER, CRAIG ERIC, and RICHARD W. BEATTY, "Developing Behaviorally-Anchored Rating Scales (BARS)," *Personnel Administrator*, September 1979, pp. 51-62.

SCHUTZ, WILLIAM C., *FIRO: A Three Dimensional Theory of Interpersonal Behavior*. New York: Rinehart & Co., 1958.

SELTZER, JOSEPH, "Discipline with a Clear Sense of Purpose," *Management Solutions*, February 1987, pp. 32-37.

SHEPPARD, JAMES A., "Productivity Loss in Performance Groups: A Motivation Analysis," *Psychological Bulletin*, January 1993, pp. 67-81.

SMITH, DAVID E., "Training Programs for Performance Appraisal: A Review," *Academy of Management Review*, January 1986, pp. 22-40.

STEINMETZ, LAWRENCE L., *The Art and Skill of Delegation*. Reading, Mass.: Addison-Wesley, 1976, p. 248.

STOFFMAN, DANIEL, "Waking Up to Great Meetings," *Canadian Business*, November 1986, pp. 75-79.

THOMAS, KENNETH W., "Conflict and Conflict Management," in Marvin Dunnette (ed.), *Handbook of Industrial and Organizational Psychology*. Chicago: Rand McNally, 1976, pp. 889-935.

TJOSVOLD, DEAN, and DAVID W. JOHNSON, *Productive Conflict Management: Perspectives for Organizations*. New York: Irvington Publishers, 1983.

VERDERBER, KATHLEEN S., and RUDOLPH F. VERDERBER, *Inter-Act: Using Interpersonal Communication Skills*, 4th ed. Belmont, Cal.: Wadsworth, 1986.

WAKIN, EDWARD, "Make Meetings Meaningful," *Today's Office*, May 1991, pp. 68-69.

WHETTEN, DAVID A. AND KIM S. CAMERON, *Developing Management Skills: Developing Self-Awareness*, New York: Harper Collins College Publishers, 1993, pp. 59-60.

WHETTTEN, DAVID A., and KIM S. CAMERON, *Developing Management Skills*, 3rd Ed. New York: HarperCollins College Publishers, 1995.

WOHLKING, WALLACE, "Effective Discipline in Employee Relations," *Personnel Journal*, September 1975, pp. 491-492.

YATES, DOUGLAS, Jr., *The Politics of Management*. San Francisco: Jossey-Bass, 1985.

YOUNG, STANLEY, "Developing Managerial Political Skills: Some Issues and Problems." Paper presented at the National Academy of Management Conference, Chicago, August 1986.